Henry James on Culture

HENRY JAMES
on Culture

Collected Essays on Politics and
the American Social Scene

Edited by Pierre A. Walker

UNIVERSITY OF NEBRASKA PRESS

Lincoln and London

⊚ The paper in this book meets the minimum requirements of American National
Standard for Information Sciences—Permanence of Paper for Printed Library Materials,
ANSI Z39.48-1984.

Library of Congress Cataloging-in-Publication Data
James, Henry, 1811–1882.
Henry James on culture: collected essays on politics and the
American social scene / edited by Pierre A. Walker.
p.   cm.
Includes bibliographical references (p.   ) and index.
ISBN 0-8032-2589-X (cl: alk. paper)
I. Walker, Pierre A.   II. Title.
PS2112.W3   1999
814'.4—dc21   98-38341
CIP

Contents

Acknowledgments

It is appropriate to begin a book designed to demonstrate something of the complexity of Henry James's relationship to the culture and society in which he lived by acknowledging my own indebtedness to the intellectual culture in which I have worked and which has helped make this book possible. I owe and hereby offer my gratitude to the following. The third edition of *A Bibliography of Henry James*, by Leon Edel and Dan Laurence (Oxford: Clarendon Press, 1982), made it possible to track down James's uncollected prose and the different original published versions of the articles in this volume. David Boxwell gave some very helpful suggestions in respect to the first essay in this volume, "The British Soldier." Martha Banta persuaded me to study James's *Harper's Bazar* essays, Beverly Haviland encouraged me to read "The Question of Our Speech" more critically, and presentations by Eric Haralson and Susan Griffin at the Midwest Modern Language Association Convention in Chicago in 1994 inspired me to investigate the World War I essays. In the Henry James sessions that they respectively chaired at the 1996 MMLA in Minneapolis and at the 1997 Michigan State University Modern Literature Conference, Eric Haralson and Sheila Teahan gave me opportunities to present some of the ideas included in the introduction to this volume. Discussions with M. J. Devaney on the postmodern subject were most engaging and suggestive. Glenn Leinbach's help as a proofreader was invaluable. Thank you too to Judith Anderson for help in preparing the manuscript. I am especially grateful to Allen Carey-Webb, Edward Jayne, Greg Zacharias, Millicent Bell, and David McWhirter, who read versions of the manuscript and provided extremely useful commentary. Lastly, I extend special thanks to Gwen, Jil, John, Allen, and Mike for fighting the good fight and thus providing hope while I worked on James's cultural criticism. To them and to their effort I dedicate this book.

Introduction

On Sunday, 18 April 1915, the British newspaper *The Observer* published a letter from a reader identified only by the initials C. L. D. The letter was about Henry James and was addressed to "those who only know Mr. Henry James as an accomplished literary artist, and who may have assumed that his way of looking at our public affairs would be that of a coldly dispassionate and cosmopolitan critic."[1] One reason this letter is interesting is that it argues against what has become a complex but inaccurate cliché about Henry James. One aspect of this cliché is the idea that James was so devoted to his art that he had little time or interest for the practical side of life. Among other things, this would explain why James's fiction is primarily about the trivial concerns of upper-class people. Furthermore, the undoubted praise that James was "an accomplished literary artist," as the letter says, implies that James's was exclusively an artistic temperament and that he was not a public figure interested in worldly affairs; as a result, the standard view has long held, James was "coldly dispassionate and cosmopolitan," not personally engaged in contemporary social and political issues.

Clichés have often some degree of truth, and such is the case here. The idea that James was devoted to his art to the point of excluding the practical side of life arises in part from the fact that James was an intensely private person who avoided the public spotlight. The "mania for publicity," he felt, was "one of the most striking signs of our times."[2] He warned that the art and the artist are not the same and fielded direct questions about his novels by referring the questioner to the fiction itself: "One's craft, one's art, is his expression, ... not one's person, as that of some great actress or singer is hers. ... Why should the public want him to splash himself, reveal his person on paper?" James made these remarks in an interview ("Henry James in the Serene Sixties," article 6) when he visited the United States in 1904–05. During that visit he resisted various efforts by one of his publishers, George Harvey, the president of Harper and Brothers, to generate publicity from James's first return to his native land in more than twenty years, but Harvey finally persuaded James to give one reluctant interview— apparently the first of only two that James ever gave—to one of Harvey's newspapers.[3]

As James had resided and traveled extensively in the United States, Britain, France, Italy, and Switzerland, the label "cosmopolitan" is not inappropriate, but it too contributes to the clichéd view of James, for as the writer of the letter to *The Observer* implies by the phrase "dispassionate and cosmopolitan critic," with so varied an exposure to places and peoples, the cosmopolitan James had no particular attachment to anyone or anyplace. This view also contributes to the tendency to perceive James only as a devoted artist and not as a man engaged in the events of his day.

The point of the letter, however, is to counter the view that James is *only* "an accomplished literary artist" and a "coldly dispassionate and cosmopolitan critic." Writing during the first year of World War I, the letter writer wants to be clear that James had always been "animated by the warmest feelings of attachment towards the country of his adoption." As proof, the letter quotes from a long passage James had written and first published in 1877, which describes James's visit to Woolwich, the location of the Royal Military College.[4] In the quoted extract, James describes his reaction to seeing the college, the Royal Artillery barracks, and the nearby arsenal, all of which he calls "a glimpse of the imperial machinery of this great country." The glimpse, says James, "stirs a peculiar sentiment. I know not what to call this sentiment unless it be simply an admiration for the greatness of England."[5] The 1915 *Observer* letter suggests that this passage proves that James had always felt British patriotic fervor. By showing that James had always shared the kind of patriotic feelings that other Englishmen and -women were assumed, in early 1915, to have always felt, the letter implies that James is "one of us" and always has been. In fact, this implication proved prophetic in at least two ways: for one, the six essays James wrote about the war during the first year of the conflict were all to some degree about being "one of us"; and for another, just over three months after the appearance of *The Observer* letter, the American-born James would literally become "one of us" when, in a gesture of solidarity with the British war effort, he would take the oath of British citizenship.

If one sees C. L. D.'s letter in light of the cliché that James was not publicly engaged, then it is an effective piece of evidence to the contrary; but if one assumes that the extent of James's public engagement consisted solely of sharing uncritical nationalistic sentiments, then the letter does James a disservice. The fact is that James felt more than jingoistic patriotic fervor in relation to World War I and other public events. He *was* capable of great personal interest and engagement in public events at the same time that he could also be an acute analyst of the political, psychological, social, and moral aspects of current affairs. One of the purposes of this collection of essays is to demonstrate firsthand the scope of James's engagement in current events.[6] Some of the essays included here have never been published before in book form, while the others have generally been available only in obscure collections. Together they present a side of James's work that has been neglected during the eight decades since his death in early 1916. Reading over them, one comes to recognize these public essays as an important part of James's published writing, and the perception of James as "only" a "dispassionate," "cosmopolitan," "accomplished artist" and not also a man of his world and his times appears as false today as it was in 1915.

The essays in this collection cover most of James's career. They are presented in four groups: essays about British geopolitics; essays on gender and the American scene; James's one metaphysical essay; and writings on World War I. James wrote all but the first of these four groups during the last eleven years of his life. In these final years, he was very productive, even though he published but one novel (*The Outcry*, 1911), one novella (*Julia Bride*, 1909), and one collection of short stories (*The Finer Grain*, 1910). During his final decade, James published two autobiographical volumes (*A Small Boy and Others*, 1913, and *Notes of a Son and Brother*, 1914), two collections of literary criticism (*Views and Reviews*, 1908, and *Notes on Novelists*, 1914), two collections of travel essays (*English Hours*, 1905, and *Italian Hours*, 1909), the twenty-four volumes and eighteen prefaces of the New York Edition—the revised and definitive version of much of his earlier fiction—(1907–09), and *The American Scene*, his report of his trip to the United States in 1904–05. The first group of essays in this collection, essays about British geopolitics, dates from 1878–79. At this point in his career, James had published five books, including the novels *Roderick Hudson* (1875) and *The American* (1877), and during 1878 he would publish his single greatest commercial success, *Daisy Miller*. But early in 1878, James's situation was not as secure as he might have wished; after all, although thirty-four years old, he still relied, at times, on loans and handouts from his father to make ends meet, and as a result, he welcomed the opportunity to publish various kinds of nonfiction writing.

When the adult James moved to Europe in the fall of 1875 (he lived in Paris for a year and then moved to England, where, for the rest of his life, he made his primary residence), the financial basis of his installation in Paris was his assignment to write a regular Paris column for the *New York Tribune*.[7] The twenty pieces he wrote for the *Tribune* are typical of all of James's nonfiction contributions to periodicals in the range of subjects they cover: literary, drama, and art criticism, travel writing, and political analysis. In fact, the range of the topics of all of James's nonfiction raises the unavoidable problem of classification, for not only do the various articles address different topics, but within the articles themselves James moves from subject to subject. As a result, it becomes impossible to categorize neatly James's nonfiction. The Parisian articles for the *Tribune* are perhaps best understood as journalism, and that may very well be what James himself thought them to be, although they are certainly not the kind of sensationalist journalism that was becoming more and more common in the late nineteenth century and that James lamented as an unfortunately pervasive characteristic of modern life. "One sketches one's age but imperfectly," he wrote in 1887, "if one doesn't touch on that particular matter: the invasion, the impudence and shamelessness, of the newspaper and the interviewer, the devouring *publicity* of life, the extinction of all sense between public and private."[8]

Whenever James established a working relationship with a popular periodical, what he wrote was as varied in content as the articles from Paris for the *Tribune*. On two later occasions, he also became a regular "correspondent" for a periodical. In 1897, he wrote a series of "London Notes" for *Harper's Weekly*, and in 1898, he wrote a series of "American Letters" for *Literature*, the precursor of the *Times Literary Supplement*. The articles written on these occasions covered as broad a range of subjects as ever. The "London Notes" range from contemporary theater and literature to events in the literary and art worlds to current political events, such as the Jubilee of Queen Victoria. While the "American Letters" are devoted solely to reviewing books, the books James discusses include dialect and military novels, fiction by William Dean Howells, Bret Harte, Mary Wilkins Freeman, and Hamlin Garland, poetry by Walt Whitman, the letters of Ulysses S. Grant, essays by Theodore Roosevelt and W. A. Dunning, and writing by Nicholas Murray Butler and others on education.[9] From the beginning of his career, James's nonfiction always had a wide range of interest. He began publishing unsigned book reviews for the bimonthly *North American Review* in 1864 and in 1865 for *The Nation*, a widely read weekly; in 1868, he was also contributing art reviews to the *North American Review*, and in 1870, travel writing to *The Nation*. *Atlantic Monthly* had been publishing fiction by James since 1865, and by 1871 the magazine was running his art and book reviews as well.

The variety of his contributions to periodicals shows that neither James nor his editors thought of him as writing any one particular kind of material, and this would always be the case during his life. He was variously labeled in letters and articles about him as a "novelist," a "critic," and a "critic and novelist."

One regular correspondence—other than the 1875–76 relationship with the *Tribune*, the 1897 one with *Harper's Weekly*, and the 1898 one with *Literature*—

occurred after James had left Paris and established what would prove to be permanent residency in London. There in 1878, he understood that he was *The Nation's* "London correspondent."[10] Most of James's 1878 contributions to *The Nation* were book reviews (including the review in this collection of Moritz Busch's memoir of Bismarck); with three exceptions, the remaining articles of 1878 and all of those of 1879 were on art, drama, and travel. The three exceptions are "The Afghan Difficulty" (14 Nov. 1878), "The Early Meeting of Parliament" (26 Dec. 1878), and "The Reassembling of Parliament" (20 March 1879), none of which have ever been reprinted since their initial appearance in *The Nation*. These three articles and a fourth, "The British Soldier," which *Lippincott's Magazine* published in August 1878, all address specific events in the British colonies and make up the first part of this collection, the essays about British geopolitics. "The British Soldier" describes British military preparedness for possible war with Russia over a crisis in the Balkans; "The Afghan Difficulty" and "The Early Meeting of Parliament" are about the outbreak of the Second Afghan War, and "The Reassembling of Parliament" concerns the political fallout from the military disaster the British suffered at the hands of the Zulus at Isandhlwana, Natal.

In each of these essays, James writes political commentary. He comments on specific, current geopolitical events for a contemporary readership whose familiarity with the events James takes for granted. Two facts probably account for the complete neglect in the twentieth century of these articles. The articles are written for a readership thoroughly informed in the details of various current events, details with which many twentieth-century readers are not likely to be familiar. Secondly, until recently, scholarship has not emphasized the significance of imperialism as a context for American or European literature of the late-Victorian and Edwardian eras. This has changed considerably during the last decade, thanks especially to the efforts of Edward Said, who has argued energetically that literary critics "can no longer ignore empires and the imperial context in [their] studies."[11] Thanks to the work of Said and other scholars, the study of empire and of postcolonialism has begun to gain prominence, and collection and republication of James's articles on the British Empire now make sense as they never did before.

The first of the essays about British geopolitics, "The British Soldier," describes James's spring 1878 visit to the military training center in Aldershot, where he was the guest of his friends General and Mrs. Pakenham and where he witnessed the review in honor of the Queen's birthday, but his commentary concerns the tension between Britain and Russia in the aftermath of Russia's defeat of Turkey in the Russo-Turkish War of 1877–78.[12] Like many contemporary politicians, James understood that Russia's expressed desire for a Bulgaria independent of Turkey was not so much motivated by an altruistic support of the Balkan independence or Pan-Slavic movements of the time as by a desire to regain the influence in the area that Russia had lost with its defeat in the Crimean War over two decades before. The immediate tension did not last much beyond James's visit to Aldershot, as diplomatic pressure brought the European powers to the negotiating table at the Congress of Berlin, which concluded in July 1878 with Russia's humiliating concessions to most of the demands of Britain and Austria. In the meantime, though, from the perspective of May 1878, when James wrote the article, a diplomatic solution to the crisis was not guaranteed, and James's interest in Britain's preparation for possible war with Russia at the time is prompted partly by his interest in the drama of the standoff between the major powers over the Balkans and by an awareness, which he also displays in the other articles in part 1 of this collection, of the complexity of the "great game," as Rudyard Kipling called the geopolitical struggle between the Russian and British empires.

The "great game" also forms the backdrop to James's two articles on Afghanistan, "The Afghan Difficulty" and "The Early Meeting of Parliament." The first of these appeared almost as the Second Afghan War (1878–80) was breaking out between Britain and Afghanistan. James realized, as have later historians, that the pretext that prompted the British to invade Afghanistan was the result both of the aggressively expansionist policy of the current, Tory-appointed viceroy of India, Edward Robert Bulwer-Lytton, Lord Lytton, and of Russian and British jockeying for position for their respective empires.

The second of the two articles appeared after the war had begun, and in it James discusses how the political parties are exploiting the war. William Gladstone, at the time leader of the opposition Liberal Party, would later use the Afghan War as the impetus for two famous campaigns, the first and second Midlothian Campaigns (of late 1879 and March 1880), which are noted as the first instance of a leading politician "stumping" nationally, a new practice that both Queen Victoria and Prime Minister Benjamin Disraeli criticized. But the Midlothian Campaigns were not entirely new, for Gladstone had already used the Conservative Party's foreign policy as a pretext for national campaigning in 1876 (after the Turkish atrocities in Bulgaria that provided Russia with a pretext to go to war with Turkey), and as James describes in "The Early Meeting of Parliament," in late 1878, Gladstone was even then using the Afghan War as a subject in a series of speeches throughout the nation. The national campaigning intensified up to the election of April 1880, in which Gladstone's Liberals brought down Disraeli's Conservative government. Anyone particularly interested in the British political history of the period should appreciate this article, but the awareness James expresses of how politicians make use of current affairs to further their political ambitions ought to strike a chord with any late-twentieth-century observer of similar practices today. The essay demonstrates James's recognition that not only are historical events important to politics but that what politicians say about them is important too. As Edward Said puts it, "The power to narrate, or to block other narratives from forming and emerging, is very important to culture and imperialism, and constitutes one of the main connections between them."[13] Gladstone's foreign policy speeches attempt to form a Liberal narrative and block a potential Tory one about the significance of the events abroad, and "The Early Meeting of Parliament" shows that James has understood this.

James's final political essay for *The Nation* was "The Reassembling of Parliament," which discusses the reaction to the disaster the Zulus inflicted on a British invasion force at Isandhlwana. In this essay, James most explicitly addresses the issues of colonialism and empire. He does not appear a total opponent of British imperialism and gives no indication that Britain should not have an empire, but he does criticize the inconsistency in the English tendency to want at the same time to have an empire and to complain about imperial policy. The English must realize, he asserts, that maintaining an empire has its costs, both in forces and expenditures, and therefore they can't have and criticize the empire at the same time. James's own position, then, is ambivalent; he describes Disraeli as a circus performer, and although the imperial policies of Disraeli's government were more interventionist and aggressive than were Gladstone's, James is also critical of the Liberal leader.

"The Reassembling of Parliament" appears on the eve of "the period of the main imperialist 'scramble for Africa'" from 1885 to 1910.[14] During the three and a half decades preceding the outbreak of World War I in 1914, the presence of the European powers in Africa went from some coastal footholds to a total partition of virtually the entire continent. Several issues motivated the European powers in their "scramble for Africa." Portugal, Germany, England, Belgium, and France were playing a veritable chess match of geopolitical containment with the various regions of the continent as spaces on the board, and raw materials were also a powerful stimulus to greed. But as the cultural critic Patrick Brantlinger has argued, the Western view of Africa was always conflicted and paradoxical.[15] In England, for example, part of the explicit rationale for British incursions into Africa was the protection of the continent's natives against the demons of slavery and paganism. However, while the rationale of protection was derived from sympathy for the conditions of African life, argues Brantlinger, "many Victorians . . . sympathized with the poor at home but not with the exploited abroad," and although the suppression of slavery was often cited as a justification for British incursion in Africa, "a sizable portion of the Victorian public sided with the South during the American Civil War."[16] The point, then, is that British attitudes toward its African empire were thoroughly ambivalent, a point which finds its parallel in the ambivalence toward the empire that James expresses in "The Reassembling of Parliament."

The interest in analyzing politics that James shows in the early essays about British geopolitics should not be so surprising, for the politics on which he comments—the showdown between Britain and Russia after the Treaty of San Stefano and before the Congress of Berlin, the political brinkmanship of Russia, Afghanistan, and Britain preceding the Second Afghan War, the uses the political parties make of the Afghan War and of the setback of the British invasion of Zululand in early 1879—all involve, at least to James, dramas of human relations not entirely unlike the dramas he represented in his novels. The conflict between Basil Ransom and Olive Chancellor, in *The Bostonians*, over the affection and political commitment of Verena Tarrant, or Christopher Newman's struggle, in *The American*, with the Bellegarde family for the opportunity to marry their daughter, Claire, involve a jockeying for position, forging of alliances, and search for influence similar to the diplomatic conflict between the viceroy of India and the emir of Afghanistan. The same could be said, probably, of just about any of James's novels.

James reviewed Moritz Busch's memoir of Bismarck during the Franco-Prussian War, which is here reprinted in its entirety for the first time, at the same time he wrote the essays about British geopolitics. One of the reasons it is interesting is that it demonstrates James's interest in international politics as "human drama." Busch's book describes Bismarck's attitudes during the war and the negotiations following it and reveals the chancellor's opinions of a number of important world figures. Thus the book stamps a character on the events, a character who, by the way, in the assured confidence of his superior abilities bears comparison to another apparently hugely self-confident world figure whom James would find both appealing and unattractive at the same time, much as he finds Bismarck: Theodore Roosevelt.[17]

The first of the essays about British geopolitics, "The British Soldier," is also interesting for what it shows about James's own relation to the military. Like his elder brother, William, but unlike his two younger brothers, Wilkie and Bob, Henry James did not serve in the Civil War, and James's biographers have believed that the avoidance of participation in the great military conflict of his youth left James with a lifelong sense of inadequacy.[18] This inadequacy and James's relation to the two great wars that bracketed his adult life (the Civil War and World War I) are particularly intriguing to students and scholars of James interested in masculinity in James's life and work, and James's remarks in "The British Soldier" are especially significant in connection to masculinity, since in the nineteenth century, the soldier was an exemplary model "of masculine identity."[19] James includes in the article several expressions of his admiration for military men, including a gushing description of the "brilliant" Life Guards in their handsome uniforms, "with their tight red jackets and tight blue trousers following the swelling lines of their manly shapes." James admits to admiring the Guards so much that whenever he chances to see a squadron marching through the streets, he is "sure to make one of the gamins who stand upon the curbstone to see them pass" (8–9). But having admitted that the sight of soldiers reduces him to the childlike state of a gamin, or street urchin, James then turns the table on the military by transforming all of the various kinds of soldiers he mentions in the article to boys: They all share "one quality in common—the appearance of extreme, of even excessive, youth. It is hardly too much to say that the British army ... is an army of boys" (10). The sight of the Life Guards diminishes James's own masculinity by turning him into to what Anthony Rotundo reminds us was in the nineteenth century the opposite of a man, a boy.[20] But James brings the challenge upon his own masculinity down to size and by contrast affirms his own masculine power by turning the entire army into a band of boys: "All the regiments are boyish" (10).

Then James turns the military parade he witnesses at Aldershot into theater: "The place looked like a 'side-scene' in a comic opera. . . . and the dragoons, hussars and lancers, the beautiful horses, the capital riders, the wonderful wagons and guns, seemed even more theatrical than military" (13). If indeed James did feel a sense of inadequacy about his noninvolvement in the Civil War, the combination of contradictory responses to the sight of soldiers, admiring and belittling at the same time, may have been his outlet for this inadequacy.

The description of the Life Guards' "swelling lines" and "manly shapes" is also unabashedly homoerotic, and this raises another important issue about James that has received considerable attention in the last decade: his sexuality. Leon Edel's landmark, five-volume biography of James treats his sexuality and bachelorhood by presenting James as essentially celibate, married to his vocation as an artist and therefore unwilling to be married to any person. However, Edel wrote his biography at a time (during the 1950s and 1960s) that would probably not have been receptive to a frank discussion of a major author's homosexuality, whether practiced or only an inclination. James's more recent biographers, Fred Kaplan and Sheldon Novick (both writing in the 1990s), however, take it for granted that James loved men, and Novick has claimed (though not without controversy) that the partner in James's first, youthful sexual experiences may have been Oliver Wendell Holmes Jr.[21]

Because James scholars now see Henry James as, at the very least, homosexually inclined, his admiration of the Life Guards' "manly shapes" and "swelling lines" becomes yet another piece of evidence in relation to his sexual inclinations. Its significance is further reinforced by considerable evidence that at the time of the article English soldiers were in fact often very willing to supplement their meager pay through prostitution. No explicit evidence exists that James was aware (or not aware) of this, but some cultural historians argue that it was common knowledge, and one, Edward Prime-Stevenson, cites Aldershot, the camp James was visiting, as one of several locations for military prostitution: one "has only to walk around London, around any English garrison-center, to stroll about Portsmouth, Aldershot, Southampton ... to find the soldier-prostitute in almost open self-marketing."[22]

While James avoided enlistment and direct involvement in the Civil War, he became involved in several activities when World War I broke out, as is clear from essays in part 4 of this edition, writings on World War I. As chairman of the American Volunteer Motor-Ambulance Corps, he solicited funds in support of the corps; from his house in Rye, he worked to help shelter the refugees from Belgium whom he describes at the end of "Refugees in England"; and from his flat in Chelsea he made regular visits both to Belgian refugees at nearby Crosby Hall, which he describes in the same article, and to wounded British soldiers in neighboring hospitals, which he describes in "The Long Wards." Furthermore, in his writing of the period, James focused almost exclusively on the war.

James's biographers have generally concluded that when World War I began, James threw himself into a frenzy of war-related activity as an act of redemption of sorts for his evasion of military service in the Civil War.[23] Although past seventy and in questionable health, James spent a very active fifteen months between the outbreak of the war in the summer of 1914 and the stroke that led to his final illness in December 1915. During those months, however, he found himself entirely unable to continue work on his fiction. He abandoned *The Ivory Tower*, the novel he was writing when the war began, and he was not able to make much progress with *The Sense of the Past*, which he had discarded some years before but on which he now attempted to resume work. With four exceptions— two commemorative articles that reminisce about associations from his early adult years (one on James T. and Annie Fields and the other on the early years of *The Nation*), an introduction to the posthumous publication of Rupert Brooke's *Letters from America*, and some progress on *The Middle Years*, the never-completed third volume of his memoirs—all of James's literary work during the war consisted of writing specifically related to the great conflict.[24]

Starting in late 1914, James wrote six substantial articles on the war, collaborated in a *New York Times Magazine* profile of himself and his activities as chairman of the American Volunteer Motor-Ambulance Corps, and published a short piece in the *New York Times* on the death of a member of the ambulance corps in the sinking of the *Lusitania*. The two *New York Times* pieces have never previously been reprinted. The six more substantial war essays have never been collected in a single volume.[25] Part 4 of this collection, writings on World War I, presents the six war essays and the two *Times* pieces as a group for the first time.

It was James himself who first suggested the connection between his activities in the Civil War and in World War I. "Within the Rim," the final essay in part 4, begins with James mentioning that the outbreak of the later war immediately reminded him "of the violence with which the American Civil War broke upon us" (177), and in the first paragraph of "The Long Wards," James recalls his one previous "intimate vision" of the "soldier ... in his ... more or less war-worn state" (169). He refers here to an event during the Civil War that he recalls in the second volume of his autobiography, *Notes of a Son and Brother*, which was published not long before the outbreak of World War I.[26] During the summer of 1861, James and his close friend, Thomas Sergeant Perry, visited "a vast gathering of invalid and convalescent troops ... at some point on the Rhode Island shore," probably Portsmouth Grove.[27] In *Notes of a Son and Brother*, James suggests a similarity between himself wandering among the wounded Union soldiers, conversing with them, giving them money, to Walt Whitman, who became famous for his many visits of merciful companionship to Civil War military hospitals. This reference to Whitman is significant, because while Whitman's Civil War nursing of the wounded acts out the pervading spirit of communion among people expressed throughout his poetry, James if anything was alienated from the scores of young men, including his two youngest brothers and many friends and acquaintances, who unlike him enlisted and served.[28] The visits James made near the end of his life to similarly stricken Allied soldiers in London inevitably recall the association to Whitman for James's biographers, but this time more to James's credit, for his visits were frequent and part of his energetic involvement in war-related activities.

His writings on World War I suggest that the war enabled James to experience a communion of sorts with those more directly involved in the fighting. Not only did he devote hours to providing a friendly ear to refugees and wounded soldiers, but in his detailed descriptions of corps exploits in "The American Volunteer Motor-Ambulance Corps in France" he repeatedly resorts to the pronoun "we," as though he himself were one of the ambulance drivers or attendants. (As one reads these vivid descriptions, recalling that James admired good war novels, like Zola's *La Débâcle* and Tolstoy's *War and Peace*, one wonders what sort of war novel James himself might have written.)[29] In "Within the Rim," James describes the view from Rye across the English Channel toward France, stressing the contrast of the beauty and tranquility of his late-summer view in Rye with the knowledge of the tragedy occurring just "beyond the rim," on the continent (179).[30] But the point of this essay, as its title implies, is to bring James within the rim of those touched by the war. James labels himself "the associated outsider" and "technical alien," but he ends the essay by expressing a sentiment present at least to some degree in all the writings on World War

I: how the shared experience of the war affirmed his sense of "partaking of shared instincts and ideals, of a communion of race and tongue, temper and tradition" with the English among whom he had lived for almost forty years (185). It is no wonder that James began to seek British citizenship at the very same time: He finally felt that he belonged; he was at last "one of us."

If James became so deeply involved in the war at least in part to redeem himself, an idea that recurs in many of the World War I essays helps suggest another reason why the outbreak of the war was important to James. In "France," "The Long Wards," "The Question of the Mind," and "Refugees in England," James points out how shaken he is by the war, that it makes him realize how much he had previously taken for granted. The works of the so-called Lost Generation, the artists of the generation that actually fought in the war, have accustomed us to the idea that World War I produced a profound sense of alienation that led to a questioning and rejection of received values. Such is usually thought to be the significance of books like Robert Graves's *Goodbye to All That*, Erich Maria Remarque's *All Quiet on the Western Front*, or Ernest Hemingway's early fiction. In his World War I essays, James questions just as deeply, but rather than resulting in a rejection, his questioning ends in a reaffirmation.

"To take a thousand things for granted," James writes at the beginning of "The Question of the Mind," "is to live comfortably, but the very first effect of great world-shocks is to blight that condition by laying bare all our grounds and our supposed roots" (151). After the war, the writers of the Lost Generation would make the same point, but according to them the generation that fought World War I realized in the midst of the carnage that precious little justified the waste of life they were witnessing. As Ezra Pound (who did not fight in the war) later put it in the often-cited fifth section of "Hugh Selwyn Mauberley" (1920):

> There died a myriad,
> And of the best, among them,
> For an old bitch gone in the teeth,
> For a botched civilization,
> . . . .
> For two gross of broken statues,
> For a few thousand battered books.[31]

The point these lines make is that those who went to war fought and died for what they believed was civilization and culture, yet they found that "civilization" was "botched"—what else could it be if its end result was a war of such magnitude?—and that culture was meaningless, simply some battered books and some broken statues.

If Pound's reaction to the war was that it was a waste of life, and if this reaction was at all representative, it was nonetheless influenced by factors that James never knew. When James suffered his debilitating stroke near the end of 1915, the war was a little more than a year old; James would never know it still had three years to run. He never knew about the bleakest moments in the war for the Allied cause, such as the battles of the Somme or Verdun, the strikes and mutinies of 1917, or the final German offensive of 1918. Nor would he live to see the realization of his hope that the United States would join the allied cause. This is perhaps why the questioning of all one took for granted did not lead James, as it did many of his successors, to a rejection of civilization and culture.

In "The Long Wards," James develops a philosophy that holds that one knows things through their absence or opposites.[32] What James admires the most in the hospitalized wounded soldiers he visits is the combination of contrasts. He finds the denizens of the hospital wards, men "of action, . . . appointed to advance and explode and destroy" (172), to be "creatures so amiable" (174) and full of "sweet reasonableness" (172). By the same token, his prewar recognition of the relative scarcity of soldiers visible in everyday American life "was a revelation of the degree" of their more frequent visibility in the streets and public places of Europe (171). Such comparisons make the recognition of absence possible. "We never know . . . how much these wanting elements have to suggest to the pampered mind till we feel it living in view of the community from which they have been simplified away" (171). In "France," James makes a similar point when he describes the good luck the British have had to live so close to France and yet to have been, heretofore, so unconscious of it: "It has never been a conscious reaction or a gathered fruition" (147). What James is describing is a law of negation. When we take things for granted, we lose consciousness of them, but we can know things through an awareness of the possibility of their absence.

James is able to use the law of negation to reaffirm what the war casts into doubt. In "The Long Wards," the amiability and "sweet reasonableness" of the soldiers, men trained to destroy, lead James to recognize that "the sore human stuff" he visits in the hospitals is "strong and sound in an extraordinary degree" (176). If the soldiers, who have experienced directly "the stress of carnage" (174), are so little embittered by their experience as they strike James as being, then how much less reason have those who have not been at the front to lose faith in humanity. This is the point of "The Long Wards," as James summarizes it in the essay's final two sentences: "If this abundance all slighted and unencouraged can still comfort us, what wouldn't it do for us tended and fostered and cultivated?

That is my moral, for I believe in Culture—speaking strictly now of the honest and of our own congruous kind" (176).

In "France," we see James offering a similar affirmation of culture. Much of the essay is a panegyric to French culture, and perhaps more than any of the other World War I essays, "France" appears to merit the label "propaganda" that the noted James scholar Adeline Tintner once bestowed, and not without reason, on all of them.[33] What does France represent to the rest of the world, James asks in "France"; why is she so important that "her name means more than anything in the world to us but just our own" (148)? France, he tells us, "takes charge of those of the interests of man which most dispose him to fraternise with himself, to pervade all his possibilities and to taste all his faculties, and in consequence to find and to make the earth a friendlier, an easier, and especially a more various sojourn" (148–49). As hyperbolic as this language may seem, James is claiming that France epitomizes Western culture and that defending France is defending Western culture, since France, he tells us, has treated the world "to the impression of genius as no nation since the Greeks has treated the watching world" (149).

Implicit to James here is a view of Western culture that has dominated the twentieth century; it holds that classical Greece was the greatest flourishing of culture, followed by Italy during the Renaissance and France in the modern era. This view has informed much of the curriculum of twentieth-century American education, especially "Great Books" courses such as the one at the University of Chicago. James's view here helps explain why, when the United States entered the war, Columbia College launched the foundation of the core curriculum still in place there today, the Contemporary Civilization course, which covers major works of philosophical, political, and social thought from Plato to Marx, as a means of explaining the war and the country's involvement in it. Implicit in the writings on World War I is James's desire that the United States enter the European conflict, just as implicit in the Contemporary Civilization course was the need to explain why Americans should be involved in the war. While James argued that the Allied cause was the defense of Western culture, for James and for many of the Lost Generation writers, the war threw the values of Western culture into doubt. Not all the younger writers rejected those cultural values and adopted, as Hemingway did, a form of existentialism; others attempted to reconstruct the modern world through a return to classical and early modern culture, as Pound did with his *Cantos*, T. S. Eliot with "The Wasteland," and James Joyce with *Ulysses*.

For James, the questioning that the war prompts leads not only to a reaffirmation of culture but also to an awareness of the basis of his fictional art. The material of James's novels and stories was first and foremost that aspect of social relations that was not obvious. In novel after novel, and perhaps most famously in *The Ambassadors*, James represented characters attempting to grasp the unspoken and the unspeakable. In one of the most famous scenes in all of James's fiction, the central character in *The Ambassadors*, Lambert Strether, becomes aware of the true nature of the relationship between two other characters in the novel. Part of the impact of the scene is that Strether realizes he had fooled himself into thinking the relationship in question was more Platonic than in fact it was. James's own reaction to World War I is not unlike Strether's in this scene, for just as Strether becomes aware of the reality behind what he had perceived, so too the outbreak of the war betrayed to James the extent of the antagonisms and aggressions that had been percolating in Europe for decades. In a letter to a close friend written in the first days of the war, James wrote:

> Black and hideous to me is the tragedy that gathers, and I'm sick beyond cure to have lived on to see it. You and I, the ornaments of our generation, should have been spared this wreck of our belief that through the long years we had seen civilization grow and the worst become impossible. The tide that bore us along was then all the while moving to *this* as its grand Niagara—yet what a blessing we didn't know it. It seems to me to *undo* everything, everything that was ours, in the most horrible retroactive way....[34]

James's biographer Leon Edel writes of this letter that James "could not avert his face. He had always lived too close to the realities behind human illusion."[35] James makes clear in the letter that he had taken for granted (and assumes that his correspondent had likewise) that civilization was getting better, that it was inexorably progressing, and that as part of this improvement, conflagrations like the Great War were less and less likely. If James, however, was supposed to be the expert on "the realities behind human illusion," how then could he have not perceived the realities behind the illusions of progress, civilization, and peace? If in fact James *prided* himself on his ability to see the reality behind the illusions, might his great shock at the outbreak of war and the brutal German invasion of neutral Belgium—what he calls "the most insolent, 'Because I choose to, damn you all!' recorded in history" (143)—not betray his frustration at his own apparent blindness? His exertions with the wounded, with refugees, with the Volunteer Ambulance Corps, and as a writer on behalf of the Allied cause might have sought to redeem not just James's nonparticipation in the Civil War but also his own embarrassment at having misjudged the political and military situation in Europe prior to August 1914.

The topic of what is not obvious but hidden appears in "The Question of the Mind," the fourth of the writings on World War I. In this essay James again verges on writing propaganda, as he presents the English mind in flattering contrast to other national minds. He argues that the French or Italian minds, for example, present themselves as a whole to the observer; "there was then nevertheless no mystery more, nothing of the unexplored" after contact with the French or the Italians. With the English the matter was altogether different, for upon contact with "the Englishman . . . you would find a vast tract of the recorded history of your relation with him unaccounted for." To illustrate his point, James turns to an eating metaphor: "Your meal, copious though it should keep on proving, was never all served at one sitting" (157).

James's description of the English mind reads like a prescription for his own works of fiction. James's novels and stories portray not the obvious but the secret; as his 1904 interviewer put it, in James's fictions, "what one sees is not bare and plain. The too literal mind need not apply here for companionship" (38). "The Question of the Mind" not only extols the English mind, but it extols it in terms that correspond to James's artistic aims; if the war helped him to reaffirm culture and civilization, it also enabled him to reaffirm the appreciation of these artistic aims.

The themes one can trace throughout the writings on World War I appear perhaps most brilliantly in "Refugees in England," the sixth article in part 4. This essay concerns itself primarily with the experience of Belgian refugees in London shortly after the German invasion of their homeland. James describes the arrangements and activities organized by the Chelsea War Refugees' Fund, especially those centered at nearby Crosby Hall. He devotes a considerable portion of his essay to describing the history of this building. It was originally built around 1466 by Sir John Crosby, on Bishopsgate Street in London, in what later became Crosby Square; in the early 1500s it was the residence of Sir Thomas More. As James explains in the article, the hall was torn down at the beginning of the twentieth century to make way for various commercial interests, but it was moved and rebuilt in Chelsea in 1908. James dwells on the history of Crosby Hall because, like the Belgians it shelters, it too is a refugee, a similarity he emphasizes by the words he chooses: "re-edify" to describe the Chelsea reconstruction of the hall (163), and "edified" to describe the Belgians (165). (Having enumerated the teas, concerts, and other activities organized at Crosby Hall for the benefit of the Belgians, James then describes the refugees as "the installed and ensconced, the immemorially edified and arranged, the thoroughly furnished and provided and nourished people" (165). If the displacement of the hall and of the Belgians does not sufficiently signal their similarity, then the subsequent edification of both should, since "re-edify" is an unusual, though literal and perfectly appropriate, term for "rebuild."

The emphasized similarity of the two edified refugees, the Belgians and

Crosby Hall, serves to express a theme familiar from the other war essays: how the war makes one recognize the comforts one had taken for granted. The British, James suggests, might feel safe on their island fortress, protected by the English Channel from the battles on the continent. But just as the continent has its war-displaced refugees, so too does England have its own refugees, not just the foreigners it shelters but the victims of commercialism like Crosby Hall in its original site. The point, then, is that things are not safe, since anything or anyone can be displaced. Culture, though, at least through its correlate, education, may be the best bulwark against the chaos of displacement. This too James emphasizes through the choice of the word "edified," if we read it now in its more common sense of "instructed," for it is through edification that the Belgian refugees can receive whatever sense of security is now possible to them. While postwar Modernist classics such as *Ulysses* and *The Cantos* sought to rebuild the modern world after the chaos and destruction of World War I, and James agrees that culture is the one defense against chaos, his play on re-edification is a reminder that a reconstruction is never perfectly solid and unthreatened.

One powerful passage in "Refugees in England" is the poignant description at its conclusion of the first group of Belgian refugees arriving in Rye.[36] James describes the largely silent refugees making their way from the train station to the church. The silence is broken by the "sobbing and sobbing cry" of one young woman, a cry that to James "was the voice itself of history." This voice, says James, "brought home to me more things than I could then quite take the measure of, and these just because it expressed for her not direct anguish, but the incredibility, as we should say, of honest assured protection" (168). This is as striking a passage as any in all of Henry James, and part of what is striking about it is the ambiguity of the word "incredibility." The structure of the phrase suggests that because the woman is not crying in "direct anguish," she is crying out of gratitude for her newfound safety, the "honest assured protection," a reading that understands "incredibility" to mean "amazement." The other and more literal sense of "incredibility"—that it is not to be believed—offers an altogether different meaning to the phrase: that "honest assured protection" even here in England is not to be believed, is not credible, is therefore perhaps not possible. This second sense fits with the recurring theme in all of the World War I essays, that the war makes people realize the degree to which they have taken their comforts for granted; it also fits with the particular point in "Refugees in England," that in common with the refugees in their midst, the English should not feel secure, neither from military threats nor from the damage rampant commercialism can incur. Like so many of James's novels and stories, this particular essay leaves its readers with a question, in this case: Can "honest . . . protection" ever be "assured"? The inability to answer such a question in itself constitutes a negative answer.

Three of James's essays on World War I (a condensation of "The American Volunteer Motor-Ambulance Corps in France," a version of "The Question of the Mind," and "Refugees in England") appeared in one form or another in American newspapers. Considering how critical James was of newspapers (his 1888 novel, *The Reverberator*, for example, is a satire of the pernicious influence of the press), his willingness to express his enthusiasm for the Allied war effort in the dailies is particularly interesting. Equally interesting is how, for the sake of the cause, James handled the interview situation he so dreaded. Part 2 of this collection includes the first known interview with James, published under the byline of a journalist of Colonel Harvey's publishing conglomerate. Included in part 4, the writings on World War I, is a profile of James published in the *New York Times* Sunday magazine section in March 1915 (in fact it is a summary of this profile in *The Observer* that inspired the letter by C. L. D.).[37]

The *New York Times* article—the full title is "Henry James's First Interview: Noted Critic and Novelist Breaks His Rule of Years to Tell of the Good Work of the American Ambulance Corps"—is a curious one. According to the papers of Theodora Bosanquet, who was James's typist and amanuensis at the time, James consented to be interviewed by the *New York Times* on the subject of the American Volunteer Motor-Ambulance Corps and on the condition that he be allowed to approve final copy.[38] The interview took place in late February, and a few days later (possibly on Feb. 25), the journalist brought James the copy-proof. This version of the article displeased James, writes Bosanquet, and he spent the next few days redictating the article to the journalist. One assumes Bosanquet's account is correct.[39] Several of the passages not in quotation marks bear the stamp of James's prose style, and so much of the text consists of direct quotation or paraphrase of his speech that (as is the case with the 1904 interview) the article is for all intents and purposes by James anyway. The article certainly emphasizes James's reluctance to become a public spectacle in a newspaper, but it shows how he was willing to sacrifice his privacy for the excellent cause he was advocating, the Ambulance Corps, and it also shows what James made of the interview situation.

Unless he really had forgotten the 1904 interview in America, James must have deliberately colluded in the inaccurate idea that he was here granting his first interview. Just as in the earlier interview, "Henry James in the Serene Sixties," James makes a great point in the 1915 *Times* profile of how much he is conceding by even granting the interview. In both interviews, he deliberately plays the role of recluse and reluctant interviewee acceding only under very special circumstances to give an interview. Furthermore, he clearly toys with the *Times* journalist in the way he repeatedly parries the reporter's attempts to turn the discussion to James's art.

Because of James's role in the creation of the article, the interview becomes a fascinating instance of role playing, in which James imagines the ideal interview and consciously plays with his public image, as for example in an exchange about punctuation. In much the same way, Glenn Gould, a brilliant artist of a later generation who also professed a love for seclusion, would write an imaginary interview of himself.[40] Like the fact that James courted the major dailies when placing his war essays, his treatment of the *Times* profile shows his relationship to newspapers was not just critical, but complex and paradoxical. While he makes a point of mentioning his dislike of publicity, he consciously manipulates both the public medium and his own public image, betraying his ability to use the medium in precisely the way that leads one to be suspicious of it.

The profile reveals that James's relation to newspapers was not all that was complex and paradoxical; in fact the whole question of identity in relationship to James is no simple matter. James's admirers since his own lifetime, as the letter by C. L. D. to *The Observer* demonstrates, have disputed his national allegiance and identity; some maintain that since he was born in the United States, he was an American, albeit an expatriated one, and others maintain that he was British because he chose to reside in England during most of his adult life and chose to apply for British citizenship in 1915. But the essays collected in this book demonstrate something of the perils of trying to reduce James's sense of himself to a single national identity and, indeed, of what follows from such an attempt—characterizing his identity as having a stable, essential core.

One motif that runs throughout most of the essays is the essayist's willingness to adopt a particular persona in response to a given situation. In "The British Soldier," for example, James discusses the divisions among his pro-Turk and pro-Russian acquaintances: "Every one about me was either a Russian or a Turk, the Turks, however, being greatly the more numerous. It appeared necessary to one's self-respect to assume some foreign personality, and I felt keenly, for a while, the embarrassment of choice. At last it occurred to me simply that as an American I might be an Englishman; and the reflection became afterward very profitable" (6).

James expresses the taking of a position supporting either the Turks or the Russians not in terms of having a political opinion but in terms of taking a national identity. He does not say, "Every one was either pro-Turkish or pro-Russian," but "Every one ... was either a Russian or a Turk." Somehow the need to adopt a national identity—and a foreign one—becomes urgent: "It appeared necessary to one's self-respect to assume some foreign personality." Therefore James assumes the identity of an Englishman, and his subsequent behavior follows from the assumption of that identity. "Once I had undertaken the part, I played it with what the French call *conviction*" (6). These passages suggest something of the fluidity and the theatricality of identity, allowing one to take up a national identity like a dramatic "rôle" (6).

Throughout the essays in this collection James adopts different identities. In "The Reassembling of Parliament," he casts himself as "a friendly American, living in England," who "is exempt from the obligation of party allegiance" and who suspects himself "a better Englishman, in the old-fashioned sense of the word" than many of his neighbors (30). He presents himself, variously in the writings on World War I, as either English or American. In "The American Volunteer Motor-Ambulance Corps in France" he speaks of "us Americans" (131), and at the end of "Within the Rim," he speaks of Americans as "those of my own fond fellowship" (185), even though he devotes much of the essay to claiming his own solidarity with wartime fortunes of the British and the Allies. In "France" and in "The Question of the Mind," however, James uses the first-person plural pronoun to associate himself to the English; in "Refugees in England," he presents himself simply as "a neighbor and an observer deeply affected" (161).

James does not limit his identity positions solely to national identities. He concludes "The Speech of American Women" by casting himself in the role of an eloping lover, making an assignation with the possibly invented young woman with whom he has carried on a dialogue for several pages (75–81). At the end of "The Manners of American Women," he includes his sexagenarian self in a group of "several young persons" (111) on a bicycle expedition. And throughout both "The Speech of American Women" and "The Manners of American Women," James places "Europe" and "America" in quotation marks, which serves to underscore the apparent intangibility of these two places and their respective societies.

The roles in which James places himself are based on difference. In the words of a prominent, modern critic of James, "the Jamesian self is," in these instances of role-playing, "perpetually negotiating an identity out of its interaction with various others."[41] Identity, in James's essays, is not a distinct thing in itself, as the mind was for Descartes, but something that exists in relation to and reaction to other things.[42] For example, in many of the essays in this book, James portrays himself as an outsider by placing himself in a different position from either his readers or his subject matter or both. Writing for American magazines about British Imperialism or to the American editor to whom he addresses "The American Volunteer Motor-Ambulance Corps in France," James makes himself the American in England, but in "The Speech of American Women" and "The Manners of American Women," he presents himself to American readers as the European critic. In the *New York Times* interview, then, there is little surprise when James presents himself in a sort of parody of his own public persona.[43]

Fundamental to such theatrical role-playing lies a perception at odds with the Cartesian view of the self as monadic and autonomous. This view, which emphasizes individual independence, unity, and homogeneity, exerted a powerful influence over many of James's intellectual contemporaries in America, from Ralph Waldo Emerson to Horatio Alger. Henry James's role-playing places him at odds with such proponents of individualism and more in line with postmodern successors who perceive the self—or the subject, to use the appropriate postmodern term—as de-centered, fragmented, heterogeneous, and not autonomous and independent but organically intertwined with other subjects. As Ross Posnock argues in one of the most influential books of the last decade on Henry James, *The Trial of Curiosity*:

> Henry [James] is less concerned with role playing organized by a centered self than with putting in question the notion of this anchoring self. Because this core self, what Henry James calls "prime identity," begins and ends "with itself" and has "no connections and suggests none," it remains static and homogeneous. In contrast, a heterogeneous, theatrical self "bristles" with the mobility and impurity of internal difference, of something not wholly itself but infiltrated by "a different mixture altogether."[44]

Contrasting James with his philosopher brother, William, Posnock argues that the two brothers differ in respect to their perception of the self. Although William had a sense of the fluidity and theatricality of his novelist brother's subject position (what Posnock calls the "mimetic quality in Henry's self-representation—his assimilation to his surroundings"), he nonetheless still believed in the individual's having a true, inner self: "William leaves unquestioned his atomistic assumption that his brother has an inner core protected by an outer shell." It is precisely this assumption, Posnock continues, that "Henry's mimetic self"—its fluidity and theatricality—"with its outward projection that collapses boundaries, contests."[45] Each time he adopts a different persona in the essays in this collection, James provides evidence for Posnock's argument. He provides evidence, too, that a fundamental component of postmodern theories of the subject—the idea that the self is not "an inner core protected by an outer shell" but a series of identity positions that exist in relation to and to at least some degree are formed by exterior influences—has been around for at least a century.[46]

James's social, political, and cultural commentary was not prompted only by war and empire. With the exception of his one essay on metaphysics (part 3), the remaining essays in this collection, the essays on gender and the American scene, result from James's visit in 1904–05 to the United States, his first return to his native land since 1883. The most significant literary result of James's visit was the publication in 1907 of *The American Scene*, his account of his 1904–05 travels. *The American Scene* is more than just a travel book, though. Like Tocqueville's *Democracy in America*, it is an incisive, close observation of American life in its time. *The American Scene* registers James's reactions to the great changes in the United States since his previous visit and serves as a record of perhaps the most formative moment in the country's transition to a modern nation. With its memorable representations of rural New England life, the sudden and burgeoning growth of skyscrapers in major cities, the waves of immigrants and the urban ethnic ghettos, and the hints of post–Civil War Southern racial tension all filtered through James's own attempt to comprehend the vastness, variety, and rapid change of his native country, much as the central reflectors of his novels seek to understand the situation in which they find themselves, *The American Scene* defies classification. It is a travel document, a work of social history, and an autobiographical memoir. As such, *The American Scene* is James's most substantial, if not most important, work of cultural criticism, and unlike the works in this collection it has begun of late to receive the attention it merits and is currently in print in more than one widely available edition.[47]

At the same time that he visited the United States and wrote *The American Scene*, James composed some essays that elaborate on the concerns he expresses in that book about various aspects of modern American life. These essays have not been widely accessible since James's lifetime. During his stay in America, James delivered several public lectures, mostly on Balzac (the text of which has been widely reproduced), but he also addressed the 1905 graduation ceremony at Bryn Mawr College with "The Question of Our Speech." Although the text of James's speech was published almost immediately after its delivery, since then it has been published only once previous to this collection.[48] After returning to England in July 1905, James wrote two long essays for *Harper's Bazar* that further explore the topic of the Bryn Mawr speech: "The Speech of American Women" and "The Manners of American Women."[49] These three essays, which are properly appendices to *The American Scene*, have been largely neglected by readers interested in James, partly because they are not easily available and partly because they can at first strike new readers as trivial, reactionary, and elitist. The initial presumption of all three essays is that Americans, and American women in particular, speak badly and have terrible manners. But this charge is not simply James's descent into a condescending and sexist righteousness; in fact it leads to his analysis of complex American social and gender relations.

The underlying assumption of "The Question of Our Speech" and of "The Speech of American Women" is that everything depends upon communication, which depends upon talk, which in turn depends upon speech; language then is the basis for everything. The basis of language, James realized even before the similar insight of Ferdinand de Saussure, the founder of structuralist linguistics, is differences, or discriminations, as James prefers to call them. Like a structuralist linguist, in "The Question of Our Speech," James discusses the mutual dependence of consonants and vowels upon each other and the importance of distinguishing—discriminating—between variations of sound. Much as many structuralist anthropologists, historians, psychoanalysts, and narratologists did fifty to sixty years later, James then used the centrality of discrimination in linguistic communication as the model for everything that matters in society.[50] Therefore the ultimate target of James's criticism in "The Speech of American Women" is not so much poor speech habits as the tendency of modern life to fail to distinguish, to render everything uniform. If language is the basis of everything, and if the basis of language is discrimination (the differentiating among sounds), a neglect of linguistic discrimination is the first step to a neglect of all other distinctions, which is James's real concern, for it will lead to uniformity.

James expresses his resistance to uniformity only two years after the formation of the Ford Motor Company and three years before the production of the first Model Ts, and although he makes no explicit mention of the assembly line, the culture made possible by the assembly line is the real target of James's criticism. One might suppose that in resisting the culture of the assembly line era, James resists the inevitable progress of technology, but this is not true. He unabashedly enjoyed several of the benefits of modernity, including the automobile itself, although he did dislike other modern products, especially advertisements and the modern newspaper, which he blamed for the trend toward uniformity.[51]

More importantly, for James distinctions are what make life and the impressions it offers interesting. Not only does this explain why James does not approve of the tendency he hears to make all sounds the same, but it also explains his disapproval of the "non-existence of any criticism" in modern America. By criticism, James means precisely the ability to discriminate, to distinguish, to perceive differences, all of which he sees missing in modern American culture. Part of the cause for the lack of criticism, in James's view, is the gendered separation of spheres in America, and part of it is the democratic impulse.

In respect to speech, uniformity and the absence of discriminations lead to the feeling James attributes to American women that they are free to speak as they please and do not have to feel "oppressed" by syllables, as his interlocutor appears to argue in the fourth part of "The Speech of American Women" (75–76). The freedom to speak as one pleases can only be a preliminary step to acting as one feels, and this is the real issue behind the examples of impolite behavior that James presents in "The Manners of American Women": the gum chewers on the train (95–96), the loud "bevy of four young, very young girls" (82–83), the surly conductor (84), the ungrateful bicyclist (111–12).[52] Freedom from oppression is an inevitable and desirable result of American democracy, James recognizes, but at the same time not all of democracy's consequences are positive. The three essays raise this issue, a question in the tradition of Tocqueville, of the relation between democratic society and hierarchy: If all people are free, are they really free to act as they please? Social order for James relies on discriminations, but discriminations are inherently hierarchical, which could put social order at odds with democracy (a criticism of democracy at least as old as Thucydides). But while James wants to preserve distinctions, he does not want to throw out democracy. What he does want is to redress the lack of exchange in America on the level of culture and society between men and women.

When James speaks in part 2 of "The Speech of American Women" of American men knowing only "the yell of the stock-exchange or the football-field" (66), he returns to a point he makes in *The American Scene* about the separation of spheres of interest between men and women.[53] James thinks that in America men have abandoned all cultural fields but business to women, and in "The Manners of American Women" he argues that this has had a negative effect on behavior. Fundamental to the view of gender relations that James expresses in "The Manners of American Women" is the sense that men and women "feed off" each other, that they need each other for a sense of how to behave. He is arguing a view of gender relations similar to his theory of language in "The Question of Our Speech" (and not unrelated to the theory of negation in "The Long Wards"), for just as speech relies on contrasts, for example of consonants and vowels, so too in James's view do gender relations rely on the contrasting engagement of men and women with each other in society. The thinking here is similar to the view of negation James presents in "The Long Wards" and "The Question of the Mind," where knowledge of things is in part possible due to an awareness of the opposite or the absence of those things; things are not known only in themselves but in reaction to other things.

While James criticizes a lack of discrimination, an absence of the appreciation of difference, he also criticizes the kind of total separation that results from too much difference. Speech that makes no distinction between what should be different sounds descends to the level of animal utterance, an unenviable prospect. But the gendered separation of spheres represents the opposite extreme, of too much difference. Successful communication depends on differences, but differences within a framework of similarity, and so too does the successful cultural interaction of men and women. As Ross Posnock argues, "James comes to regard the polarized relations between the sexes as an index of American society's limited capacity for mutuality within difference, the tolerating of otherness that responsible citizenship and a vital democratic public life require."[54]

The problem for James with the gendered separation of spheres in the United States is that men and women have no influence on each other in their own, separate domains of business for men and everything else for women. In Europe, men and women correct and inspire each others' social behavior, but American men have abdicated their role as exemplars in anything other than business. There is, therefore, no interchange of behavior or of culture between the genders in America, and James finds this highly lamentable. By publicly indicting American manners with the publication of "The Manners of American Women," James takes upon himself the role that American men have abandoned, making himself the "real" man, the kind of man who can set a corrective example, which in turn incites women to provide further corrections of their own. By presuming to correct American manners, James turns the tables on the more typical American man, the man of business, and asserts his own version of exemplary masculinity, much as he turns the tables on the "manly" British soldiers in "The British Soldier" by transforming them into comic-opera boys.

"The Speech of American Women" begins most deferentially, enumerating and praising the accomplishments of American women, mentioning their marriages to foreign nobles and their fearlessness. By the end of "The Manners of American Women," James has come full circle and contradicts the praise he offered at the beginning of the earlier essay with his example of an ungrateful American bicyclist who fails to show any gratitude for her fellow cyclist's impromptu roadside repair of her bicycle. For every fearless Daisy Miller who wins the hand of a foreign noble, there is also a self-centered "queen" (to use the word James uses, and for which late-twentieth-century Americans would use "princess") like the bicyclist. It is an audacious and perhaps deliberately ironic turn to take in a "woman's magazine" like *Harper's Bazar*.

In the essays occasioned by the 1904–05 trip to America, James frequently mentions the importance of criticism. The examples of careless speech that James presents in "The Speech of American Women" serve to prove the "universal non-existence of any criticism, worthy of the name" (72) in America, and the general "immunity from comment, from any shadow of criticism" (70). He began his public lecture on Balzac by emphasizing the beneficence of the "play of criticism" and defines criticism as "the particular judgment,'... that quantity of opinion, ... that is capable of giving some intelligible account of itself..., this element of the lucid report of impressions received, of estimates formed, of intentions understood, of values attached."[55]

What James means by criticism bears some consideration, for the meaning of the word has evolved during the last century. Today, when academic literary critics "do" criticism, they interpret, and criticism has come to mean the kind of analysis that contributes to interpretation. In the nineteenth century, criticism usually meant evaluation, and it is certainly at least a major part of what criticism meant to James. That the task of criticism was evaluation explains part of the importance to James of discrimination, since evaluation requires the ability to distinguish the value of one object in relation to others. If no differences were distinguishable, then everything would seem uniform, and James holds uniformity in horror. But while James champions an appreciation of a discriminatory kind of criticism, in the articles in this collection he also engages in analysis that leads to interpretation. When he considers the various moves of the major and minor players in the chess match of British geopolitics, they lead him to an understanding of the nature of national and international politics and to the connections among, for example, military events in Africa and Asia and political campaigning at home. When he examines particular habits of speech and manners, his examination leads him to conclusions about the nature and the disadvantages of the gendered separation of spheres in American society. The events of World War I lead James to a number of conclusions that we could call interpretative: the nature of his own relation to the English nation, the value of culture, and the inevitable uncertainty of anything. Even James's one published metaphysical essay, "Is There a Life After Death?," which is part 3 of this collection, is an act of interpretation.[56] This much-neglected essay (and one rarely understood when it is not neglected) is an interpretation that leads to the conclusion that there are different degrees of life, for one can be alive and yet not really live. (Here James repeats the underlying sentiment to the famous admonition in *The Ambassadors:* "Live all you can; it's a mistake not to.")[57] Who's to say that when no longer alive one is no longer living? Both life and the afterlife are matters of personal interpretation.

When James examines the various topics he addresses in the essays in this collection, he analyzes and interprets them and ultimately interprets society itself. This is what he does in his novels and stories too, in fact doubly so, since in his fiction he often portrays characters interpreting the situations in which they find themselves at the same time that he presents to his reader an interpretation of the society represented in the fiction.[58]

One of the best examples of James as a cultural interpreter occurs in the fourth section of "The Manners of American Women." James wonders how the members of the poor, rural societies represented in the stories of Sarah Orne Jewett and Mary Wilkins Freeman could have been so good-natured toward each other as this literature presents them to be. His answer—that a relative equality of economic conditions makes people more friendly to each other—relies on a grasp of the economic and historical situation.

The explanation, when it comes, is touching; since it consists apparently in the fact of the so prolonged and so equal participation of every one in the essential hardness and grimness of the old American condition. Life was long bare and strenuous and difficult, but was so for all alike, with the fortunate exceptions, the representatives of privilege and exemption, few in number, and not so remarkably fortunate, after all, nor so armed with resources. People could thus have the sense and the imagination of each other's states in a much more unbroken way than in "Europe," where great differences of state had long since grown up, and where, accordingly, with the danger of taking liberties operating as a check to spontaneity, the reflective and calculated freedoms were much more numerous, but both the independence and the dependence much less acute. (106–7)

In this passage James's many interests most strikingly coalesce. James addresses a social matter—manners—but in relation to literature—Jewett's stories—and explains the behavior that intrigues him through an attention to economics (the comparative leveling of wealth in "the old American condition"), to class differences (or rather the relative lack of them), and to social history (the difficulty of early American life). Since James grounds the differences in behavior in America and Europe in social and economic conditions, this passage is perhaps the clearest example in this collection of essays of James writing what we today call cultural criticism, which as some cultural critics define it, "should show works in reference to other works, economic contexts, or broad social discourses (about childbirth, women's education, rural decay, etc.) within whose contexts the work makes sense."[59] This is precisely what James does.

If evaluation and interpretation are both components of the task of criticism for James, one must also ask what, for him, is the object of criticism, on what does one perform criticism? One goal of this collection of essays is to demonstrate that James performed criticism on a range of subjects: world politics, the relation between gender roles and speech and behavior, the impact of war, and metaphysics. Today when James is called a critic, the assumption is that he was a literary critic who dabbled in art and drama criticism and wrote a few forgotten, miscellaneous articles on other subjects. But this is not how James saw himself, for critics of his time did not necessarily perceive their subject matter as so rigidly categorized and demarcated.

Matthew Arnold, perhaps the foremost critic in late nineteenth-century English letters, exemplifies the scope of criticism at that time. But today Arnold is a controversial figure, for while he saw that what we today call history, philosophy, literature, religion, and art as all subjects for criticism, he also believed that there was a self-evident distinction between the best of culture and all the rest.[60] One of the results of the evolution of the university during the last century has been the increased compartmentalization of the subjects of criticism, as a result of which history, art, literature, political science, economics, and sociology have become increasingly distinct and specialized. One significant backlash against this trend has been the growth of cultural studies, and although the proponents of cultural studies, or cultural criticism as it is sometimes called, vary considerably in their actual methods, they share a disregard for the high culture/low culture divide and for academic disciplinary boundaries, both of which they seek to break down. For his formative role in establishing the distinction between high and low culture, Arnold often is the bogeyman of the cultural critics, but it is also true that the cultural critics share with Arnold a sense of the variety and range of appropriate subjects for criticism.

It has often been tempting but never entirely accurate to perceive James as a close copy of Arnold, and as a proponent of high culture over low. Some recent James scholars have demonstrated that the high culture/low culture distinction does not apply to his fiction, for James composed his novels and stories in the context of both popular and eclectic fictional traditions.[61] Furthermore, as a critic, James's professed goals are not quite the same as Arnold's. In a famous statement, Arnold pronounced that the "business" of criticism was "to know the best that is known and thought in the world, and by in its turn making this known, to create a current of true and fresh ideas."[62] Many historians of criticism today find this statement controversial because Arnold seems to think that what makes "the best that is known and thought" is self-evident. It is no surprise, then, that many see Arnold as an elitist.

For James the function of criticism is not the same; it is to tease out the great variations that life offers, so while he may have made hierarchical distinctions, he would not have viewed culture narrowly. It is not the object of criticism that is self-evident to James but the pleasure derived from it. He makes no pronouncements limiting the range of the critics' attention; he takes it for granted that the impressions life offers, and the more varied the better, are what make life most interesting. The value of the idea of France, we remember in the passage quoted above from "France," is that it helps us "to make the earth a friendlier, an easier, and *especially a more various sojourn*" (148–49, emphasis added). What enhances the appreciation of variety, of distinctions, against the modern tendency toward uniformity—but without going to the opposite extreme of total differ-ence—is what matters to James in criticism.

James's most significant impact as a literary critic was in his championing of prose fiction as an art form as worthy of attention and acclaim as poetry or the fine arts. Championing this cause is the explicit aim of "The Art of Fiction" (1884), one of James's best-known literary essays. While it is tempting to think today of James as exemplary of "high" art, the fact is that the art he championed was not at the time universally accepted as "high." The perception of the novel during most of the nineteenth century was not unlike the perception today, in the late twentieth century, of movies or television shows. Just as these today are condescendingly considered entertainment more than art, so too, a hundred and fifty years ago, novels were thought of as entertainment. That the perception of the novel as a valid art form has changed to the extent it has is at least in part a result of James's efforts (both as literary critic and as fiction writer). Yet it is important to remember that in proselytizing for fiction as an art, James was at the time in a position not too unlike that today of a cultural critic who, like Terry Eagleton, "rejects the dogmatism which would insist that Proust is always more worthy of study than television advertisements" and to whom "it may seem best to look at Proust and *King Lear*, or at children's television programmes or popular romances or avant-garde films."[63]

The kinds of distinctions that cultural critics today are committed to dismantling were in fact not operative for James in his time; other distinctions were. Just as cultural critics of today argue that what is often and derisively categorized as popular entertainment deserves the same consideration as what is generally acknowledged as art, so James argued in his day that prose fiction deserved as much consideration as the acknowledged art forms.

A difference between "high" and "low" art has little relevance for the essays in this collection. A glimpse at the range of periodicals in which James published them and at some of the other contributions juxtaposed against James's would be surprising to anyone believing the cliché of Henry James as the "great," high-minded artist. James contributed the writings on World War I not just to the *New York Times* and the *Times Literary Supplement*, but also to the *New York Sun*, the *New York World*, and the *Boston Herald*. The version of "The Question of the Mind" published in the *New York Sun*, for example, appeared opposite a horrific account of Russian mistreatment of Jewish war refugees. It might seem unusual to read Henry James in such a context, even so coincidental a one as this, but part of the point of this collection of essays is to suggest that such a context is not all that surprising. While *The Nation*, to which James contributed most of the early essays in this collection, was at the time quite prestigious, "Is There a Life After Death?," "The Speech of American Women," and "The Manners of American Women" all appeared in the "women's" magazine *Harper's Bazar*. The final sentences of "Is There a Life After Death?" appear on the same page as an article about "A Novel Sewing-Chair" that features two illustrations of a "pretty little brocade chair" and advertisements for *Harper's Bazar* dress patterns and embroidery designs, boys' books from Harper and Brothers, infant wear, "the new French turban style of hair dressing," and ostrich feathers.[64] The end of the second installment of "The Manners of American Women" appears on the same page as a poem by Mary J.

Serrano entitled "Love."[65] Constance Johnson's poem "Experience" shares the same page as the conclusion of "The Speech of American Women."[66]

The essays in this collection appear in highly varied juxtapositions even in book publications. "The Question of the Mind" was published in England in a pamphlet that also included A. Clutton-Brock's essay, "England," reprinted from the *Times Literary Supplement*, which argues that the English tendency toward self-criticism is in fact one of the great values of the English character that distinguishes Englishmen from Germans.[67] "France" appears in Winifred Stephens's collection, *The Book of France*, which includes another essay called "France," by Rudyard Kipling, and essays in French by such contributors as Anatole France, Rémy de Gourmont, Pierre Loti, Anna de Noailles, Maurice Barrès, and André Gide, with accompanying translations into English by Thomas Hardy, H. G. Wells, Lady Randolph Churchill, Henry James, Edmund Gosse, and others. "The Long Wards" appears in Edith Wharton's collection *The Book of the Homeless*, along with contributions by Wharton herself, Barrès, Sarah Bernhardt, Paul Bourget, Rupert Brooke, Paul Claudel, Jean Cocteau, Joseph Conrad, Eleonora Duse, John Galsworthy, Edmund Gosse, Thomas Hardy, William Dean Howells, Francis Jammes, Maurice Maeterlinck, Anna de Noailles, Theodore Roosevelt, Edmond Rostand, George Santayana, Igor Stravinsky, Mrs. Humphrey Ward, Barrett Wendell, and W. B. Yeats, among others. And the collection *In After Days: Thoughts on the Future Life*, included along with "Is There a Life After Death?" essays on the same subject by Howells, Thomas W. Higginson, Julia Ward Howe (the author of "The Battle Hymn of the Republic"), the novelist Elizabeth Stuart Phelps, the one-time owner of the *New York Evening Post*, John Bigelow, and Henry Alden, the editor of *Harper's Monthly*. The point of mentioning these juxtapositions for James's contributions is to show how varied were the contexts in which his essays found their way into print.

The overall purpose of this collection of essays is to provide evidence that Henry James should be thought of as a cultural critic, as that term is understood by academic scholars today. James's nonfiction is often classified as literary criticism, drama criticism, art criticism, travel writing, biography, and autobiography, but I have tried to suggest—and the essays in this collection should underscore—that the variety of subjects and interests in James's non-fiction strains the usual definitions of such classifications, definitions which were not as restrictive a century ago. The critics of James's time who are still widely read today (Thomas Carlyle, John Ruskin, Matthew Arnold, Oscar Wilde, to cite only a few British ones) saw culture more broadly defined as the object of criticism, and in no case is this more true than with Henry James, who subjected literature of all types, painting and sculpture, travel, politics, gender, and religion to his analytical gaze. Since James's death, his writing on literature, art, and travel has been accessible through modern reprints, but the writing on politics, gender, and religion has not. This volume serves to correct that deficiency.

NOTES

1. C. L. D., "Mr. Henry James on England," *The Observer* 18 Apr. 1915: 14.

2. *The Complete Notebooks of Henry James*, ed. Leon Edel and Lyall H. Powers (New York: Oxford Univ. Press, 1987) 40.

3. See Leon Edel's *Henry James: The Master, 1901–1916* (Philadelphia: Lippincott, 1972) 237–38, 241–42.

4. Henry James, "London at Midsummer," *Lippincott's Magazine* Nov. 1877: 603–11. James reprinted this article in both *Portraits of Places* (London: Macmillan, 1883) and *English Hours* (London: Heinemann, 1905).

5. "London at Midsummer," *Collected Travel Writings: Great Britain and America: English Hours; The American Scene; Other Travels* (New York: Library of America, 1993) 144–45.

6. A major inspiration for this collection is Ross Posnock's work, *The Trial of Curiosity: Henry James, William James, and the Challenge of Modernity* (New York: Oxford Univ. Press, 1991), which argues that the "procedures of literary canonization" have enshrined "a reified image of James the master formalist" and that this canonization "has repressed" a perception of "Henry James as the peripatetic cultural critic animated by restless curiosity" and as "the cultural analyst of modernity" (21–22). The fourth and the beginning of the sixth chapters of Posnock's book (80–104, 141–55) provide excellent accounts of the historical development in James criticism of what I am calling the clichéd view of Henry James of today.

7. James's Paris contributions to the *Tribune* were collected as *Parisian Sketches* (New York: New York Univ. Press, 1957; rpt. New York: Collier, 1961, and Westport CT: Greenwood, 1978).

8. Edel and Powers, eds. *Complete Notebooks* 40.

9. The complete "American Letters" for *Literature* are included in *The American Essays* (New York: Vintage, 1956; rpt. Princeton: Princeton Univ. Press, 1989) and in *Literary Criticism: Essays on Literature, American Writers, English Writers* (ed. Leon Edel [New York: Library of America, 1984]). Two of the nine "London Notes" James wrote for *Harper's Weekly* in 1897 were first reprinted during James's life in *Notes on Novelists* (London: Dent, 1914; New York: Scribner's, 1914) as "London Notes, July 1897" and "London Notes, August 1897." One was reprinted as "The Blight of the Drama" in *The Scenic Art: Notes on Acting and Drama, 1872–1901* (ed. Allan Wade [New Brunswick NJ: Rutgers Univ. Press, 1948]); and two, dated 15 January and 3 March, were collected for the first time in Edel's *Literary Criticism: Essays on Literature*. Parts of the other four "London Notes" have been reprinted in *Notes on Novelists*, Wade's *Scenic Art*, *The Painter's Eye* (ed. John L. Sweeney [London: Rupert Hart-Davis, 1956]) and Edel's *Literary Criticism: Essays on Literature*, but they are available in their entirety only in their original periodical appearance. The nine articles have never been collected together in a single volume.

10. Henry James to Alice James, 15 Sept. 1878, *Henry James Letters*, ed. Leon Edel, 4 vols. (Cambridge MA: Harvard Univ. Press, 1974–84) 2:186.

11. Edward Said, *Culture and Imperialism* (New York: Knopf, 1993) 6.

12. In a 29 May 1878 letter to his father, James wrote: "I went down to Aldershot the other day to spend forty-eight hours at the Pakenhams'—they are situated there in a 'hut'—and to assist at the review on the Queen's birthday. It was a charming episode; but I have written something about Aldershot, so I won't descant" (Edel, ed., *Henry James Letters* 2:176).

13. Said, *Culture and Imperialism* xiii.

14. Patrick Brantlinger, "Victorians and Africans: The Genealogy of the Myth of the Dark Continent," *"Race," Writing, and Difference*, ed. Henry Louis Gates, Jr. (Chicago: Chicago Univ. Press, 1986) 211.

15. Brantlinger, "Victorians and Africans" 185–222.

16. Brantlinger, "Victorians and Africans" 193–94.

17. During his 1905 visit to Washington, James dined at the White House, where he was seated two seats to the right of the incumbent, Theodore Roosevelt. The evening is supposed to have passed pleasantly, but James and Roosevelt had previously engaged in a war of words. Roosevelt had called James a "miserable little snob" and an "undersized man of letters who … with his delicate, effeminate sensitiveness … cannot play a man's part among men" (Fred Kaplan, *Henry James: The Imagination of Genius* [New York: Morrow, 1992] 488), while James, in his 23 April 1898 "American Letter," had complained of Roosevelt's "puerility" (Edel, ed., *Literary Criticism: Essays on Literature* 665) and, in a letter of 1901 to Jessie Allen, wrote that Roosevelt was "a dangerous and ominous Jingo" (Edel, ed., *Henry James Letters* 4:202).

18. Adeline Tintner calls the sense of inadequacy "a burden of guilt" from which James could only "partially relieve himself" at the end of his life ("Henry James and the First World War: The Release from Repression," in *Literature and War: Reflections and Refractions*, Papers of the 1984 Monterey Institute of International Studies Symposium on Comparative Literature and International Studies, ed. Elizabeth W. Trahan [Monterey: Monterey Institute of International Studies, 1985] 169–70). Leon Edel writes that for the young Henry James the Civil War "call to arms provoked an acute conflict. Temperamentally unsuited for soldiering, unable to endure violence, he had long ago substituted acute and close observation of life for active participation in it" (Leon Edel, *Henry James: The Untried Years, 1843–1870* [Philadelphia: Lippincott, 1953] 170). Edel adds: "To remain at home…, while the great hurricane of the fratricidal war swept over the nation, could indeed 'in no light pass for graceful.' Henry James felt acutely that he had to 'make some show of life'" (190). Fred Kaplan, in his biography of James, argues in a vein similar to Edel's that a back injury sustained while helping put out a fire early in the war allowed James "to create an interesting personal history to substitute for the war experience that apparently he preferred not to engage directly" (*Imagination of Genius* 56). Kaplan adds that in respect to World War I, James felt "none of the ambivalence that he had felt … about the American Civil War" (556).

19. James Eli Adams, *Dandies and Desert Saints: Styles of Victorian Masculinity* (Ithaca NY: Cornell Univ. Press, 1995) 2.

20. E. Anthony Rotundo, *American Manhood: Transformations in Masculinity from the Revolution to the Modern Era* (New York: Basic Books, 1993) 20. By calling himself a "gamin" and the British soldiers "boys," James further undermines the soldiers' masculinity in comparison to his own. "Gamin" found its way from an eighteenth-century eastern French dialect (*Petit Robert: Dictionnaire de la langue française*) into English in the second half of the nineteenth century (*Oxford English Dictionary*). Its most famous use in French, a use that James would have known, is in describing Gavroche, the resourceful, independent child of the streets in Victor Hugo's *Les Misérables*. Hugo offers twelve general chapters on "le gamin," emphasizing his resourceful street smarts and his centrality to the greatness of Paris, as an introduction to Gavroche (*Les Misérables*, 3 vols. [Paris: Garnier-Flammarion, 1967–79] 2:104–22). By making himself a "gamin" and the soldiers only "boys," James puts himself above them, for as a gamin he is not just any boy.

21. Sheldon M. Novick, *Henry James: The Young Master* (New York: Random House, 1996) 109–11. Novick's hypothesis has been hotly contested. See Millicent Bell's *Times Literary Supplement* review of Novick's biography, "The Divine, the Unique: A Suggestion of 'Active Love' in Henry James's Attachments to Men," 6 Dec. 1996, 3–4; Novick's response in the same magazine, "Henry James's Life and Work," 20 Dec. 1996, 17; Edel's review of Novick in the online publication *Slate*, "Henry James Henry James," 11 Dec. 1996 (http://www.slate.com); and the acrimonious exchanges among Novick, Kaplan, and Edel that followed in *State* under the title "Henry James's Love Life," 18 Dec. 1996, 20 Dec. 1996, 30 Dec. 1996, 6 Jan. 1997, 12 Jan. 1997, 17 Jan. 1997, 23 Jan. 1997, 29 Jan. 1997.

22. Edward Prime-Stevenson (aka Xavier Mayne), *The Intersexes: A History of Simisexualism as a Problem in Social Life* (London, 1908; rpt. New York: Arno, 1975) 220. For general comments on soldiers' moonlighting as prostitutes, see Prime-Stevenson 212–23; J. R. Ackerley, *My Father and Myself* (New York: Poseidon, 1968) 135–40; James Gardiner, *A Class Apart: The Private Pictures of Montague Glover* (London: Serpent's Tail, 1992) 50–53; Havelock Ellis and John Addington Symonds, *Sexual Inversion* (1897; rpt. New York: Arno, 1975) 9–10; Neil Bartlett, *Who Was That Man? A Present for Mr. Oscar Wilde* (London: Serpent's Tail, 1988) 126–27; David A. Boxwell, " 'Between Idealism and Brutality': Desire, Conflict, and the British Experience of the Great War," Ph.D. diss., Rutgers, 1995, 311–16.

23. Kaplan sums up an account of James's busy activities thus: "At last he did his Civil War service" (*Imagination of Genius* 555).

24. *Cornhill Magazine* published "Mr. & Mrs. Fields" in England in its July 1915 issue (29–43), and *Atlantic Monthly* published it in the United States as "Mr. and Mrs. James T. Fields" the same month (21–31). The July 1915 *Nation* included "The Founding of the 'Nation': Recollections of the 'Fairies' that Attended Its Birth" (44–45). All three of these essays have been reprinted in recent collections of James's prose. The unfinished version of *The Middle Years* was published in late 1917 (*Scribner's Magazine*, Oct. 1917: 465–76, Nov. 1917: 608–15; New York: Scribner's, 1917; London: Collins, 1917). Brooke's *Letters*

from America, with James's introduction, appeared in America (New York: Scribner's) and in England (London: Sidgwick and Jackson) in 1916.

25. "Within the Rim," "Refugees in Chelsea" (the English newspaper version of "Refugees in England"), "The American Volunteer Motor-Ambulance Corps in France," "France," and "The Long Wards" were collected in *Within the Rim and Other Essays, 1914–15* (London: Collins, 1918; rpt. Freeport NY: Books for Libraries, 1968). "The Question of the Mind," "Refugees in England," "Within the Rim," and "The Long Wards" were published together in *Collected Travel Writings: Great Britain and America; English Hours, The American Scene, Other Travels* (New York: Library of America, 1993), and "The American Volunteer Motor-Ambulance Corps in France" and "France" were published in *Collected Travel Writings: The Continent; A Little Tour in France, Italian Hours, Other Travels* (New York: Library of America, 1993).

26. Henry James, *Notes of a Son and Brother, Autobiography*, ed. Frederick W. Dupee (Princeton: Princeton Univ. Press, 1983) 420–27.

27. James, *Notes of a Son and Brother* 421.

28. See Edel, *Untried Years* 167–73, and Kaplan, *Imagination of Genius* 53–56. For comments particularly on the similarity of James's wartime visits to soldiers to Whitman's, see Edel, *The Master* 516; Kaplan, *Imagination of Genius* 53, 555; Novick, *Young Master* 81–82; and Tintner, "Henry James and the First World War" 174, 179.

29. Of Zola's novel of the Franco-Prussian War of 1870–71, James wrote in 1903: "It takes its place with Tolstoi's very much more universal but very much less composed and condensed epic as an incomparably human picture of war.... I recall the effect [reading *La Débâcle*] then produced on me as a really luxurious act of submission" (Henry James, "Emile Zola," *Literary Criticism: French Writers, Other European Writers, The Prefaces to the New York Edition*, ed. Leon Edel [New York: Library of America, 1984] 898).

James wrote "The American Volunteer Motor-Ambulance Corps in France" between Nov. 21 and Nov. 24, according to his amanuensis, Theodora Bosanquet; see "Some Dates from my Diary which may serve as tacks for the picture of Henry James at Work," Theodora Bosanquet Papers, Houghton Library, Harvard Univ. (bMS Eng 1213.2 [3]) 20.

30. James began writing "Within the Rim" in early March 1915 and continued to work on it until July of that same year, according to Theodora Bosanquet; see Bosanquet, "Some Dates from my Diary" (bMS Eng 1213.2 [3]) 21–22.

31. Ezra Pound, "Hugh Selwyn Mauberley," *Selected Poems* (New York: New Directions, 1957) 64.

32. According to Theodora Bosanquet, James wrote "The Long Wards" between May and July 1915; see Bosanquet, "Some Dates from my Diary" (bMS Eng 1213.2 [3]) 22.

33. Tintner, "Henry James and the First World War" 170, 173, 174.

34. Henry James to Rhoda Broughton, 10 Aug. 1914, Edel, ed., *Henry James Letters* 4:713.

35. Edel, *The Master* 512.

36. According to the diary of Theodora Bosanquet, this occurred on Thursday, 24 Sept. 1914; see the Theodora Bosanquet diary, Theodora Bosanquet Papers, Houghton Library, Harvard Univ. (bMS Eng 1213.1 [10]).

37. "Mr. Henry James and the War." *The Observer* 11 Apr. 1915: 6.

38. See the Theodora Bosanquet Papers, Houghton Library, Harvard Univ. The two passages on the *Times* interview appear in "Diary Notes 1912–1916" for 1 March 1915 (bMS Eng 1213.2 [1]) and "Some Dates from my Diary" (bMS Eng 1213.2 [3]) 21.

39. The only reason to doubt Bosanquet's account of the interview is that the two passages in her papers about the interview appear in typed summaries she made for Leon Edel about half a century later (Edel's account appears in *The Master*, 527); the original diary entries are not part of the Harvard collection and apparently have not survived.

40. "Glenn Gould Interviews Glenn Gould About Glenn Gould," *The Glenn Gould Reader*, ed. Tim Page (New York: Knopf, 1984) 313–28.

41. Posnock, *Trial of Curiosity* 136.

42. René Descartes, *Meditations on First Philosophy*, in *Discourse on Method and Meditations on First Philosophy*, trans. Donald A. Cress (Indianapolis: Hackett, 1985) 50, 52–53.

43. Posnock, who speaks of "the heterodox audacity of [James's] self-representation" (*Trial of Curiosity* 168), labels as "mimetic" what I am describing here as the fluidity and theatricality of identity (167–93).

44. Posnock, *Trial of Curiosity* 58; for more on the Cartesian vs. the Postmodern self, see also *Trial of Curiosity* 168–74, 221–23.

45. Posnock, *Trial of Curiosity* 59.

46. Indeed Posnock cites C. S. Peirce as an important nineteenth-century opponent of the Cartesian, monadic self and Henry James Sr. as an influence on Peirce; see *Trial of Curiosity* 174, 295 n.15.

47. *The American Scene* is available in *Collected Travel Writings: Great Britain and America: English Hours; The American Scene; Other Travels* (New York: Library of America, 1993) and *The American Scene* (New York: Penguin, 1994).

48. "The Question of Our Speech" was published in *Appleton's Booklovers Magazine* 6 (Aug. 1905): 199–210, and in *The Question of Our Speech; The Lesson of Balzac: Two Lectures* (Boston: Houghton Mifflin–Riverside Press, 1905) 3–52. (Haskell House of New York reprinted the Houghton Mifflin edition in 1972.) Its only other book publication is in *French Writers and American Women*, ed. Peter Buitenhuis (Branford CT: Compass, 1960) 18–31.

49. The two *Harper's Bazar* essays have been reprinted twice: first in Buitenhuis's *French Writers and American Women* (32–53, 54–80) and then in *The Speech and Manners of American Women*, ed. E. S. Riggs, introd. Inez Martinez (Lancaster PA: Lancaster House, 1973). For a history of James's relations with *Harper's Bazar* and his letters to its editor, Elizabeth Jordan, on the subject of the two essays (among other things), see Leon Edel and Lyall H. Powers, "Henry James and the *Bazar* Letters," *Bulletin of the New York Public Library* 62 (1958): 75–103.

50. It is no coincidence that Tzvetan Todorov refers to the same point in "The Question of Our Speech" to support his point in *Introduction à la littérature fantastique* that language is "the structuring agent" of human relations ([Paris: Seuil, 1970] 147).

51. Martha Banta's *Taylored Lives: Narrative Productions in the Age of Taylor, Veblen, and Ford*

(Chicago: Univ. of Chicago Press, 1993) gives an excellent account of the homogeneity of assembly line culture, and particularly in relation to Henry James (esp. 274–77).

52. John Ruskin offers an account similar to James's of two unruly young American women on a train in Italy in letter 20 (August 1872) of *Fors Clavigera: Letters to the Workmen and Labourers of Great Britain*, 4 vols. (1886; rpt. New York: Greenwood, 1968) 1:269–70.

53. Rotundo explains the importance of the doctrine of the separation of spheres in *American Manhood*, esp. 22–25.

54. Posnock, *Trial of Curiosity* 259.

55. Henry James, "The Lesson of Balzac," in Edel, ed., *Literary Criticism: French Writers* 115.

56. This essay has only been republished once since its original 1910 periodical and book publications. F. O. Matthiessen included the book version of the essay (with two corrections) in *The James Family: Including Selections from the Writings of Henry James, Senior, William, Henry, and Alice James* (1947; rpt. New York: Vintage, 1980) 602–14.

57. Henry James, *The Ambassadors*, ed. S. P. Rosenbaum (New York: Norton, 1964) 132.

58. See, for example, William W. Stowe's *Balzac, James, and the Realistic Novel* (Princeton NJ: Princeton Univ. Press, 1983) for the centrality of the protagonist's interpretation in James's novels.

59. Ross C. Murfin, "What is Cultural Criticism?" *The House of Mirth: A Case Study in Contemporary Criticism*, ed. Shari Benstock (New York: Bedford–St. Martin's, 1994) 327.

60. See Gerald Graff and Bruce Robbins, "Cultural Criticism," *Redrawing the Boundaries: The Transformation of English and American Literary Studies*, ed. Stephen Greenblatt and Giles Gunn (New York: Modern Language Association of America, 1992) 427–28.

61. See Marcia Jacobson, *Henry James and the Mass Market* (University: Univ. of Alabama Press, 1983), Anne T. Margolis, *Henry James and the Problem of Audience: An International Act* (Ann Arbor MI: UMI Research Press, 1985), Michael Anesko, *"Friction With the Market": Henry James and the Profession of Authorship* (New York: Oxford Univ. Press, 1986), and my own *Reading Henry James in French Cultural Contexts* (DeKalb: Northern Illinois Univ. Press, 1995). Posnock's *Trial of Curiosity* argues throughout that James did not belong to a "genteel" intellectual tradition associated with Arnold but in fact "seems closer to the younger generation of self-conscious modernists who declared 'the futility of the Arnoldian ideal' " (146).

62. Matthew Arnold, "The Function of Criticism at the Present Time," *Lectures and Essays in Criticism* (Ann Arbor: Univ. of Michigan Press, 1962), vol. 3 of *The Complete Prose Works of Matthew Arnold*, ed. R. H. Super (1960–77) 270.

63. Terry Eagleton, *Literary Theory: An Introduction* (Minneapolis: Univ. of Minnesota Press, 1983) 211.

64. *Harper's Bazar* 44 (Feb. 1910): 129.

65. *Harper's Bazar* 41 (May 1907): 458.

66. *Harper's Bazar* 41 (Feb. 1907): 117.

67. A. Clutton-Brock, "England," *Times Literary Supplement* 19 Nov. 1914, 1.

Henry James on Culture

I

Essays about British Geopolitics,
1878–1879

The British Soldier

I allude to the British soldier, more especially, as I lately observed and admired him at Aldershot, where, just now, he appears to particular advantage; but at any time during the past twelvemonth—since England and Russia have stood glaring at each other across the prostrate body of the expiring yet reviving Turk—this actually ornamental and potentially useful personage has been picturesquely, agreeably conspicuous. I say "agreeably," speaking from my own humble point of view, because I confess to a lively admiration of the military class. I exclaim, cordially, with Offenbach's Grand Duchess, "Ah, oui, j'aime les militaires!" Mr. Ruskin has said somewhere, very naturally, that he could never resign himself to living in a country in which, as in the United States, there should be no old castles. Putting aside the old castles, I should say, like Mr. Ruskin, that life loses a certain indispensable charm in a country destitute of an apparent standing army. Certainly, the army may be too apparent, too importunate, too terrible a burden to the state and to the conscience of the philosophic observer. This is the case, without a doubt, just now in the bristling empires of the Continent. In Germany and France, in Russia and Italy, there are many more soldiers than are needed to make the taxpayer thrifty or the lover of the picturesque happy. The huge armaments of continental Europe are an oppressive and sinister spectacle, and I have rarely derived a high order of entertainment from the sight of even the largest masses of homesick conscripts. The *chair à canon*—the cannon-meat—as they aptly term it in French, has always seemed to me dumbly, appealingly conscious of its destiny. I have seen it in course of preparation—seen it salted and dressed and packed and labelled, as it were, for consumption. In that

From *Lippincott's Magazine* 22 (Aug. 1878): 214-21.

marvellous France, indeed, which bears all burdens lightly, and whose good spirits and absence of the tragic *pose* alone prevent us from calling her constantly heroic, the army scarcely seems to be the heavy charge that it must be in fact. The little red-legged soldiers, always present and always moving, are as thick as the field-flowers in an abundant harvest, and amid the general brightness and mobility of French life they strike one at times simply as cheerful tokens of the national exuberance and fecundity. But in Germany and Italy the national levies impart a lopsided aspect to society: they seem to drag it under water. They hang like a millstone round its neck, so that it can't move: it has to sit still, looking wistfully at the long, forward road which it is unable to measure.

England, which is fortunate in so many things, is fortunate in her well-fed mercenaries, who suggest none of the dismal reflections provoked by the great foreign armies. It is true, of course, that they fail to suggest some of the inspiring ones. If Germany and France are burdened, at least they are defended—at least they are armed for conflict and victory. There seems to be a good deal of doubt as to how far this is true of the nation which has hitherto been known as the pre-eminently pugnacious one. Where France and Germany and Russia count by hundreds, England counts by tens; and it is only, strictly speaking, on the good old principle that one Englishman can buffet a dozen foreigners that a very hopeful view of an Anglo-continental collision can be maintained. This good old principle is far from having gone out of fashion: you may hear it proclaimed to an inspiring tune any night in the week in the London music-halls. One summer evening, in the country, an English gentleman was telling me about his little boy, a rosy, sturdy, manly child whom I had already admired, and whom he depicted as an infant Hercules. The surrounding influences at the moment were picturesque. An ancient lamp was suspended from the ceiling of the hall; the large door stood open upon a terrace; and outside the big, dense treetops were faintly stirring in the starlight. My companion dilated upon the pluck and muscle, the latent pugnacity, of his dear little son, and told me how bravely already he doubled his infant fist. There was a kind of Homeric simplicity about it. From this he proceeded to wider considerations, and observed that the English child was of necessity the bravest and sturdiest in the world, for the plain reason that he was the germ of the English man. What the English man was we of course both knew, but, as I was a stranger, my friend explained the matter in detail. He was a person whom, in the ordinary course of human irritation, every one else was afraid of. Nowhere but in England were such men made—men who could hit out as soon as think, and knock over persons of inferior race as you would brush away flies. They were afraid of nothing: the sentiment of hesitation to inflict a blow under rigidly proper circumstances was unknown to them. English soldiers and sailors in a row carried everything before them:

foreigners didn't know what to make of such fellows, and were afraid to touch them. A couple of Englishmen were a match for a foreign mob. My friend's little boy was made like a statue: his little arms and legs were quite of the right sort. This was the greatness of England, and of this there was an infinite supply. The light, as I say, was dim in the great hall, and the rustle of the oaks in the park was almost audible. Their murmur seemed to offer a sympathetic undertone to the honest conversation of my companion, and I sat there as humble a ministrant to the simple and beautiful idea of British valor as the occasion could require. I made the reflection—by which I must justify my anecdote—that the ancient tradition as to the personal fighting-value of the individual Englishman flourishes in high as well as in low life, and forms a common ground of contact between them; with the simple difference that at the music-halls it is more poetically expressed than in the country-houses.

I am grossly ignorant of military matters, and hardly know the names of regiments or the designations of their officers; yet, as I said at the beginning of these remarks, I am always very much struck by the sight of a uniform. War is a detestable thing, and I would willingly see the sword dropped into its scabbard for ever. Only I should plead that in its sheathed condition the sword should still be allowed to play a certain part. Actual war is detestable, but there is something agreeable in possible war; and I have been thankful that I should have found myself on British soil at a moment when it was resounding to the tread of regiments. If the British army is small, it has during the last six months been making the most of itself. The rather dusky spectacle of British life has been lighted up by the presence in the foreground of considerable masses of that vivid color which is more particularly associated with the protection of British interests. The sunshine has appeared to rest upon scattered clusters of red-coats, while the background has been enveloped in a sort of chaotic and fuliginous dimness. The red-coats, according to their number, have been palpable and definite, though a great many other things have been inconveniently vague. At the beginning of the year, when Parliament was opened in the queen's name, the royal speech contained a phrase which that boisterous organ of the war-party, the *Pall Mall Gazette*, pronounced "sickening" in its pusillanimity. Her Majesty alluded to the necessity, in view of the complications in the East, of the government taking into consideration the making of "preparations for precaution." This was certainly an ineffective way of expressing a thirst for Russian blood, but the royal phraseology is never very felicitous; and the "preparations for precaution" have been extremely interesting. Indeed, for a person conscious of a desire to look into what may be called the psychology of politics, I can imagine nothing more interesting than the general spectacle of the public conduct of England during the last two years. I have watched it with a good deal of the same sort of entertainment with which one watches a five-act drama from a comfortable place in the stalls. There are moments of discomfort in the course of such a performance: the theatre is hot and crowded, the situations are too prolonged, the play seems to drag, some of the actors have no great talent. But the piece, as a whole, is intensely dramatic, the argument is striking, and you would not for the world leave your place before the dénouement is reached. My own pleasure all winter, I confess, has been partly marred by a bad conscience: I have felt a kind of shame at my inability to profit by a brilliant opportunity to make up my mind. This inability, however, was extreme, and my regret was not lightened by seeing every one about me set an admirable example of decision, and even of precision. Every one about me was either a Russian or a Turk, the Turks, however, being greatly the more numerous. It appeared necessary to one's self-respect to assume some foreign personality, and I felt keenly, for a while, the embarrassment of choice. At last it occurred to me simply that as an American I might be an Englishman; and the reflection became afterward very profitable.

When once I had undertaken the part, I played it with what the French call *conviction*. There are many obvious reasons why the rôle, at such a time as this, should accommodate itself to the American capacity. The feeling of race is strong, and a good American could not but desire that, with the eyes of Europe fixed upon it, the English race should make a passable figure. There would be much fatuity in his saying that at such a moment he deemed it of importance to give it the support of his own striking attitude, but there is at least a kind of filial piety in this feeling moved to draw closer to it. To see how the English race would behave, and to hope devoutly it would behave well,—this was the occupation of my thoughts. Old England was in a difficult pass, and all the world was watching her. The good American feels in all sorts of ways about Old England: the better American he is, the more acute are his moods, the more lively his variations. He can be, I think, everything but indifferent; and, for myself, I never hesitated to let my emotions play all along the scale. In the morning, over the *Times*, it was extremely difficult to make up one's mind. The *Times* seemed very mealy-mouthed—that impression, indeed, it took no great cleverness to gather—but the dilemma lay between one's sense of the brutality and cynicism of the usual utterances of the Turkish party and one's perception of the direful ills which Russian conquest was so liberally scattering abroad. The brutality of the Turkish tone, as I sometimes caught an echo of it in the talk of chance interlocutors, was not such as to quicken that race-feeling to which I just now alluded. English society is a tremendously comfortable affair, and the crudity of the sarcasm that I frequently heard levelled by its fortunate members at the victims of the fashionable Turk was such as to produce a good deal of resentful meditation. It was provoking to hear a rosy English gentleman, who had just been into Leicestershire for a week's hunting, deliver the opinion that the vulgar Bulgarians had really not been massacred half enough; and this in spite of the fact that one had long since made the observation that for a good plain absence of mawkish sentimentality a certain type of rosy English gentleman is nowhere to be matched. On the other hand, it was not very comfortable to think of the measureless misery in which these interesting populations were actually steeped, and one had to admit that the deliberate invasion of a country which professed the strongest desire to live in peace with its invaders was at least a rather striking anomaly. Such a course could only be justified by the most gratifying results, and brilliant consequences as yet had not begun to bloom upon the blood-drenched fields of Bulgaria.

To see this heavy-burdened, slow-moving Old England making up her mind was an edifying spectacle. It was not over-fanciful to say to one's self, in spite of the difficulties of the problem and the (in a certain sense) evenly-balanced scales, that this was a great crisis in her history, that she stood at the crossing of the ways, and that according as she put forth her right hand or her left would her greatness stand or wane. It was possible to imagine that in her huge, dim, collective consciousness she felt an oppressive sense of moral responsibility, that she too murmured to herself that she was on trial, and that, through the mists of bewilderment and the tumult of party cries, she begged to be enlightened. The sympathetic American to whom I have alluded may be represented at such an hour as making a hundred irresponsible reflections and indulging in all sorts of fantastic visions. If I had not already wandered so far from my theme, I should like to offer a few instances here. Very often it seemed natural to care very little whether England went to war with Russia or not: the interest lay in the moral struggle that was going on within her own limits. Awkward as this moral struggle made her appear, perilously as it seemed to have exposed her to the sarcasm of some of her neighbors—of that compact, cohesive France, for instance, which even yet cannot easily imagine a great country sacrificing the substance of "glory" to the shadow of wisdom—this was the most striking element in the drama into which, as I said just now, the situation had resolved itself. The Liberal party at the present hour is broken, disfigured, demoralized, the mere ghost of its former self. The opposition to the government has been, in many ways, factious and hypercritical: it has been opposition for opposition's sake, and it has met, in part, the fate of such immoralities. But a good part of the cause that it represented appeared at times to be the highest conscience of a civilized country. The aversion to war, the absence of defiance, the disposition to treat the emperor of Russia like a gentleman and a man of his word, the readiness to make concessions, to be conciliatory, even credulous, to try a great many expedients before resorting to the showy argument of the sword,—these various attributes of the peace party offered, of course, ample opportunity to those scoffers at home and abroad who are always prepared to cry out that England has sold herself, body and soul, to "Manchester." It was interesting to attempt to feel what there might be of justice in such cries, and at the same time feel that this looking at war in the face and pronouncing it very vile was the mark of a high civilization. It is but fair to add, though it takes some courage, that I found myself very frequently of the opinion of the last speaker. If British interests were in fact endangered by Russian aggression—though, on the whole, I did not at all believe it—it would be a fine thing to see the ancient might of this great country reaffirm itself. I did not at all believe it, as I say; yet at times, I confess, I tried to believe it, pretended I believed it, for the sake of this inspiring idea of England's making, like the lady in *Dombey & Son*, "an effort." There were those who, if one would listen to them, would persuade one that that sort of thing was quite out of the question; that England was no longer a fighting power; that her day was over; and that she was quite incapable of striking a blow for the great empire she had built up—with a good deal less fighting, really, than had been given out—by taking happy advantage of weaker states. (These hollow reasoners were of course invidious foreigners.) To such talk as this I paid little attention—only just enough to feel it quicken my desire that this fine nation, so full of private pugnacity and of public deliberation, might find in circumstances a sudden pretext for doing something gallant and striking.

Meanwhile I watched the soldiers whenever an opportunity offered. My opportunities, I confess, were moderate, for it was not often my fortune to encounter an imposing military array. In London there are a great many red-coats, but they rarely march about the streets in large masses. The most impressive military body that engages the attention of the contemplative pedestrian is the troop of Life Guards or of Blues which every morning, about eleven o'clock, makes its way down to Whitehall from the Regent's Park barracks. (Shortly afterward another troop passes up from Whitehall, where, at the Horse Guards, the guard has been changed.) The Life Guards are one of the most brilliant ornaments of the metropolis, and I never see two or three of them pass without feeling shorter by several inches. When, of a summer afternoon, they scatter themselves abroad in undress uniform—with their tight red jackets and tight blue trousers following the swelling lines of their manly shapes, and their little visorless caps perched neatly askew on the summit of their six feet two of stature—it is impossible not to be impressed, and almost abashed, by the sight of such a consciousness of neatly-displayed physical advantages and by such an air of superior valor. It is true that I found the other day in an amusing French book (a little book entitled *Londres pittoresque*, by M. Henri Bellenger) a description of these majestic warriors which took a humorous view of their grandeur. A Frenchman arriving in London, says M. Bellenger, stops short in the middle of the pavement and stares aghast at this strange apparition—"this tall lean fellow, with his wide, short torso perched upon a pair of grasshopper's legs and squeezed into an adhesive jacket of scarlet cloth, who dawdles himself along with a little cane in his hand, swinging forward his enormous feet, curving his arms, throwing back his shoulders, arching his chest, with a mixture of awkwardness, fatuity and stiffness the most curious and the most exhilarating.... In his general aspect," adds this merciless critic, "he recalls the circus-rider, minus the latter's flexibility: skin-tight garments, simpering mouth, smile of a dancing-girl, attempt to be impertinent and irresistible which culminates only in being ridiculous."

This is a very heavy-handed picture of those exaggerated proportions and that conquering gait which, as I say, render the tall Life Guardsman one of the most familiar ornaments of the London streets. But it is when he is armed and mounted that he is most picturesque—when he sits, monumentally, astride of his black charger in one of the big niches on either side of the gate of the Horse Guards, cuirassed and helmeted, booted and spurred. I never fail to admire him as I pass through the adjacent archway, as well as his companions, equally helmeted and booted, who march up and down beside him, and, as Taine says, alluding in his *Notes sur l'Angleterre* to the scene, "posent avec majesté devant les gamins." If I chance to be in St. James's street when a semi-squadron of these elegant warriors are returning from attendance upon royalty after a Drawing-Room or a Levee, I am sure to make one of the gamins who stand upon the curbstone to see them pass. If the day be a fine one at the height of the season, and London happen to be wearing otherwise the brilliancy of supreme fashion—with beautiful dandies at the club-windows, and chariots ascending the sunny slope freighted with wigged and flowered coachmen, great armorial hammercloths, powdered, appended footmen, dowagers and débutantes—then the rattling, flashing, prancing cavalcade of the long detachment of the Household troops strikes one as the official expression of a thoroughly well-equipped society. It must be added, however, that it is many a year since the Life Guards or the Blues have had harder work than this. To escort their sovereign to the railway-stations at London and Windsor has long been their most arduous duty. They were present to very good purpose at Waterloo, but since their return from that immortal field they have not been out of England. Heavy cavalry, in modern warfare, has gone out of fashion, and in case of a conflict in the East those nimble, pretty fellows the Hussars, with their tight, dark-blue tunics so brilliantly embroidered with yellow braid, would take precedence of their majestic comrades. The Hussars are indeed the prettiest fellows of all, and if I were fired with a martial ambition I should certainly enlist in their ranks. I know of no military personage more agreeable to the civil eye than a blue-and-yellow hussar, unless indeed it be a young officer in the Rifle Brigade. The latter is perhaps, to a refined and chastened taste, the most graceful, the most truly elegant, of all military types. The little riflemen, the common soldiers, have an extremely useful and durable aspect: with their plain black uniforms, little black Scotch bonnets, black gloves, total absence of color, they suggest the rigidly practical and business-like phase of their profession—the restriction of the attention to the simple specialty of "picking off" one's enemy. The officers are of course more elegant, but their elegance is sober and subdued. They are dressed all in black, save for a broad, dark crimson sash which they wear across the shoulder and chest, and for a very slight hint of gold lace upon their small, round, short-visored caps. They are furthermore adorned with a small quantity of broad black braid discreetly applied to their tight, long-skirted surtouts. There is a kind of severe gentlemanliness about this costume which, when it is worn by a tall, slim, neat-waisted young Englishman with a fresh complexion, a candid eye and a yellow moustache, is of quite irresistible effect. There is no such triumph of taste as to look rich without high colors and picturesque without accessories. The imagination is always struck by the figure of a soberly-dressed gentleman with a sword.

The little riflemen, the Hussars, the Life Guards, the Foot Guards, the artillerymen (whose garments always look stiffer and more awkwardly fitted than those of their *confrères*) have all, however, one quality in common—the appearance of extreme, of even excessive, youth. It is hardly too much to say that the British army, as a stranger observes it now-a-days, is an army of boys. All the regiments are boyish: they are made up of lads who range from seventeen to five-and-twenty. You look almost in vain for the old-fashioned specimen of the British soldier—the large, well-seasoned man of thirty, bronzed and whiskered beneath his terrible bearskin and with shoulders fashioned for the heaviest knapsack. This was the ancient English grenadier. But the modern grenadier, as he perambulates the London pavement, is for the most part a fresh-colored lad of moderate stature, who hardly strikes one as offering the elements of a very solid national defence. He enlists, as a general thing, for six years, and if he leave the army at the end of this term his service in the ranks will have been hardly more than a juvenile escapade. I often wonder, however, that the unemployed Englishman of humble origin should not be more often disposed to take up his residence in Her Majesty's barracks. There is a certain street-corner at Westminster where the recruiting-sergeants stand all day at the receipt of custom. The place is well chosen, and I suppose they drive a tolerably lively business: all London sooner or later passes that way, and whenever I have passed I have always observed one of these smart apostles of military glory trying to catch the ear of one of the dingy London *lazzaroni*. Occasionally, if the hook has been skilfully baited, they appear to be conscious of a bite, but as a general thing the unfashionable object of their blandishments turns away, after an unillumined stare at the brilliant fancy dress of his interlocutor, with a more or less concise declaration of incredulity. In front of him stretches, across the misty Thames, the large commotion of Westminster Bridge, crowned by the huge, towered mass of the Houses of Parliament. To the right of this, a little *effaced*, as the French say, is the vague black mass of the Abbey; close at hand are half a dozen public-houses, convenient for drinking a glass to the encouragement of military aspiration; in the background are the squalid and populous slums of Westminster. It is a characteristic congregation of objects, and I have often wondered that among so many eloquent mementos of the life of the English people the possible recruit should not be prompted by the sentiment of social solidarity to throw himself into the arms of the agent of patriotism. Speaking less vaguely, one would suppose that to the great majority of the unwashed and unfed the condition of a private in one of the queen's regiments would offer much that might be supremely enviable. It is a chance to become, relatively speaking, a gentleman—more than a gentleman, a "swell"— to have the grim problem of existence settled at a stroke. The British soldier always presents the appearance of scrupulous cleanliness: he is scoured, scrubbed, brushed beyond reproach. His hair is enriched with pomatum and his shoes are radiantly polished. His little cap is worn in a manner determined by considerations purely aesthetic. He carries a little cane in one hand, and, like a gentleman at a party, a pair of white gloves in the other. He holds up his head and expands his chest, and bears himself generally like a person who has reason to invite rather than to evade the fierce light of modern criticism. He enjoys, moreover, an abundant leisure, and appears to have ample time and means for participating in the advantages of a residence in London—for frequenting gin-palaces and music-halls, for observing the beauties of the West End and cultivating the society of appreciative housemaids. To a ragged and simple-minded rustic or to a young Cockney of vague resources all this ought to be a brilliant picture. That the picture should seem to contain any shadows is a proof of the deep-seated relish in the human mind for our personal independence. The fear of "too many masters" weighs heavily against the assured comforts and the opportunity of cutting a figure. On the other hand, I remember once being told by a communicative young trooper with whom I had some conversation that the desire to "see life" had been his own motive for enlisting. He appeared to be seeing it with some indistinctness: he was a little tipsy at the time.

I spoke at the beginning of these remarks of the brilliant impressions to be gathered during a couple of days' stay at Aldershot, and I have delayed much too long to attempt a rapid and grateful report of them. But I reflect that such a report, however friendly, coming from a visitor profoundly uninitiated into the military mystery, can have but a relative value. I may lay myself open to contempt, for instance, in making the simple remark that the big parade held in honor of the queen's birthday, and which I went down more particularly to see, struck me, as the young ladies say, as perfectly lovely. I will nevertheless hazard this confession, for I should otherwise seem to myself to be grossly irresponsive to a delightful hospitality. Aldershot is a very charming place—an example the more, to my sense, if examples were needed, of the happy variety of this wonderful little island, its adaptability to every form of human convenience. Some twenty years ago it occurred to the late prince consort, to whom so many things occurred, that it would be a good thing to establish a great camp. He cast his eyes about him, and instantly they rested upon a spot as perfectly adapted to his purpose as if Nature from the first had had an eye to pleasing him. It was a matter of course that the prince should find exactly what he looked for. Aldershot is at but little more than an hour from London—a high, sunny, breezy expanse surrounded by heathery hills. It offers all the required conditions of liberal space, of quick accessibility, of extreme salubrity, of contiguity to a charming little tumbled country in which the troops may indulge in ingenious imitations of difficult manoeuvres; to which it behooves me to add the advantage of enchanting drives and walks for the entertainment of the impressible visitor. In winter, possibly, the great circle of the camp is rather a prey to the elements, but nothing can be more agreeable than I found it toward the end of May, with the light fresh breezes hanging about, and the sun-rifts from a magnificently cloudy sky lighting up all around the big yellow patches of gorse.

At Aldershot the military class lives in huts, a generic name given to certain low wooden structures of small dimensions and a single story, covering, however, a good many specific variations. The oblong shanty in which thirty or forty common soldiers are stowed away is naturally a very different affair from the neat little bungalow of an officer. The buildings are distributed in chessboard fashion over a very large area, and form two distinct camps. There is also a substantial little town, chiefly composed of barracks and public-houses; in addition to which, at crowded seasons, far and near over the plain there is the glitter of white tents. "The neat little bungalow of an officer," as I said just now: I learned, among other things, what a charming form of habitation this may be. The ceilings are very low, the partitions are thin, the rooms are all next door to each other; the place is a good deal like an American "cottage" by the seaside. But even in these narrow conditions that homogeneous English luxury which is the admiration of the stranger blooms with its usual amplitude. The specimen which suggests these observations was cushioned and curtained like a pretty house in Mayfair, and yet its pretensions were tempered by a kind of rustic humility. I entered it first in the dark, but the next morning, when I stepped outside to have a look at it by daylight, I burst into pardonable laughter. The walls were of plain planks painted a dark red: the roof, on which I could almost rest my elbow, was neatly endued with a coating of tar. But, after all, the thing was very pretty. There was a matting of ivy all over the front of the hut, thriving as I had never known ivy to thrive upon a wooden surface: there was a tangle of creepers about all the windows. The place looked like a "side-scene" in a comic opera. But there was a serious little English lawn in front of it, over which a couple of industrious red-coats were pulling up and down a garden-roller; and in the centre of the drive before the door was a tremendous clump of rhododendrons of more than operatic brilliancy. I leaned on the garden-gate and looked out at the camp: it was twinkling and bustling in the morning light, which drizzled down upon it in patches from a somewhat agitated sky. An hour later the camp got itself together and spread itself, in close battalions and glittering cohorts, over a big green level, where it marched and cantered about most effectively in honor of a lady living at a quiet Scotch country-house. One of this lady's generals stood in a corner, and the regiments marched past and saluted. This simple spectacle was in reality very brilliant. I know nothing about soldiers, as the reader must long since have discovered, but I had, nevertheless, no hesitation in saying to myself that these were the handsomest troops in the world. Everything in such a spectacle is highly picturesque, and if the observer is one of the profane he has no perception of weakness of detail. He sees the long squadrons shining and shifting, uncurling themselves over the undulations of the ground like great serpents with metallic scales, and he remembers Milton's description of the celestial hosts. The British soldier is doubtless not celestial, but the extreme perfection of his appointments makes him look very well on parade. On this occasion at Aldershot I felt as if I were at the Hippodrome. There was a great deal of cavalry and artillery, and the dragoons, hussars and lancers, the beautiful horses, the capital riders, the wonderful wagons and guns, seemed even more theatrical than military. This came, in a great measure, from the freshness and tidiness of their accessories— the brightness and tightness of uniforms, the polish of boots and buckles, the newness of leather and paint. None of these things were the worse for wear: they had the bloom of peace still upon them. As I looked at the show, and then afterward, in charming company, went winding back to camp, passing detachments of the great cavalcade, returning also in narrow file, balancing on their handsome horses along the paths in the gorse-brightened heather, I allowed myself to wish that since, as matters stood, the British soldier was clearly such a fine fellow and a review at Aldershot was such a delightful entertainment, the bloom of peace might long remain.

H. James, Jr.

The Afghan Difficulty

II

LONDON, OCTOBER 28, 1878.

London may be said just now to be both agitated and tranquil. On the one hand the air is filled with the smell of gunpowder wafted from Himalayan regions, and there is every appearance that the country is about to have a considerable war upon its hands. On the other, the "dead" season has not yet come to life again, and the powers that be are more or less conspicuous by their absence. The Queen is at Balmoral, inhaling the fine Scotch weather of incipient November; the Cabinet, though it held a partial meeting a few days since, is scattered—one of its members being in Scotland with the Queen, and two others embarked for Cyprus in order to examine that much-discussed island and talk over the famous "purchase" on the spot. The Prince of Wales, even, is in Paris, helping to close the Exhibition. This latter personage is not usually regarded as what it is at present the fashion to call a "factor" in English public affairs; but I hardly feel it proper to forbear to mention him, rising as I have just done from the perusal of the extraordinary puff (there is no other word for it) published in this morning's *Times* by M. de Blowitz, the remarkable Parisian correspondent of that journal. The Prince, ever since the opening of the Exhibition, in which he takes a great interest, has been a great deal in Paris, where, according to M. de Blowitz, he has endeared himself to the inhabitants to a degree which, if he were only a Frenchman, would render him fatal to the prospects of the Republic. The panegyric is a "portrait" in the old-fashioned French sense of the term. It represents the Prince of Wales as having so charmed and captivated the

From *The Nation* 27.698 (14 Nov. 1878): 298–99.

French imagination by his reproduction of the temperament and manners of Francis I. and Henry IV.—by his "love of beauty in every form"—that if, instead of being a safe young Englishman, he were a claimant of the French crown, he would carry everything before him on the shoulders of popular enthusiasm. The Prince of Wales is considered in England a very good-natured, pleasure-loving personage, of whose characteristics it would be indiscreet to attempt an elaborate analysis; and I cannot but think that, laid upon English breakfast-tables, the singular effusion in the *Times* will provoke a great many honest British smiles— smiles at the idea of his being regarded in foreign parts as a possible saviour of society. The British public loves a prince, assuredly; but in this case it would seem really to have been entertaining an angel unawares. There is more important news in the papers, however, than M. de Blowitz's opinion of the Prince of Wales. The war-cloud in India is daily growing larger, and if the season had been less advanced and the Viceroy more prepared it would doubtless already have burst. The public is very much in the dark, and it hardly adds to its illumination to suspect that this is also the case with the Government.

The Amir's reply to the English demand that he should receive a mission, despatched by the native agent whom the Indian Government already had at Cabul, after the rebuff of Sir Neville Chamberlain's very military embassy, has been received, but has not been made known. It is known, however, that if it is not absolutely defiant it is quite uncompromising, and that it makes no amends for the much-discussed "insult." The justice and the wisdom, the necessity and the profit, of making war upon Afghanistan are the theme of perpetual discussion. The papers are filled with letters on the subject, some of which are much to the point, and others not at all. Lord Lawrence, the ex-Viceroy, Lord Grey, Sir Bartle Frere, Sir Henry Havelock, Sir John Adye, Sir Charles Trevelyan, Sir James Stephen, have all committed themselves to print, and have expressed themselves in various senses. A good deal of the discussion I speak of has borne upon the point whether the famous insult offered to Major Cavagnari by the Amir's deputy was really an insult. The ultimate impression appears to be that it was an insult tempered by civility—or rather, perhaps, more correctly, that the interview consisted of a good deal of civility tempered by impertinence. A correspondent of the *Pall Mall Gazette*, who professes to furnish the most absolutely authentic account, affirms that the Afghan officer concluded by remarking if it were not for his personal esteem for Major Cavagnari he would shoot him. This can hardly pass muster even as a dry compliment. This, however, is a mere detail, and it is not, strictly speaking, because the terms on which Major Cavagnari escaped with his life were not more liberal that England is going to war. If I say this it is by no means because I am prepared to lay down the grounds of such a course. The war has all but come, is felt to be almost inevitable, is believed to be to a considerable degree necessary, and yet no one here, I suspect—no group of persons—has a grain of enthusiasm on the subject.

The Chancellor of the Exchequer has just been "stumping" the midland counties, and making at Birmingham, Wolverhampton, Dudley, etc., a series of the longest and dullest speeches it has lately been my fortune to read. (At Birmingham, I may say in parenthesis, he on one occasion divided the honors of the evening with the doughty Captain Burnaby, who came to the point in a very short speech—Captain Burnaby reduces the political views of the Tory party to their simplest expression—with a violent dig at Mr. Gladstone for his "un-English and unpatriotic" conduct in writing an article in the *North American Review.*) Sir Stafford Northcote appears to have taken upon himself the mission to keep the country in good-humor, to talk it out of ill-humor, with the present Government, and to explain and justify, so far as might very discreetly be done, the actual, very incoherent state of affairs. But Sir Stafford Northcote's discretion was greatly in excess of his eloquence; he was extremely shy of the Afghan difficulty, and he made no attempt whatever to strike a spark from the public conscience. The public conscience, interrogating itself and the situation, says that England is coming down on the Amir, first, because he refused to receive a mission, and, second, because the Russians are trying to "get round" him. It is, of course, not as a quarrel with Afghanistan pure and simple that the present complications are serious, but because Russia has made herself very frankly a party to the dispute. She has done nothing, indeed, as yet but send an embassy to Cabul (in spite of a "positive assurance" made to the English Foreign Office in 1875 that she would thenceforth "consider Afghanistan as entirely outside of her sphere of action"); but since the Indian Government has begun to prepare to extract penalties from Shir Ali, the Russian press has certainly been allowed to express itself with startling crudity. The "sphere of action" of Russia has enlarged itself considerably since Prince Gortchakoff's promise in 1875. A year ago it was possible to ridicule the idea that her expansive tendencies would bring her, within any calculable time, into juxtaposition with India; but to-day, certainly, the alarmist organs have a slightly better show of reason. It is not necessary to say with the Conservative press that, because there are three or four Russian officers at Cabul, she is actually at the gates of India; but it is perfectly true that within a much shorter period than was to have been expected the strengthening of the northwestern frontier has become a practical question. So quickly, just now, does history seem to make itself.

Nevertheless, I should say the country at large is not at all alarmed, but that it is a good deal irritated and disgusted. It cannot rid itself of a feeling that the Amir might perfectly well have been let alone. After all, what had he done? This is the policy satirically characterized by the bellicose party as "masterly inactivity";

but it may certainly be said that in this matter, up to the present moment, there has been nothing masterly in the conduct of the Government. Why should a mission have been tentatively forced upon a potentate, small though he is, who had positively refused several times over to receive one? The demands that were to have been made of the Amir have not yet been made known; but the fact that they are withheld strengthens the presumption that they were such as the Amir might very properly and naturally decline. Why should he be bullied into concessions which no other ruler in his place would have been the least likely to make? And why, furthermore, if the Indian Government was to put itself in a position to receive a resounding rebuff, should it not first have taken care to be ready to resent it? A few weeks since, when the belief in the "insult" was general, there was something almost grotesque in the prospect of the great Indian Empire having to nurse its outraged dignity all winter in the absence of the proper appliances for inflicting chastisement. The chastisement was intended to show to Indian dependencies that the might of England could not be made light of with impunity, but the lesson was to be postponed until the thunder could be manufactured. After the delay that has already taken place there is a growing belief that it is not at all a case for thunder. The retort made to the objections to Lord Lytton's proceedings is that in a case of self-defence it is out of place to be punctilious, and that, with the security of the beneficent Indian Empire at stake, it is absurd for the Government to let their hands be tied by misplaced scruples. Have international usages any force as between "imperial" considerations and such a ruler as the Amir of Cabul, and has the latter any rights which, with the Russians looming in the distance, England is bound to respect? Every one is agreed that India must be defended in the best possible way, but there is a wonderful strife of opinions as to what that way consists in.

Lord Lawrence, who may be presumed to speak with a good deal of authority, is almost passionately of the opinion that the actual frontier is the most defensible; other reasoners hold that it is indispensable to make a new frontier by the absorption of certain portions of the Amir's territory, and that there is no time like the present, before Russia has fixed herself. An extreme mistrust of the necessity, in general, of new frontiers forms so large an element in English public opinion to-day that I suspect it will take a livelier sense of the aggressive ability (I don't say disposition) of Russia than yet, on the whole, prevails to make the present undertaking seem anything but an ill-disguised calamity. In two or three very weighty and judicial letters that he has addressed to the *Times* Sir James Stephen sets forth the weakness of the "international" view of Shir Ali. He makes out, I think, a very fair case. Sir James Stephen is never mawkish or transcendental; but on this point he can probably not be said to be gratuitously brutal. If the Russians were thundering at the northern frontier of Afghanistan, it is tolerably certain that Shir Ali's independence would stand a poor chance even in those minds now most occupied with the moral view of it. Sir James Stephen thinks, however, with a good many other people, that there is no danger, even of a remote kind, of Russia being able to "thunder" in this region. He believes in her advance, but he believes in its taking place by other means—by the slow, gradual activity of traders and colonists, which, if sufficiently prolonged and sufficiently clever, will practically Russianize the country. If it be asked, What then? have we not still an eminently defensible frontier? Sir James Stephen answers that this may be; that it is a question for military experts to settle; that it is to be supposed that the Government, with a tremendous sense of its responsibilities, will settle it by the pure light of science, and that to attempt to question and overhaul the Government while it is so engaged is a course to be strongly deprecated. It must be confessed that such a recommendation to reserve as this is at present completely wasted upon the more demonstrative section of the Liberal party. There are signs abroad of a theory that the Liberal party has begun to "come up," though I must say I think it slightly premature. The Government is certainly not as popular as it was when Lord Beaconsfield brought home "peace with honor" from Berlin, both the peace and the honor having been observed to be of a slightly inferior quality. But the Liberal tone appears to represent too little else than heterogeneous criticism of an embarrassed administration to be spoken of just yet as a revival. It declines, however, to stay its hand for an hour, and, whatever doubts there may be, the Government certainly has not the benefit of them. Meanwhile the poor Amir remains a somewhat pathetically interesting figure. He is in the situation of a man deprived of the right of choosing his friends—of the right, indeed, of choosing none at all, if it suits him. If he wished to have nothing to do with the English, he was also by no means sociably inclined to the Russians, his hospitality toward the latter being purely comparative. Between the two parties, apparently, he is about to be reduced to the impalpable. If England overwhelms and obliterates him it will be essentially as an anticipatory measure. In the present improved state of English political morality an anticipatory war has an ugly look. Twist the thing about as one will, the Amir is about to be invaded not because he, but because Russia, is aggressive. If Russia were very imminently or effectively aggressive, this anomaly would doubtless seem less striking. But, making proper allowance—evidently a very large one—for bravado and "bounce," is the danger great enough to warrant a possibly unremunerative deviation from the path of virtue?

Review of
Graf Bismarck und seine Leute während des Krieges mit Frankreich. Nach Tagebuchsblättern,

BY MORITZ BUSCH

III

—The London *Times* lately published, in three instalments, a series of copious extracts from a publication which has excited no little attention in Germany—'Graf Bismarck und seine Leute während des Krieges mit Frankreich. Nach Tagebuchsblättern, von Dr. Moritz Busch.' M. Émile de Lave-leye, in the December *Fortnightly*, devotes an entertaining article to the same record, which we shall see before long in an English translation. The book is only just out in Germany, where it has produced no small agitation and scandal; and while we await a more complete acquaintance with it we may find some profit in the specimens with which we have already been furnished. Dr. Moritz Busch, who appears to be a veritable Teutonic Boswell, was a practised journalist, in the employ of the Berlin Foreign Office, when he accompanied the great Chancellor, in the summer of 1870, to the seat of war. It may be added that his name figures as the translator of those American tales (by Messrs. Bret Harte, Howells, Aldrich, H. James, jr., etc.) which have lately been introduced in such profusion to German readers. He appears to have noted down, indefatigably, the conversation of his illustrious chief, and his book offers an almost complete record of Prince Bis-marck's table-talk and small-talk during the momentous months of the Franco-German war. The result is an extraordinary portrait, which, whether pleasing or not, has evidently the merit of minute fidelity. The Chancellor, in fact, paints

From *The Nation* 27.703 (19 Dec. 1878): 384–85.

himself, and his devoted diarist has done nothing but suspend the picture. It has presumably been given to the world with Prince Bismarck's own sanction, and this proceeding is only the conclusive, crowning instance of that tremendous audacity which is the most salient feature in the personality of the model. As regards everything and every one, Prince Bismarck is unsparingly, exhaustively, brutally frank. His opinion of the French nation is of the lowest; he speaks lightly even of M. Thiers:

> "He is a clever, attractive gentleman, witty, spirited, intellectual, but without talent for diplomacy. He is far too sentimental for the profession. Though more manly and dignified then M. Favre, he is altogether unfit for the trade. He came to me as a negotiator when he had not gumption enough to know how to set about selling a horse. He is easily staggered, and he shows it."

Elsewhere, however, he is reported as having said to M. Thiers: "It is a pleasure to talk with so civilized a human being as you." In regard to the French love of phrases he says: "You may lay twenty-five lashes on a Frenchman's back with impunity, if only delivering the while a speech upon liberty and the dignity of mankind; the imaginative victim will not know he is being flogged." And the world will be interested to learn that, for every defect of the French, the Germans have a corresponding merit: "I am quite sure that the expression *politesse de coeur* is not French, but a translation from the German. This is a peculiar sort of politeness which I have met nowhere but in Germany. . . . The French certainly know nothing of the kind, being polite only from hatred or envy." One may be pardoned for wondering whether it was from *politesse de coeur* (even in the German original) that, as the Chancellor relates, the Princess Bismarck, in the autumn of 1870, "would have the French exterminated root and branch, only excepting the little children, who cannot be held responsible for having such atrocious parents." This edifying wish is one of those numerous passages for which it is almost inconceivable that Prince Bismarck should have desired the honors of publicity.

—A great many of Dr. Busch's notes are autobiographic and relate to the Prince's personal idiosyncrasies and physical exploits—his duels, his bouts of beer-drinking, his endurance of fatigue, his extraordinary capacity for work. His physical endowments are evidently quite on the same grand scale as his intellectual, and his iron will has had at its service a temperament of iron. Dr. Busch, like a faithful Boswell, represents his capacity of consuming food as Johnsonian, and quotes the Prince's own assertion that "the German nation is determined to have a corpulent Chancellor." It would appear that in all these details there was, on the Chancellor's part, a sort of bravado, of grossness, and animalism. And yet he is also represented as extremely spiritual, and he affirms on several occasions the intensity of his religious belief. "A plain, God-fearing man"—that old-fashioned phrase is about Prince Bismarck's description of himself.

> "If I ceased to be a Christian, I should not remain at my post another hour.... If I had not been rigorously orthodox the German nation would never have had its present Chancellor.... How willingly would I go away! I love the life of the fields, of woods, of nature. Take away from me my belief in God, and to-morrow morning I pack my portmanteau and set off for Varzin to grow my corn."

Of course there are great numbers of political judgments, many of which are very curious—some for their striking felicity, some for what may be fairly called their absurdity. (We may mention in this latter class the Prince's prophecy that France would shortly be decomposed into various states, under Legitimist, Republican, Radical, and Imperialist governments respectively.) He points out with cruel definiteness what Napoleon III., had he been a wiser man, *might* have done with certain success in 1866:

> "At the beginning of hostilities against Austria he ought to have seized what he wished to obtain by the Benedetti treaty [a projected treaty for the freedom, as far as Prussia was concerned, to lay Bonapartist hands on Belgium, granted in exchange for the cession of Landau, Saarbrück, etc., and withdrawal from the duchy of Luxembourg] and to have kept it as a pledge against future events. We could not have stopped him, and it is not very likely that England would have done so. In any case he could have awaited her with a firm foot. If we proved victorious he ought to have led us to push on our advantages even to excess. But he has never been anything but a dreamer."

It is highly displeasing, at any rate, to perceive how perpetually the late Emperor of the French dreamed of doing violence to Belgium. In the case of so formidable a personage as the Chancellor it is agreeable for us to learn, under date of September 12, 1870, that "Prince Bismarck has long been well disposed towards the Americans." He is very frank as regards the ideal form of political power. "After all, a benevolent, rational absolutism is the best form of government. Unless strengthened by some of this salutary tonic any government must fall to pieces. But, alas! we have no real absolutists left; the race has died out." The violently repressive measures now taking place in Germany would seem to disprove this last clause, though perhaps even Prince Bismarck himself would hardly pretend that the strong military régime at Berlin is a "benevolent, rational" absolutism.

The Early Meeting of Parliament

================

IV

LONDON, DEC. 11, 1878.

Politically speaking, we are in the midst of a season of recrimination. Parliament met, for a short and extraordinary session, upwards of a week ago, and both for some time before it and ever since the air has been dark with mutual inculpations. The Afghan war has begun in earnest, and has thus far been substantially successful. Whatever opposition may still await the English advance, there has been none, as yet, of a formidable character. Parliament has been called to be put *au courant*, as it were, of the affair, and for some nights past has been actively discussing it. It was only a few days before the Queen's speech that the very voluminous papers relating to the whole Afghan episode were made public; but though the Opposition has bitterly complained of this delay and of the insufficient time allowed for looking into them, I cannot perceive that they have been oppressed by these bewildering documents or have overlooked any choice morsels of evidence that might serve to feather their arrows. I cannot pretend to have even partially kept an account of the charges and counter-charges that have been extracted from this rich repository, and I must confess that the whole spectacle seems to me a not particularly edifying one. It is, perhaps, of the absolute essence of an Opposition to make an arrow, as the French say, of any wood—to invent occasions when none offer themselves, to cultivate agitation for agitation, just as people nowadays cultivate art for art. If this be the case, the Liberal party, in so far as it is represented by most of its official spokesmen, may flatter itself on conforming to its ideal. It is certainly

From *The Nation* 27.704 (26 Dec. 1878): 397–98.

true that there are a good many natural occasions for criticising the Government, but I suspect that, to the country at large, they are not such completely happy ones as they appear to Mr. Gladstone and his friends. Mr. Gladstone has, apparently, a very good case against the present Cabinet, in fixing upon them the responsibility of that change in the attitude of the Afghan ruler which has led to the actual complications. The Government has attempted, with a good deal of resolution and ingenuity, to rebut, or, rather, to anticipate, the charge of having put the Amir off—of having thrown him into the arms of the Russians. Just before the Afghan papers were published Lord Cranbrook, the present Secretary for India, issued a despatch, nominally addressed to Lord Lytton, but in reality addressed to the newspapers. This document contains a summary of the intercourse between the Amir and Lord Lytton's predecessor in office, and in a certain 9th paragraph—it is always spoken of now as the "famous" 9th paragraph—Lord Cranbrook attempted by insinuation to establish the fact that Mr. Gladstone's Cabinet refused in 1873 to give Shir Ali those assurances of protection against Russian aggression which were necessary for keeping on good terms with him. This intimation was promptly and indignantly refuted—first by the Duke of Argyll, who was Secretary for India during a large part of the last Liberal administration, and then by Mr. Gladstone, in the powerful (not to say the violent) and characteristic speech which he delivered to his Greenwich constituents a few days before the opening of Parliament. The late Government appears to have given Shir Ali rigidly reasonable satisfaction on the subject of his liability to Russian approaches; this comes out clearly enough in the papers submitted to Parliament. If a change took place in his feelings and conduct, it coincides with the coming into power of the present Administration and the adoption of a new and aggressive policy by Lord Lytton. Such, at least, is the contention of the present critics of the Government and the charge brought with vehement elaboration by Mr. Gladstone. According to this theory Lord Lytton, as soon as he got to India, began, in harmony with the tendencies of an "imperial" policy, to bully Shir Ali and to urge that demand to which the latter had always consistently refused to give a moment's hearing—the admission into his dominions of permanent British representatives. The Amir had made it clear that concession on this point was hopeless; is it, therefore, true that Lord Lytton's purpose was simply to pick a quarrel—to drive the Amir, by insisting on the impossible, into an offensive act which would offer a pretext for an invasion? It is not necessary to adopt this hypothesis, which has become one of the commonplaces of Liberal criticism. If Lord Lytton had been in so truculent a mood it is probable that he would have been better prepared to carry out his policy than the incident of three months ago found him.

By the terms of the Queen's speech Parliament has been called to discuss the

Afghan question alone; her Majesty makes no mention of anything else, not even of the great distress prevailing throughout the country, and which in the manufacturing districts, at the beginning of a winter which threatens to be a much severer one than either of the two that have preceded it, has reached terrible proportions. This reticence has been made a reproach to the royal address, but it is highly probable that it springs from an amiable cause. The Government had a natural desire to conciliate the large body of gentlemen whom it has brought up to town at a period at which town is extremely unpleasant to the mind of the governing classes, deprived suddenly of the recreations and luxuries in which their rural retreats are so prolific. It shrank from laying before them a long list of *agenda*, and confined itself to what was necessary for the moment. Later in the winter, when Parliament reassembles, there is to be another Queen's speech, when other questions more or less embarrassing will be presented. The present lively episode will very soon come to an end; as far as the House of Lords is concerned it has already practically done so. The Lords divided last night on the vote of censure on the Government which had been moved by Lord Halifax, with the result of 65 in the Opposition against 201 with the Cabinet; thus giving the latter a majority of 136. The amendment moved in the House of Commons (that it "disapproves the conduct of her Majesty's Government which has resulted in the war with Afghanistan") is still under discussion, but it is not to be expected that it will have a very different issue. In writing six weeks ago I said that the theory that the Liberal party was "coming up" seemed, on the whole, to be premature; and it is probable that the fate of the present attempt to discredit the Cabinet will confirm this impression. This is the more remarkable because the conduct of the Government appears in several particulars distinctly discreditable. Mr. Gladstone charges them with duplicity of the deepest dye, besides the misdemeanor of having prevented the country from speaking its mind about the war. This, however, is only part of the duplicity—the charge being that Lord Beaconsfield had set his heart upon taking a slice of Afghanistan long before the last session was over, and that in spite of these criminal designs he wore an innocent face and never gave a hint of Lord Lytton's little game. If he had given such a hint and the country could have spoken earlier, would it have spoken very differently? I must incline to doubt it; I suspect that the country is most disposed just now to make the best of what it has. The Government has a word which is not perhaps of absolutely magical influence, but which is still a better name to conjure with than anything in the possession of its adversaries. The Government can always say "Russia"; the Opposition can say nothing so good as that. The Government does not tell a straight story, nor does it act, by any means, a straight part. There have been in its deportment half a dozen of those flagrant contradictions to which it is easy to call attention. Lord Beaconsfield, in his

Guildhall speech, five weeks ago, announced that his purpose in proceeding against Afghanistan was to secure a "scientific frontier." The expression, like several other of Lord Beaconsfield's expressions, has become classical, and is a very good specimen of that gift of plausible phrase-making by means of which he renders a not strikingly intellectual band of followers the brilliant service of supplying it with formulas after the fact. In other communications of the Government, however, and notably in the Queen's speech, we hear nothing whatever about a frontier, scientific or otherwise; her Majesty declaring that she has gone to war with the Amir simply because he was hostile, and because he repulsed a friendly mission. In the same way the Government affirms at one time that they have never departed from the line of the late Administration in their relations with Shir Ali; and at another time they make it a virtue that they *have* so departed, in order to keep off the Russians.

The most damaging inconsistency, however, of which the Cabinet has been guilty is the disparity between its course in holding Shir Ali to account, and its acceptance, as against Russia directly, of the Czar's mission to Cabul. Lord Salisbury applied to the Russian Government for an explanation of this step and received an almost ludicrously insufficient one. He was told that it was merely a mission of courtesy, and he made the best of this piece of irony, but at the same time the Cabinet prepared to fall upon the Amir for having received the delegation. The strong, active power enjoys impunity, and a penalty is to be extorted from the weak, passive one. This is a fact of which even a feeble opposition could easily make capital, and I am surprised that it has not actually been turned to account by the Liberal leaders. It figures effectively in Mr. Gladstone's passionate diatribes, but one is a little startled at its finding even moderate tolerance with an English public. It involves the sort of accusation of which the English spirit is, justly, least patient—the charge of choosing an adversary with an eye to his size, and striking a blow only where it is safe. But the patience I speak of here is doubtless less real than it appears; the country takes very little pleasure and finds very little glory in the idea of getting the better of poor Shir Ali. It has not the least desire to obliterate or annex him; it only believes, in a general way, that sentimental considerations should not allow him to interfere with the safety of India. The Government for the time believes, or affirms that it believes, that it is in his power so to interfere, and the country is willing to assent. The fierce discussions of the last month—the papers have been flooded with letters on the subject—must strike a good many reasonable people as to a considerable extent a mere beating of the air. Whether Mr. Gladstone's Government were a little more or a little less alive to the dangers of Russian expansion—a little more or a little less ready to listen to Shir Ali's fears on this subject; whether Lord Lytton has pressed the Amir overmuch and occasionally been too emphatic in his diction—all this seems ancient history.

Mr. Gladstone's taunts about truckling to Russia and bullying the Amir lose part of their force from his failure to convey any inspiring, or even definite, notion of what, given the circumstances, he himself would do. Would he demand satisfaction of Russia? Mr. Gladstone is far from saying so. Given the circumstances, I say; for the country perforce accepts the circumstances. The question of who produced them may have a psychological interest, but cannot be said to have any practical bearing. If one is not pledged to look at the matter through partisan spectacles one may perhaps be free to conjecture that, like many other disagreeable things, they came about very naturally. Like Topsy in the novel, they "growed." One may safely believe that Shir Ali was never very fond of his English neighbors, and that it required no great bungling to put him out of conceit of them. It would have required great positive tact and liberality to keep him consistently well disposed, and it is certainly evident that neither under the last Administration nor the present did these virtues superabound. If Lord Lytton has been too harsh, as incontestably he has, his predecessors were curiously meagre and stingy. There is a real "imperial" policy as well as a false one, and from the point of view of the former strictly it is not consoling to see, in retrospect, Mr. Gladstone's Government bargaining and haggling over their assurances of support to the Amir—or, at least, measuring them out with such almost pedantic minuteness. That Russia even now is acutely sensible of a check at this point I very much doubt; but since the Russian question was always looming larger Shir Ali was worth spending some ingenuity upon. It would have been so much gained. Now that decidedly he is being treated in another fashion there is a natural dread of making any more mistakes. Therefore, though the treatment allotted to him is not at all popular, there is an equally natural feeling that it is most patriotic not to interfere with it; and it will be from a vague, shapeless, not especially self-complacent reason of this sort that the Government will escape any degree of censure that it needs to take into account. It will not perhaps have been strengthened by the calling of Parliament, but it will certainly not have been weakened.

The Reassembling of Parliament

V

Parliament met again three weeks ago, but I have not written before to call attention to the fact because I was waiting for something to happen which would justify such a proceeding. Up to the present moment I have waited in vain, and I must now content myself with remarking that the session is characterized by extreme vacuity. The course of legislation is dull, and there is nothing exciting in prospect. It seems probable that the remainder of the session will be very humdrum, and that its interest will have been exhausted in those lively debates upon the Afghan war (if lively is the word) which took place before the recess. There was no second Queen's speech, as it had been thought possible there might be, and the national legislators have settled down to the discussion of domestic measures more or less substantial indeed, but not calculated to renew the strife of parties or to agitate the public mind. The Opposition, for the moment, is not aggressive, and the Government is not jubilant. There is just now no particular reason for jubilation, and whatever excitement exists in the country is outside of Parliament. It carries the minds of Englishmen very far from the Westminster shore to that remote South African territory, of its connection with which the country has never before had so acute a consciousness. This consciousness has become, all of a sudden, terribly painful, and we have got some time to wait before it can be transmuted into something brighter. Even then, too, the brightness will be questionable, for it will simply mean that a large number more of young English lives have been expended in castigating

From *The Nation* 28.716 (20 Mar. 1879): 197–99.

a multitude of brutal savages. You will long since have heard all the details of the military disaster in South Africa, and have learned that the public suspense, since it occurred, has been greater than on any occasion since the first news of the Indian mutiny reached England twenty-two years ago. Telegraphic communication with Natal is only partial, thanks to the economical principles of successive governments ambitious of achieving the remarkable feat of reconciling the possession of great and distant dependencies with comfortable ideas of cheapness. After the almost complete destruction of the Twenty-fourth Regiment at Isandula, and the momentary paralyzation of Sir Bartle Frere's aggressive movement, it seemed very likely that the whole colony of Natal lay at the mercy of the victorious Zulus. There was no means of knowing in what degree the Zulus had followed up their victory, so that for many days after the news of the massacre of Lord Chelmsford's troops arrived the anxiety was of the most painful sort. Little by little it has abated, and as successive mails have shown that Cetewayo, in spite of his horrible triumph and of the panic he had produced at Natal, was still holding off, there is every reason to hope that he will not have followed up his advantage before the arrival of the reinforcements which, with all the speed that has been found possible, are now embarking for the Cape. It is assumed without unwarrantable fatuity that the six regiments now despatched from England will promptly turn the tables upon the Zulus.

It cannot be said, however, that there is any great comfort in this assumption, or that the outlook in this and in several other directions is particularly gratifying. People are glad to be able to feel that a tragic accident like the hopeless resistance at Isandula and the defence at Rorke's Drift serves at least to remind them of the solid quality of English courage. There has been, inevitably, a considerable flourish of journalistic trumpets over this exhibition. One would almost have thought at moments that it had been supposed that the great tradition of British bravery had got mislaid. In fact, it is evidently in excellent keeping. The British soldier, as one observes him in the streets of garrison towns, is apt to seem rather slim and juvenile; but if his resolution in putting the best face upon imminent slaughter by an overwhelming force of bloodthirsty savages be taken as a measure, his fighting qualities in the gross are still such as a great nation may count upon. No one, however, has ever seriously doubted the capacity of contemporary Englishmen, in case of absolute necessity, for drinking, as Tennyson says, delight of battle. But the country is averse to fighting, and it has formed the habit—an eminently proper one—of looking very hard at the occasion or the provocation before enjoying itself. Exercising at the present moment this scrutinizing faculty, it is by no means gratified by what it perceives. Sir Bartle Frere has all the appearance of having undertaken a Zulu war upon his own responsibility, and as the affair has opened with a deplorable catastrophe, it is obvious that he will not be let off so easily as if he had made a more impressive beginning. At the time I write Sir Charles Dilke is moving in the House of Commons a vote of censure upon the whole business. It remains to be seen with what cordiality the motion will be taken up by the Opposition. I think I may say, without speaking cynically, that the Liberals will lack the incentive of feeling, in this case, that they shall embarrass the Government. The case is a very different one from that of the Afghan war, which afforded a much more convenient handle for making out a grievance. This is not a Governmental war. The Cabinet has already done a great deal towards washing its hands of Sir Bartle Frere's performances, and it is not impossible that it may completely cleanse them by sacrificing him altogether upon the altar of popular indignation. If it does so, however, I cannot help thinking that it will pay to this irritated divinity a tribute unduly large. It may be thought that nothing less will serve to propitiate the public conscience, for the Cabinet is slightly compromised in the matter by the fact that only six months since it went altogether with Sir Bartle Frere in his showing cause why the Afghan war was an eminently desirable enterprise. It was upon the demonstration drawn up by Sir Bartle that the Government avowedly took its stand. He has apparently a weakness for colonial aggression—or, in politer terms, expansion—and a relish for conflict with dusky races. However this be, the Government had distinctly differed with him as regards the policy he was preparing to institute in his new governorship. He was eager for an anticipatory war; he was alarmed at the growth of the Zulu power and the facility with which the subjects of the corpulent Cetewayo appeared to assimilate European military notions. He wished to do what Prussia has the credit of having desired to do some five years since with regard to France—to fall upon his menacing neighbor and crush him before he should grow stronger. Sir Theophilus Shepstone had begun by annexing the Transvaal—it will be remembered that this little transaction took place, rather awkwardly, more than a year ago, at the moment that the outcry against the absorbent tendencies of Russia was at its height—and Sir Bartle Frere, appointed for the purpose of imparting an official gloss to a rather rough proceeding, appears to have found no better way of regularizing, as the French say, the situation than to take up the quarrel of the Dutch settlers, whose policy with regard to the natives had made hostilities chronic.

It may have been that he has behaved very improperly, and in the happy consciousness of immunity from telegraphic control has snapped his fingers at the home Government. As I said just now, the tone that the Government ˙has already taken in Parliament points to this; but I cannot help repeating that even if he has been a trifle precipitate in taking for granted that hostilities were inevitable, there is a point of view from which it would not be especially inspiring to see him sacrificed. This point of view is perhaps a little too much that of the disinterested stranger, the irresponsible spectator of English public affairs; but it coincides with that of a certain type of British patriot quite closely enough to make it defensible. I am almost tempted to say that a friendly American, living in England, suspects himself at times of being a better Englishman, in the old-fashioned sense of the word, than a certain proportion of her Majesty's subjects. He is fortunate, at any rate, in this respect, that he is exempt from the obligation of party allegiance—he is at liberty to contemplate philosophically, among numbers of his friends and of the nation at large, the moral ravages of party passion. He is at liberty to say to himself, and to passive listeners across the sea, that it sometimes narrows down rather pitifully the proud consciousness of being an Englishman. The hatred of Lord Beaconsfield and all his ways and works has a regrettable as well as an estimable side. It is, very properly, displeasing to many honorable minds to see a charlatan of genius at the head of affairs—a gentleman who irresistibly suggests the performer at a circus, in the spangled *caleçon*, turning somersaults upon a piebald courser and leering mechanically at the spectators. It is certainly disagreeable that the British nation should be assimilated to a piebald courser. But Lord Beaconsfield is an accident, and those idiosyncrasies of the British Empire which have given him his chance are, it is to be hoped, a permanence. These idiosyncrasies are an "imperial" spirit (the word is in dreadfully bad odor, but if we are free to use the substantive I don't see why we shouldn't use the adjective), a collection of great colonies and dependencies, an immense artificial cohesion, the need to keep things up, to spend money, the liability to fight. It can hardly fail to strike an American observer that the attitude of a great many very reasonable and sensible Englishmen with regard to these points is extremely illiberal. I hardly know what to call it without using invidious epithets; it is stingy, grudging, parsimonious. I have lived in various countries, but I have never heard so much about the "taxpayer" as since I have lived in this opulent and comfortable London. And I have heard about him in the most unexpected places; I have heard pathetic appeals made for him at luxurious firesides in South Kensington, in circumstances which seemed the last expression of the tendencies of a luxurious generation. I have been startled in the midst of five-o'clock tea by indignant allusions to the increase of a penny in the pound on the income-tax. There is scarcely a nation in the civilized world which of late years has not been obliged to enter more or less cheerfully upon a great national war, and to accommodate itself to the pecuniary burdens of the case. Have the English lost this useful faculty, and are they weaker in this respect than the French and the Germans, the Russians, the Italians, ourselves? Have they been corrupted by making themselves the most comfortable nation in the world, and their country the most convenient to live in—by their immense elaboration of the arts of peace, of leisure, of extracting large enjoyment from large incomes?

I am far from believing it or from saying it; and yet I cannot help saying that a good sympathetic American cannot help feeling a little alarmed at times, and wishing, in a friendly way, that the country might be thrown on its back, suddenly, for half an hour, by some incalculable accident, so that it might give a little play to unused muscles in the effort to sit upright again. It is a theory of a good many positive people who don't all go with the Opposition just now as an opposition, that the Liberal party had completely forgotten the existence of colonies, of foreign nations, of "imperial" responsibilities, and that its present ill-humor arises from having been too abruptly reminded of them. However this may be, it certainly appears to the perhaps rather vague-minded speculators with whom I here identify myself, that the British Empire is an immense artificial structure which can only be sustained by very handsome arrangements—by a large army, a large expenditure, and a considerable confidence in the powers, whoever they be for the time, administering colonial affairs. The British Empire is an heroic creation, and it seems to me there must be a grain of heroism in the usual management of it. It is on those general impressions—I will not do them the honor of calling them principles—that I should deprecate that sort of agitation of which the precipitate condemnation of Sir Bartle Frere would be an example. It may perfectly well be that in this case such a catastrophe is well merited. But none the less one might almost regret the encouragement it would give to a fashion of which it would be hard to foresee the outcome—the fashion of contesting and overhauling in detail, at home, every step taken by the Government abroad, of compelling it to account, on the instant, for every motion of its foreign policy at the bar of the daily papers. It is impossible to eat one's cake and have it, and it is out of the question to administer the British Empire on what the *Pall Mall Gazette* is so fond of denouncing as "parochial" principles. If the English people establish their dominion in a land of bellicose savages, it is surely conceivable that hostile relations with such savages should be on the cards.

II

Essays on Gender and the American Scene,
1904–1907

Henry James in the Serene Sixties

VI

*A chat with the American novelist. In a New England setting after
an absence of twenty years. Some views on life, letters and critics.
Of taking up his residence in England.*

Mr. Henry James, long absent from his native land, returned the other
day from England. He is the subject of great interest for many reasons.
His life of seclusion for twenty years in England and on the Continent
has kept him personally out of the public eye, which he very much prefers to
the amiable habit we have of advertising celebrity.

The great author landed in New York quietly and retired at once to the
background—merged himself, as it were, in the misty green of the peaceful New
England landscape. Crowds either curious or critical have not yet seen him,
hidden as he is in the gentle hills, inaccessible, removed from railway, from all
publicity in the heart of New England, miles north of Boston.

The particular shrine that holds this rare object of unusual devotion is a
comfortable frame country house of a simple "L" shape, two stories high, with
verandas. It is off the track of travellers, on a natural road frequented only by
the gentle country people, near one of the beautiful New England lakes.

Back of the house at the edge of the slight grassy slope a forest encircles the
place, full of suggestions, of dreams, of rest and forgetfulness. On the other hand
are glimpses from the roadway of the chain of perfect little lakes lying in the
laps of the purplish hills.

Henry James, of middle height, slightly bald, his black hair turned iron gray

From an interview by Florence Brooks, *New York Herald*, 2 Oct. 1904: magazine section (sec. 4), p. 1.

at the sides, was found here after a most varied journey by trains, stage and hired carriages. He is not so different in mere appearance from other people as his fiction is different from other fiction.

He wears in these simple wilds a plain rough morning sack suit of dark gray. His face is long and strong, broad of cheekbone and jaw, narrower in the high doming forehead. There is no childlike appeal in the eyes, which are yet the reverse of sharp or keen—they have seen, rather than seem to see. His nose is massive and fine, his mouth large and tender, and the childlike quality that all artists manifest in some feature because they are so in certain phases is in the delicate, young expression of the chin—the lower lip.

THE FIRST IMPRESSION

It is a face the peculiarity of which lies in the unusual combination of expressions. For rapidly and superficially one would not count the whole as striking. Roughly speaking, strength and mellowness, shyness and kindness, are the mingling traits. In a mere quick glance no ordinarily dull person could feel a trace of hyperdelicacy, disquieting subtlety.

Blue gray, his eyes do not seem to penetrate. It is a wonder how those opaque eyes could have seen such subtleties, pierced such disguises of soul. And the manner of Mr. James, given that he is a distinguished man, is really more American than it might have been if he had not lived in England for so many years. It is absolutely natural, absolutely unremiss—all there. But one may say that the refinement of courtesy does not come so easily even after long practice without the right feelings to back it up.

Henry James was found in a comfortable low ceiled room, where the dreamy space of grass surmounted by a rim of trees made through each window a similar panorama. His welcome was simple and without stiffness.

The presence was not formidable. Instead, the smallest person might feel more so. And, after a kindly if bewildered welcome from this man who is called intensely shy, he was found to relinquish himself with delightful confidence to that profane rite, an interview. But this is not an interview, only a glimpse and a chat.

Henry James has never been "interviewed." It has been one of his cherished habits to keep out of the sort of gaze that follows the limelight. The marvel is how he has escaped. It is not because he does not understand the journalistic life; he has done it wonderfully in a bit of fiction called "The Papers." So we must think it is because he does understand. "What," he asks of newspaper fame, "is queerer, less human, than to be formed for offence, for injury, by the mere inherent play of the spirit of observation, of criticism, by the inextinguishable flame—in fine, of the ironic passion?"

Our great author's qualities not yet turned cold on paper, he speaks of his feelings in this respect:—

"One's craft, one's art, is his expression," he holds, "not one's person, as that of some great actress or singer is hers. After you have heard a Patti sing why should you care to hear the small private voice of the woman?"

Henry James, as if in all corroboration of his habit of privacy, speaks exactly as he writes, with extreme care as to the choice of a word, a phrase. Therefore he seems pathetically to make you wonder:—Why should he not be left to his mere vocal silence? Why should the public want him to splash himself, reveal his person on paper?

The kindly manner of the author, then, refutes his demand to be let alone. His courtesy in some way flows all between the interstices of the conversation, easing its effort, its keenness.

AS TO INTERVIEWS

"One rather discounts mere talk," he continues, but here the interviewer could find no application. "In such a matter, too, the artist is practically helpless, practically at the mercy of the hearer."

He added to the illumination. "The author in his work has meant something perhaps, but if he had to express this meaning in a different way it would never have been written."

Here is a disclosure of a literary creed, and the author refined it. "I try to express my subject. If I do so express it as I apprehend it, it is enough."

A question as to purpose arose. His stories leave the reader with a question of "moral purpose" "tendency" at the end.

"What if it leave you with that question at the end?" asked the author. Personal illumination has no place in this. "Ah, is not that the trick that life plays? Life itself leaves you with a question—it asks you questions."

To take one of Mr. James' stories, read it with a true taste of every word, every combination, every omission, is a delicate joy. But, as he expresses it of life, the story leaves you with a question—not what happens to the story, to the characters, but a question about what the situation, put with rare truth as it is, means in life.

In a broad acceptance Mr. James in his art is neither moral nor immoral. He enforces no brutal lesson. His regard for worldly convention and the scene of its enactment is only a mode. Beneath the polished gleams, where his subject is scarcely touched, is something real. Under the finished surface, as in a trimmed garden, the life processes must be understood to be. The whole art in detail of Henry James is a tribute to the true expression of shades, of tints, too changing, too slight, too delicate to be roughly handled, ungraciously splashed on the canvas.

So, his avowed purpose being to "express his subject," the question of tendency, inartistically obvious, is kept under. With other elementary foundations, the mere person, the unessential word, the grosser manifestation—this is thrust beneath. He gives only that which shows a trait, a tinge of individual coloring. That with which he builds up to the point where his edifice first strikes the light, he told me, finally, in his own words are:—

"Facts—facts," he repeats; "facts are the basis upon which I build."

He gives these facts a solid grouping as basis. His observations, really solid, appear to be fancifully clothed because what one sees is not bare and plain. The too literal mind need not apply here for companionship. Nor need the seeker for remedies. This is no hospital, no public place of entertainment.

In the house which he has built are comfortable, mellow places, shaded places, the flower which has grown from the roots of the whole labor. In these perfected places, his dramas, his idylls, his romances live in the guise of fancies and impressions. The manner is eliminated of all but suggestion.

AN APPRECIATION

He calls himself "a painter of life."

I should hardly have used this metaphor, but it is his. The work of Henry James has often a monochrome, a black and white effect, or, when more tender, a Corot like spirit. Greenish, misty gray is often what one sees. He uses color—not the color words, but the sense of color—in the oddest places.

To pursue his own illustration of himself as "a painter of life" he has, as well as impressions, a beautiful "line." This has been denied. Outline he does not present continuously. But to his "line"—nothing more exquisite is drawn—he is not only not a slave but a negligent master. He can also paint chiaroscuros, he can accentuate with glints of sharp light, he can use all too rare color in strange mad glows, he can blur his object, or he can etch it.

He is a stylist, a psychologist, in his manner of "painting from life."

One of Henry James' friends told me, before I saw him, that he also calls himself a realist. In this sense he is said to deal "only with phenomena which are visible; only so much as one would see."

This leads the casual reader to think that his work is of the surface only. But the wonder is that he reads so deeply in these open signs. Every person is a book written in a strange symbolism. He simply translates the symbols into ordinary words. No really intimate scene does he touch upon, no crisis, revealed at the height of its flame.

For instance, in "The Other House" he never tells who drowned the child in the beautiful river dividing the perfect gardens of the two country places. This event, which is the climax of the story, though it haunt one afterward, the reader is brought to so gently that he scarcely knows what has happened. The unfortunate little girl, whom we saw adorned for her birthday, petted, beloved, one sees but once. One does not know why in the world, it is totally unexpected that she should be drowned, totally out of the surroundings. Only afterward, through the hurried, astonished talk of the characters in twos or threes in the other rooms of one house, is it made plain who did it, the motive, the act, how and when, and only in significant touches. No bare fact obtrudes. Henry James would as soon present one of his characters as one of his facts unclothed.

Only Maurice Maeterlinck is so shy of the violent, of that which is not seen. He, like Henry James, likes to keep the unseen where it belongs. Few of us have seen horrid things—it is so much more terrible to know them without! The glimpse of a rare mystery the more brings art to the highest level.

With no determined lesson to teach Henry James offers to the reader a delight for his taste. And with no direct appeal to the intellect he offers yet a stimulus to thought. His work, like life, "asks questions."

High currents of stimulus thread and rend the nerves. Mr. James' work makes one think. It is—a bit of one of his novels—like a page of science. It is a tonic rather than an intoxicant.

HIS NATIVE COUNTRY

When questioned about his views of American literature Mr. James would only speak in general. "The mass of writing is so great," he explained, "and so unguided. Never yet has such a mass of literature been put forth so unwarned, so unprotected, so unguided by any adequate criticism." He spoke rather sadly, rather aghast, of the effects of the demands of the American "publics," which he considers so intermingled, so almost inseparable in their parts, as to be unsusceptible to division into classes of tastes.

We have such a vast number of dissolute readers—omnivorous, gulping read-ers—those who, fortunately, cannot remember what they read and ought not to care to. They are either ignorant or weary, they read either to soothe or to indulge. People in general in America do not like to think. For an average reader our author's rapidity of delicate thrusts, as one piercing revelation after another—his tremendous power of rapid fire—leaves such a one, to quote from "The Sacred Fount," "struck with more things than" he can "take up."

Mr. James thinks that well defined differences of public desire are to be noted in old civilizations, where are "conditions that have time to accumulate and so to be observed."

But besides an added delicacy from the French, a mellowness absorbed in England, I think we can call Henry James essentially American. He has read our souls a little, maybe much, and he has displayed them, sometimes queerly, in worldly environments, without the hackneyed word, with epithets inevitable, inimitable. Each drawing has been so brilliant as to make another of necessity a tour d'ésprit. "The Bostonians," "The Americans," "Daisy Miller," to mention a few, and two women in the beautiful "Wings of the Dove," and innumerable fine line-drawings, etchings, impressionist washes out of many short stories, show that he has not forgotten us either in irony or affection.

"I have had too many American contacts both in my earlier years and abroad to forget my country, to ignore it. For purposes of material these contacts have been sufficient.

"One must not overdo the English and American distinction," he continues; "we are all one literary tradition."

It was in France twenty odd years ago that as a young man Mr. James had the chance to seek how to do these things. With that famous group, Alphonse Daudet, Zola, De Maupassant, the Goncourts, Turgenieff, those who gathered at the house of Gustave Flaubert, he had the inestimable privilege of interchange of discussion, comradeship.

These authors were, as Mr. James remarked, "descendants of a much stronger group. And I wish to say that an author for whom I entertain a great esteem is Balzac."

Balzac, in a sense a "painter of life" in the "Comedie Humaine," is something of a literary ancestor. Henry James has lost the romance which Balzac inherited and gained the subtlety of the French analysts which Flaubert's realism in "Madame Bovary" prefigured and which waned in Bourget's feebleness of fibre.

All these artists, small and great, have been for our countryman as a fund of experience. His own individuality he has had the courage and strength to preserve. The physical frankness of England and the psychological frankness of the French have done a good deal for Henry James. These influences, to be translated by him, through his temperament, are enriching. If, as Americans, we are not one in culture with foreign peoples, we have still links with the world literature.

If his art is too comprehensive in culture for most of us, yet we may flatter ourselves no other country could have produced him. We find this root in his sense of humor, his avoidance of emotional appeal, his very delicacy.

LOYALTY TO AMERICA

A great many persons prefer the earlier works of Henry James. The more "precious" work of later periods inspires distrust. But this is not to call Mr. James a better writer in the former—only, perhaps, from their point of view, a better American. There will be many who will contradict this—those who prefer his perfected flavor, who delight in the most "Jamesy" things possible, but these are, just now, the connoisseurs.

Whether we admire Mr. James or not, whether outside the scattered ring of his disciples the literary critic thoroughly enjoys his work, he is not now too sure of himself. A certain self distrust is perhaps the best thing that our author has taught us.

This is one of the first notes of that which is growing into a superb public recognition, a superb literary influence. Honors cannot possibly be delayed, however little Mr. James desires fuss—personal publicity. We are really glad that our greatest author is going to take us in hand again. He may not have admitted that he intends to, but how can he help it? Because he has not lived with us, he has seemed to say that we cannot have him. Yet suddenly he has come back.

Our country is so large in area that Mr. James can find unsuspected material for great creations. His intention is to remain here for several months, visiting the South and the Pacific coast. To touch a good deal of American ground, if only suggestively, is not too much to hope for in his future work.

We need Henry James more than we deserve him. But perhaps he will turn the tables and make us deserve him before he is done with us.

Florence Brooks.

The Question of Our Speech

VII

I am offered the opportunity of addressing you a few observations on a subject that should content itself, to my thinking, with no secondary place among those justly commended to your attention on such a day as this, and that yet will not, I dare say, have been treated before you, very often, as a matter especially inviting that attention. You will have been appealed to, at this season, and in preparation for this occasion, with admirable persuasion and admirable effect, I make no doubt, on behalf of many of the interests and ideals, scholarly, moral, social, you have here so happily pursued, many of the duties, responsibilities, opportunities you have learned, in these beautiful conditions, at the threshold of life, to see open out before you. These admonitions, taken together, will have borne, essentially, upon the question of culture, as you are expected to consider and cherish it; and some of them, naturally, will have pressed on the higher, the advanced developments of that question, those that are forever flowering above our heads and waving and rustling their branches in the blue vast of human thought. Others, meanwhile, will have lingered over the fundamentals, as we may call them, the solid, settled, seated elements of education, the things of which it is held, in general, that our need of being reminded of them must rarely be allowed to become a desperate or a feverish need. These underlying things, truths of tradition, of aspiration, of discipline, of training consecrated by experience, are understood as present in any liberal course of study or scheme of character; yet they permit of a certain renewed reference and slightly ceremonial insistence,

From Henry James, *The Question of Our Speech; The Lesson of Balzac: Two Lectures* (Boston: Houghton Mifflin, Riverside Press, 1905). The following footnote appeared on the first page of the essay: "Address to the graduating class at Bryn Mawr College, Pennsylvania, June 8, 1905; here printed with the restoration of a few passages omitted on that occasion."

perhaps, on high days and holidays; without the fear, on the part of any one concerned, of their falling too much into the category of the commonplace. I repeat, however, that there is a prime part of education, an element of the basis itself, in regard to which I shall probably remain within the bounds of safety in declaring that no explicit, no separate, no adequate plea will be likely to have ranged itself under any one of your customary heads of commemoration. If there are proprieties and values, perfect possessions of the educated spirit, clear humanities, as the old collegiate usage beautifully named them, that may be taken absolutely for granted, taken for granted as rendering any process of training simply possible, the indispensable preliminary I allude to, and that I am about to name, would easily indeed present itself in that light; thus confessing to its established character and its tacit intervention. A virtual consensus of the educated, of any gathered group, in regard to the *speech* that, among the idioms and articulations of the globe, they profess to make use of, may well strike us, in a given case, as a natural, an inevitable assumption. Without that consensus, to every appearance, the educative process cannot be thought of as at all even beginning; we readily perceive that without it the mere imparting of a coherent culture would never get under way. This imparting of a coherent culture is a matter of communication and response—each of which branches of an understanding involves the possession of a common language, with its modes of employment, its usage, its authority, its beauty, in working form; a medium of expression, in short, organized and developed. So obvious is such a truth that even at these periods of an especially excited consciousness of your happy approximation to the ideal, your conquest, so far as it has proceeded, of the humanities aforesaid, of the great attainable amenities, you would not think of expecting that your not having failed to master the system of mere vocal sounds that renders your fruitful association with each other a thinkable thing should be made a topic of inquiry or of congratulation. You would say if you thought about the point at all: "Why, of course we speak in happy forms; we arrive here, arrive from our convenient homes, our wonderful schools, our growing cities, our great and glorious States, speaking in those happy forms in which people speak whose speech promotes the refinements (in a word the success) of intercourse, intellectual and social—not in any manner in which people speak whose speech frustrates, or hampers, or mocks at them. That conquest is behind us, and we invite no discussion of the question of whether we are articulate, whether we are intelligibly, or completely, expressive—we expose ourselves to none; the question of whether we are heirs and mistresses of the art of making ourselves satisfactorily heard, conveniently listened to, comfortably and agreeably understood."

Such, I say, is the assumption that everything must always have ministered to your making: so much as to stamp almost with a certain indecorum, on the face of the affair, any breach of the silence surrounding these familiar securities and serenities. I can only stand before you, accordingly, as a breaker of the silence; breaking it as gently, of course, as all the pleasant proprieties of this hour demand, but making the point that there is an element of fallacy—in plain terms a measurable mistake—in the fine confidence I am thus feeling my way to impute to you. It is needless to make sure of the basis of the process of communication and intercourse when it is clear, when it is positive, that such a basis exists and flourishes; but that is a question as to which the slightest shade of doubt is disquieting, disconcerting—fatal indeed; so that an exceptional inquiry into the case is then prescribed. I shall suggest our making this inquiry altogether—after having taken it thus as exceptionally demanded; making it rapidly, in the very limited way for which our present conditions allow us moments; but at least with the feeling that we are breaking ground where it had not hitherto, among us, strangely enough, been much broken, and where some measurable good may spring, for us, from our action.

If we may not then be said to be able to converse before we are able to talk (and study is essentially, above all in such a place as this, your opportunity to converse with your teachers and inspirers), so we may be said not to be able to "talk" before we are able to speak: whereby you easily see what we thus get. We may not be said to be able to study—and *a fortiori* do any of the things we study *for*—unless we are able to speak. All life therefore comes back to the question of our speech, the medium through which we communicate with each other; for all life comes back to the question of our relations with each other. These relations are made possible, are registered, are verily constituted, by our speech, and are successful (to repeat my word) in proportion as our speech is worthy of its great human and social function; is developed, delicate, flexible, rich—an adequate accomplished fact. The more it suggests and expresses the more we live by it— the more it promotes and enhances life. Its quality, its authenticity, its security, are hence supremely important for the general multifold opportunity, for the dignity and integrity, of our existence.

These truths, you see, are incontestable; yet though you are daughters, fortunate in many respects, of great commonwealths that have been able to render you many attentions, to surround you with most of the advantages of peace and plenty, it is none the less definite that there will have been felt to reign among you, in general, no positive mark whatever, public or private, of an effective consciousness of any of them; the consciousness, namely—a sign of societies truly possessed of light—that no civilized body of men and women has ever left so vital an interest to run wild, to shift, as we say, all for itself, to stumble and flounder, through mere adventure and accident, in the common dust of life, to pick up a living, in fine, by the wayside and the ditch. Of the degree in which a society is civilized the vocal form, the vocal tone, the personal, social accent and sound of its intercourse, have always been held to give a direct reflection. That sound, that vocal form, the touchstone of manners, is the note, the representative note—representative of its having (in our poor, imperfect human degree) achieved civilization. Judged in this light, it must frankly be said, our civilization remains strikingly *un*achieved; the last of American idiosyncrasies, the last by which we can be conceived as "represented" in the international concert of culture, would be the pretension to a tone-standard, to our wooing comparison with that of other nations. The French, the Germans, the Italians, the English perhaps in particular, and many other people, Occidental and Oriental, I surmise, not excluding the Turks and the Chinese, have for the symbol of education, of civility, a tone-standard; we alone flourish in undisturbed and—as in the sense of so many other of our connections—in something like sublime unconsciousness of any such possibility.

It is impossible, in very fact, to have a tone-standard without the definite preliminary of a *care* for tone, and against a care for tone, it would very much appear, the elements of life in this country, as at present conditioned, violently and increasingly militate. At one or two reasons for this strange but consummate conspiracy I shall in a moment ask you to glance with me, but in the meanwhile I should go any length in agreeing with you about any such perversity, on the part of parents and guardians, pastors and masters, as their expecting the generations, whether of young women or young men, to arrive at a position of such comparative superiority alone—unsupported and unguided. There is no warrant for the placing on these inevitably rather light heads and hearts, on any company of you, assaulted, in our vast vague order, by many pressing wonderments, the *whole* of the burden of a care for tone. A care for tone is part of a care for many other things besides; for the fact, for the value, of good breeding, above all, as to which tone unites with various other personal, social signs to bear testimony. The idea of good breeding—without which intercourse fails to flower into fineness, without which human relations bear but crude and tasteless fruit—is one of the most precious conquests of civilization, the very core of our social heritage; but in the transmission of which it becomes us much more to be active and interested than merely passive and irresponsible participants. It is an idea, the idea of good breeding (in other words, simply the idea of *secure* good manners), for which, always, in every generation, there is yet more, and yet more, to be done; and no danger would be more lamentable than that of the real extinction, in our hands, of so sacred a flame. Flames, however, even the most sacred, do not go on burning of themselves; they require to be kept up; handed on the torch needs to be from one group of patient and competent watchers to another. The possibility, the preferability, of people's speaking as people speak when their speech has had for them a signal importance, is a matter to be kept sharply present; from that comes support, comes example, comes authority—from that comes the inspiration of those comparative beginners of life, the hurrying children of time, who are but too exposed to be worked upon, by a hundred circumstances, in a different and inferior sense. You don't speak soundly and agreeably, you don't speak neatly and consistently, unless you *know* how you speak, how you may, how you should, how you shall speak, unless you have discriminated, unless you have noticed differences and suffered from violations and vulgarities; and you have not this positive consciousness, you are incapable of any reaction of taste or sensibility worth mentioning, unless a great deal of thought of the matter has been taken *for* you.

Taking thought, in this connection, is what I mean by obtaining a tone-standard—a clear criterion of the best usage and example: which is but to recognize, once for all, that avoiding vulgarity, arriving at lucidity, pleasantness, charm, and contributing by the mode and the degree of utterance a colloquial, a genial value even to an inevitably limited quantity of intention, of thought, is an art to be acquired and cultivated, just as much as any of the other, subtler, arts of life. There are plenty of influences round about us that make for an imperfect disengagement of the human side of vocal sound, that make for the confused, the ugly, the flat, the thin, the mean, the helpless, that reduce articulation to an easy and ignoble minimum, and so keep it as little distinct as possible from the grunting, the squealing, the barking or the roaring of animals. I do not mean to say that civility of utterance may not become an all but unconscious beautiful habit—I mean to say, thank goodness, that this is exactly what it *may* become. But so to succeed it must be a collective and associated habit; for the greater the number of persons speaking well, in given conditions, the more that number will tend to increase, and the smaller the number the more that number will tend to shrink and lose itself in the desert of the common. Contact and communication, a beneficent contagion, bring about the happy state—the state of sensibility to tone, the state of recognizing, and responding to, certain vocal sounds *as* tone, and recognizing and reacting from certain others as negations of tone: negations the more offensive in proportion as they have most enjoyed impunity. You will have, indeed, in any at all aspiring cultivation of tone, a vast mass of assured impunity, of immunity on the wrong side of the line, to reckon with. There are in every quarter, in our social order, impunities of aggression and corruption in plenty; but there are none, I think, showing so unperturbed a face—wearing, I should slangily say, if slang were permitted me here, so impudent a "mug"—as the forces assembled to make you believe that no form of speech is provably better than another, and that just this matter of "care" is an affront to the majesty of sovereign ignorance. Oh, I don't mean to say that you will find in the least a clear field and nothing but favor! The difficulty of your case is exactly the ground of my venturing thus to appeal to you. That there is difficulty, that there is a great blatant, blowing dragon to slay, can only constitute, as it appears to me, a call of honor for generous young minds, something of a trumpet-sound for tempers of high courage.

And now, of course, there are questions you may ask me: as to what I more intimately mean by speaking "well," by speaking "ill;" as to what I more definitely mean by "tone" and by the "negation" of tone; as to where you are to recognize the presence of the exemplary rightness I have referred you to—as to where you are to see any standard raised to the breeze; and above all, as to my reasons for referring with such emphasis to the character of the enemy you are to overcome. I am able, I think, to satisfy you all the way; but even in so doing I shall still feel our question to be interesting, as a whole, out of proportion to any fractions of an hour we may now clutch at; feel that if I could only treat it with a freer hand and more margin I might really create in you a zeal to follow it up. I mean, then, by speaking well, in the first place, speaking under the influence of *observation*—your own. I mean speaking with consideration for the forms and shades of our language, a consideration so inbred that it has become instinctive and well-nigh unconscious and automatic, as all the habitual, all the inveterate amenities of life become. By the forms and shades of our language I mean the innumerable differentiated, discriminated units of sound and sense that lend themselves to audible production, to enunciation, to intonation: those innumerable units that have, each, an identity, a quality, an outline, a shape, a clearness, a fineness, a sweetness, a richness, that have, in a word, a value, which it is open to us, as lovers of our admirable English tradition, or as cynical traitors to it, to preserve or to destroy.

Many of these units are, for instance, our syllables, emphasized or unemphasized, our parts of words, or often the whole word itself, our parts of sentences, coming in *for* value and subject to be marked or missed, honored or dishonored—to use the term we use for checks at banks—as a note of sound. Many of them are in particular our simple vowel-notes and our consonantal, varying, shifting—shifting in relation and connection, as to value and responsibility and place—and capable of a complete effect, or of a complete absence of effect, according as a fine ear and a fine tongue, or as a coarse ear and a coarse tongue, preside at the use of them. All our employment of constituted sounds, syllables, sentences, comes back to the way we say a thing, and it is very largely by saying, all the while, that we live and play our parts. I am asking you to take it from me, as the very moral of these remarks, that the way we say a thing, or fail to say it, fail to learn to say it, has an importance in life that it is impossible to overstate—a far-reaching importance, as the very hinge of the relation of man to man. I am asking you to take that truth well home and hold it close to your hearts, setting your backs to the wall to defend it, heroically, when need may be. For need will be, among us, as I have already intimated, and as I shall proceed in a moment, though very briefly, to show you further: you must be prepared for much vociferous demonstration of the plea that the way we say things—the way we "say" in general—has as little importance as possible. Let the demonstration proceed, let the demonstration abound, let it be as vociferous as it will, if you only meanwhile hug the closer the faith I thus commend to you; for you will very presently perceive that the more this vain contention does make itself heard, the more it insists, the sooner it shall begin to flounder waist-high in desert sands. Nothing, sayable or said, that pretends to expression, to value, to consistency, in whatever interest, but finds itself practically confronted, at once, with the tone-question: the only refuge from which is the mere making of a noise—since simple noise is the sort of sound in which tone ceases to exist. To simple toneless noise, as an argument for indifference to discriminated speech, you may certainly then listen as philosophically as your nerves shall allow. But the term I here apply brings me meanwhile to my second answer to your three or four postulated challenges—the question of what I mean by speaking badly. I might reply to you, very synthetically, that I mean by speaking badly speaking as millions and millions of supposedly educated, supposedly civilized persons—that is the point—of both sexes, in our great country, habitually, persistently, imperturbably, and I think for the most part all unwittingly, speak: that form of satisfaction to you being good enough—is n't it?—to cover much of the ground. But I must give you a closer account of the evil against which I warn you, and I think none is so close as this: that speaking badly is speaking with that want of attention to speech that we should blush to see any other of our personal functions compromised by—any other controllable motion, or voluntary act, of our lives. Want of attention, in any act, results in a graceless and unlighted effect, an effect of accident and misadventure; and it strikes me in this connection that there is no better comprehensive description of our vocal habits as a nation, in their vast, monotonous flatness and crudity, than this aspect and air of unlightedness— which presents them as matters going on, gropingly, helplessly, empirically, almost dangerously (perilously, that is, to life and limb), in the dark. To walk in the dark, dress in the dark, eat in the dark, is to run the chance of breaking our legs, of misarranging our clothes, of besmearing our persons; and speech may figure for us either as the motion, the food, or the clothing of intercourse, as you will. To do things "unlightedly" is accordingly to do them without neatness or completeness—and to accept that doom is simply to accept the doom of the slovenly.

Our national use of vocal sound, in men and women alike, *is* slovenly—an absolutely inexpert daub of unapplied tone. It leaves us at the mercy of a medium that, as I say, is incomplete; which sufficiently accounts, as regards our whole vocal manifestation, for the effect of a want of finish. Noted sounds have their extent and their limits, their mass, however concentrated, and their edges; and what is the speech of a given society but a series, a more or less rich complexity, of noted sounds? Nothing is commoner than to see throughout our country, young persons of either sex—for the phenomenon is most marked, I think, for reasons I will touch on, in the newer generations—whose utterance can only be indicated by pronouncing it destitute of any approach to an emission of the consonant. It becomes thus a mere helpless slobber of disconnected vowel noises—the weakest and cheapest attempt at human expression that we shall easily encounter, I imagine, in any community pretending to the general instructed state. Observe, too, that the vowel sounds in themselves, at this rate, quite fail of any purity, for the reason that our consonants contribute to the drawing and modeling of our vowels—just as our vowels contribute to the coloring, to the painting, as we may call it, of our consonants, and that any frequent repetition of a vowel depending for all rounding and shaping on another vowel alone lays upon us an effort of the thorax under which we inevitably break down. Hence the undefined noises that I refer to when consonantal sound drops out; drops as it drops, for example, among those vast populations to whose lips, to whose ear, it is so rarely given to form the terminal letter of our "Yes," or to hear it formed. The abject "Yeh-eh" (the ugliness of the drawl is not easy to represent) which usurps the place of that interesting vocable makes its nearest approach to deviating into the decency of a final consonant when it becomes a still more questionable "Yeh-ep."

Vast numbers of people, indeed, even among those who speak very badly, appear to grope instinctively for some restoration of the missing value even at the cost of inserting it between words that begin and end with vowels. You will perfectly hear persons supposedly "cultivated," the very instructors of youth sometimes themselves, talk of vanilla-r-ice-cream, of California-r-oranges, of Cuba-r-and Porto Rico, of Atalanta-r-in Calydon, and (very resentfully) of "the idea-r-of" any intimation that their performance and example in these respects may not be immaculate. You will perfectly hear the sons and daughters of the most respectable families disfigure in this interest, and for this purpose, the pleasant old names of Papa and Mamma. "Is Popper-up stairs?" and "is Mommer-in the parlor?" pass for excellent household speech in millions of honest homes. If the English say throughout, and not only sometimes, Papa and Mama, and the French say Papa and Maman, they say them consistently—and Popper, with an "r," but illustrates our loss, much to be regretted, alas, of the power to emulate the clearness of the vowel-cutting, an art as delicate in its way as gem-cutting, in the French word. You will, again, perfectly hear a gentle hostess, solicitous for your comfort, tell you that if you wish to lie down there is a sofa-r-in your room. No one is "thought any the worse of" for saying these things; even though it be distinct that there are circles, in other communities, the societies still keeping the touchstone of manners, as I have called our question, in its place, where they would be punctually noted. It is not always a question of an *r*, however—though the letter, I grant, gets terribly little rest among those great masses of our population who strike us, in the boundless West perhaps especially, as, under some strange impulse received toward consonantal recovery of balance, making it present even in words from which it is absent, bringing it in everywhere as with the small vulgar effect of a sort of morose grinding of the back teeth. There are, you see, sounds of a mysterious intrinsic meanness, and there are sounds of a mysterious intrinsic frankness and sweetness; and I think the recurrent note I have indicated—fatherr and motherr and otherr, waterr and matterr and scatterr, harrd and barrd, parrt, starrt, and (dreadful to say) arrt (the repetition it is that drives home the ugliness), are signal specimens of what becomes of a custom of utterance out of which the principle of taste has dropped.

If I speak, as to these matters of tone, I may add, of intrinsic meanness and intrinsic sweetness, there is also no doubt that association, cumulation, the context of a given sound and the company we perceive it to be keeping, are things that have much to say to our better or worse impression. What has become of the principle of taste, at all events, when the *s*, too, breaks in, or breaks out, all unchecked and unchided, in such forms of impunity as Some-wheres-else and Nowheres-else, as A good ways-on and A good ways-off?—vulgarisms with which a great deal of general credit for what we good-naturedly call "refinement" appears so able to coexist. Credit for what we good-naturedly call refinement— since our national, our social good nature is, experimentally, inordinate—appears able to coexist with a thousand other platitudes and poverties of tone, aberrations too numerous for me to linger on in these very limited moments, but in relation to which all the flatly-drawling group—gawd and dawg, sawft and lawft, gawne and lawst and frawst—may stand as a hint. Let me linger only long enough to add a mention of the deplorable effect of the almost total loss, among innumerable speakers, of any approach to purity in the sound of the *e*. It is converted, under this particularly ugly blight, into a *u* which is itself unaccompanied with any dignity of intention, which makes for mere ignoble thickness and turbidity. For choice, perhaps, "vurry," "Amurrica," "Philadulphia," "tullegram," "twuddy" (what becomes of "twenty" here is an ineptitude truly beyond any alliteration), and the like, descend deepest into the abyss. It is enough to say of those things that they substitute limp, slack, passive tone for clear, clean, active, tidy tone, and that they are typical, thereby, of an immense body of limpness and slackness and cheapness. This note of cheapness—of the cheap and easy—is especially fatal to any effect of security of intention in the speech of a society—for it is scarce necessary to remind you that there are two very different kinds of ease: the ease that comes from the facing, the conquest of a difficulty, and the ease that comes from the vague dodging of it. In the one case you gain facility, in the other case you get mere looseness. In the one case the maintenance of civility of speech costs what it must—which is a price we should surely blush to hear spoken of as too great for our inaptitude and our indolence, our stupidity and our frivolity, to pay.

I must invite you indeed to recognize with me, at whatever cost to any possible share in our national self-complacency, that we encounter in all this connection a certain portent in our sky, a certain lion in our path, complications duly to be reckoned with; encounter them in the circumstance of the *voice* of our people at large, our people abundantly schooled and newspapered, abundantly housed, fed, clothed, salaried and taxed—which happens to fall on no expert attention you may easily note, as the finest or fullest or richest of the voices of the nations: this, moreover, least of all among our women, younger and older, as to whom in general, and as to the impression made by whom, the question of voice ever most comes up and has most importance. The *vox Americana* then, frankly, is for the spectator, or perhaps I should say for the auditor of life, as he travels far and wide, one of the stumbling blocks of our continent—having no claim to be left out of account in any discussion of the matter before us. It remains for the moment, this collective vocal presence, this preponderant vocal sign, what a convergence of inscrutable forces (climatic, social, political, theological, moral, "psychic") has made it and failed to make it: so that I shall ask you to let it stand for you thus as a *temporarily-final* fact—so stand long enough to allow me to say that, whatever else it is, it has been, among the organs of the schooled and newspapered races, perceptibly the most abandoned to its fate. That truth about it is more to our purpose than any other, and throws much light, I am convinced, on the manner in which it affects and afflicts us. I shall go so far as to say that there is no such thing as a voice pure and simple: there is only, for any business of appreciation, the voice *plus* the way it is employed; an employment determined here by a greater number of influences than we can now go into— beyond affirming at least, that when such influences, in general, have acted for a long time we think of them as having made not only the history of the voice, but positively the history of the national character, almost the history of the people.

It would take thus too long to tell you why the English voice, or why the French, or why the Italian, is so free to strike us as *not* neglected, not abandoned to its fate; as having much rather been played upon, through the generations, by a multitude of causes which have finally begotten, in each of these instances, as means to an end, a settled character, a certain ripeness, finality and felicity. I cannot but regard the unsettled character and the inferior quality of the colloquial *vox Americana*—and I speak here but of the poor dear distracted organ itself— as in part a product of that mere state of indifference to a speech-standard and to a tone-standard on which I have been insisting. The voice, I repeat, is, as to much of its action and much of its effect, not a separate, lonely, lost thing, but largely what the tone, the conscious, intended, associated tone, makes of it— and what the tone that has none of these attributes falls short of making; so that if we here again, as a people, take care, if we take even common care, of the question, for fifty years or thereabout, I have no doubt we shall in due course find the subject of our solicitude put on, positively, a surface, find it reflect and repay the enlightened effort. We shall find that, while we have been so well occupied, the vocal, the tonic possibilities within us all, grateful to us for the sense of a flattering interest, of the offer of a new life, have been taking care, better care, excellent care, of *themselves*. The experiment, absolutely, would be worth trying—and perhaps not on so formidable a scale of time either. We see afresh, at any rate, into what interesting relations and ramifications our topic opens out—if only as an illustration of what we may do for ourselves by merely *raising* our question and setting it up before us. With it verily we raise and set up the question of our manners as well, for that is indissolubly involved. To discriminate, to learn to find our way among noted sounds, find it as through the acquisition of a new ear; to begin to prefer form to the absence of form, to distinguish color from the absence of color—all this amounts to substituting manner for the absence of manner: whereby it is *manners themselves*, or something like a sketchy approach to a dim gregarious conception of them, that we shall (delicious thought!) begin to work round to the notion of.

I should also not fail to remind you, for keeping all things clear, that I refer here not specifically, in fact not directly at all, to our handling of the English language as such—even though wonderful enough the adventure may be to which, in our so unceremonious, so simplified and simplifying conditions, we are treating that ancient and battered but still nobly robust and at the same time tenderly vulnerable idiom. I am not doing so, because this matter of the use and abuse of our mother-tongue would be another theme altogether, in spite of its close alliance with the question before us. Yet I cannot wholly forget that the adventure, as I name it, of our idiom and the adventure of our utterance have been fundamentally the same adventure and the same experience; that they at a given period migrated together, immigrated together, into the great raw world in which they were to be cold-shouldered and neglected together, left to run wild and lose their way together. They have suffered and strayed together, and the future of the one, we must after all remember, is necessarily and logically the prospect or the doom of the other. Keep in sight the so interesting historical truth that no language, so far back as our acquaintance with history goes, has known any such ordeal, any such stress and strain, as was to await the English in this huge new community it was so unsuspectingly to help, at first, to father and mother. It came *over*, as the phrase is, came over originally without fear and without guile— but to find itself transplanted to spaces it had never dreamed, in its comparative humility, of covering, to conditions it had never dreamed, in its comparative innocence, of meeting; to find itself grafted, in short, on a social and political order that was both without previous precedent and example and incalculably expansive.

Taken on the whole by surprise it may doubtless be said to have behaved as well as unfriended heroine ever behaved in dire predicament—refusing, that is, to be frightened quite to death, looking about for a *modus vivendi*, consenting to live, preparing to wait on developments. I say "unfriended" heroine because that is exactly my point: that whereas the great idioms of Europe in general have grown up at home and in the family, the ancestral circle (with their migrations all comfortably prehistoric), our transported maiden, our unrescued Andromeda, our medium of utterance, was to be disjoined from all the associations, the other presences, that had attended her, that had watched for her and with her, that had helped to form her manners and her voice, her taste and her genius. It is the high modernism of the conditions now surrounding, on this continent, the practice of our language that makes of this chapter in its history a new thing under the sun; and I use that term as the best for expressing briefly ever so many striking actualities. If you reflect a moment you will see how unprecedented is in fact this uncontrolled assault of most of our circumstances—and in the forefront of them the common school and the newspaper—upon what we may call our linguistic *position*. Every language has its position, which, with its particular character and genius, is its most precious property—the element in it we are most moved (if we have any feeling in the connection at all) to respect, to confirm, to consecrate. What we least desire to do with these things is to give them, in our happy phrase, "away;" and we must allow that if this be none the less what has really happened in our case the reason for the disaster resides in the seemingly overwhelming (for the time at least) forces of betrayal. To the American common school, to the American newspaper, and to the American Dutchman and Dago, as the voice of the people describes them, we have simply handed over our property—not exactly bound hand and foot, I admit, like Andromeda awaiting her Perseus, but at least distracted, dishevelled, despoiled, divested of that beautiful and becoming drapery of native atmosphere and circumstance which had, from far back, made, on its behalf, for practical protection, for a due tenderness of interest.

I am perfectly aware that the common school and the newspaper are influences that shall often have been named to you, exactly, as favorable, as positively and actively contributive, to the prosperity of our idiom; the answer to which is that the matter depends, distinctly, on what is meant by prosperity. It is prosperity, of a sort, that a hundred million people, a few years hence, will be unanimously, loudly—above all loudly, I think!—speaking it, and that, moreover, many of these millions will have been artfully wooed and weaned from the Dutch, from the Spanish, from the German, from the Italian, from the Norse, from the Finnish, from the Yiddish even, strange to say, and (stranger still to say) even from the English, for the sweet sake, or the sublime consciousness, as we may perhaps put it, of speaking, of talking, for the first time in their lives, *really* at their ease. There are many things our now so profusely imported and, as is claimed, quickly assimilated foreign brothers and sisters may do at their ease in this country, and at two minutes' notice, and without asking any one else's leave or taking any circumstance whatever into account—any save an infinite uplifting sense of freedom and facility; but the thing they may best do is play, to their heart's content, with the English language, or, in other words, dump their mountain of promiscuous material into the foundations of the American. As to any claim made for the newspapers, there would be far more to say than I can thus even remotely allude to; it will suffice, however, if I just recall to you that contribution to the idea of expression which you must feel yourselves everywhere getting, wherever you turn, from the mere noisy vision of their ubiquitous page, bristling with rude effigies and images, with vociferous "headings," with letterings, with black eruptions of print, that we seem to measure by feet rather than by inches, and that affect us positively as the roar of some myriad-faced monster—as the grimaces, the shouts, shrieks and yells, ranging over the whole gamut of ugliness, irrelevance, dissonance, of a mighty maniac who has broken loose and who is running amuck through the spheres alike of sense and of sound. So it is, surely, that our wonderful daily press *most* vividly reads us the lesson of *values*, of just proportion and just appreciation, lights the air for this question of our improvement.

The truth is that, excellent for diffusion, for vulgarization, for simplification, the common schools and the "daily paper" define themselves before us as quite below the mark for discrimination and selection, for those finer offices of vigilance and criticism in the absence of which the forms of civility, with the forms of speech most setting the example, drift out to sea. Our case is accordingly not that we should indulge in jealousy, in care, less than other communities, but that we are the community in the world who should precisely most indulge in them.

We should rather sit up at night with our preoccupation than close our eyes by day as well as by night. All the while we sleep the vast contingent of aliens whom we make welcome, and whose main contention, as I say, is that, from the moment of their arrival, they have just as much property in our speech as we have, and just as good a right to do what they choose with it—the grand right of the American being to do just what he chooses "over here" with anything and everything: all the while we sleep the innumerable aliens are sitting up (*they* don't sleep!) to work their will on their new inheritance and prove to us that they are without any finer feeling or more conservative instinct of consideration for it, more fond, unutterable association with it, more hovering, caressing curiosity about it, than they may have on the subject of so many yards of freely figured oilcloth, from the shop, that they are preparing to lay down, for convenience, on kitchen floor or kitchen staircase. Oilcloth is highly convenient, and our loud collective medium of intercourse doubtless strikes these new house-holders as wonderfully resisting "wear"—with such wear as it gets!—strikes them as an excellent bargain: durable, tough, cheap.

Just here it is that I may be asked, meanwhile—or that you are likely to be asked in your turn, so far as you may be moved to make anything of these admonitions—whether a language be not always a living organism, fed by the very breath of those who employ it, whoever these may happen to be; of those who carry it with them, on their long road, as their specific experience grows larger and more complex, and who need it to help them to meet this expansion. The question is whether it be not either no language at all, or only a very poor one, if it have not in it to respond, from its core, to the constant appeal of time, perpetually demanding new tricks, new experiments, new amusements of it: so to respond without losing its characteristic balance. The answer to that is, a hundred times, "Yes," assuredly, so long as the conservative interest, which should always predominate, remains, equally, the constant quantity; remains an embodied, constituted, inexpugnable thing. The conservative interest is really as indispensable for the institution of speech as for the institution of matrimony. Abate a jot of the quantity, and, much more, of the quality, of the consecration required, and we practically find ourselves emulating the beasts, who prosper as well without a vocabulary as without a marriage-service. It is easier to overlook any question of speech than to trouble about it, but then it is also easier to snort or neigh, to growl or to "meaow," than to articulate and intonate.

With this hint, for you, of the manner in which the forces of looseness are in possession of the field, you may well wonder where you are to meet the influences of example and authority, as we can only call them, my failure to undertake to indicate same attesting presence of which would leave me in such sore straits. Well, I grant you here that I am at a loss to name you particular and unmistakable, edifying and illuminating groups or classes, from which this support is to be derived; since nothing, unfortunately, more stares us in the face than the frequent failure of such comfort in those quarters where we might, if many things were different, most look for it. When you have heard a fond parent remark, in jealous majesty, to a conscientious instructor of youth, that there is no call for "interference" with the vocal noises of a loved son or daughter whose vocal noises have been unmoderated and uncontrolled since the day of birth, and that these graces quite satisfy the sense of the home-circle; and when, to match such an attitude, you have heard an unawakened teacher disclaim responsibility for any such element as the tone-element and the voice-element in the forming of a young intelligence: when you have been present at such phenomena you will not unnaturally feel that the case is bewildering, feel yourselves perhaps even tragically committed to a doom. Cling, none the less, always, to a working faith, and content yourselves—if you can't encounter complete pleasantly-speaking companies, in any number—with encountering, blessedly, here and there, articulate individuals, torch-bearers, as we may rightly describe them, guardians of the sacred flame. It is not a question, however, so much of simply meeting them, as of attending to them, of making your profit of them, when you do meet. If they be at all adequate representatives of some decent tradition, you will find the interest of a new world, a whole extension of life, open to you in the attempt to estimate, in the habit of observing, in their speech, all that such a tradition consists of. Begin to exercise your attention on that, and let the consequences sink into your spirit. At first dimly, but then more and more distinctly, you will find yourselves noting, comparing, preferring, at last positively emulating and imitating.

Imitating, yes; I commend to you, earnestly and without reserve, as the first result and concomitant of observation, the imitation of formed and finished utterance wherever, among all the discords and deficiencies, that music steals upon your ear. The more you listen to it the more you will love it—the more you will wonder that you could ever have lived without it. What I thus urge upon you, you see, is a consciousness, an acute consciousness, absolutely; which is a proposition and a name likely enough to raise among many of your friends a protest. "Conscious, imitative speech—is n't that more dreadful than anything else?" It's not "dreadful," I reply, any more than it's ideal: the matter depends on the stage of development it represents. It's an awkwardness, in your situation, that your own stage is an early one, and that you have found, round about you— outside of these favoring shades—too little help. Therefore your consciousness will now represent the phase of awakening, and that will last what it must. Unconsciousness is beautiful when it means that our knowledge has passed into our conduct and our life; has become, as we say, a second nature. But the opposite state is the door through which it has to pass, and which is, inevitably, sometimes, rather straight and narrow. This squeeze is what we pay for having revelled too much in ignorance. Keep up your hearts, all the same, keep them up to the pitch of confidence in that "second nature" of which I speak; the perfect possession of this highest of the civilities, the sight, through the narrow portal, of the blue horizon across the valley, the wide fair country in which your effort will have settled to the most exquisite of instincts, in which you will taste all the savor of gathered fruit, and in which perhaps, at last, *then*, "in solemn troops and sweet societies," you may, sounding the clearer notes of intercourse as only women can, become yourselves models and missionaries, perhaps a little even martyrs, of the good cause.

The Speech of American Women

VIII

PART I

I seem to recognize it as one of the commonplaces of journalism, certainly of American journalism, that the American woman more and more presents herself as a great success in the world; and it is evident enough that for a long time she has been abundantly assured of this. She has had at her service an unequalled system of publicity—that of the journalism in question, taking the term in its largest sense—and not to have been quite at its mercy she must much have veiled her face and stopped her ears. The great agency of her fame has not always treated, and still does not inveterately treat, her with high consideration in particular cases—it may be noted, in truth, over the land, as often taking strange liberties with her; but it at least trumpets, in its brazen voice, from sea to sea, every motion she makes, every step she takes, every dress she wears, every friend she visits or receives, the color of her hair, the number of her gloves, the names of her lap-dogs, the parties to her flirtations and matrimonial engagements; and so on from the cradle to the grave. This tribute is rendered in virtue of her high importance—in other words of the intensity and immensity of her presence, regarded everywhere as so promptly effective and triumphant. The publicity it is that attests her success, for what is success, at this time of day and in the conditions I refer to, but to be as public as possible? It is the most universal state, then, of the American woman, who enjoys it with fewer restrictions, fewer discriminations as from Mrs. Brown to Mrs. Smith, let alone

From *Harper's Bazar* 40.11 (Nov. 1906): 979–82; 40.12 (Dec. 1906): 1103–06; 41.1 (Jan. 1907): 17–21; 41.2 (Feb. 1907): 113–17.

from maiden to maiden, in either clan, than her sisters elsewhere under the sun; and it has ended as with a practical invitation to us to swell the appreciative chorus. Good-naturedly, irreflectively, the vague observer is prone, no doubt, to do so; the last thing he thinks of, that is, is to challenge so seemingly overwhelming a consensus. It is borne in upon him that if mankind at large has become acutely conscious of the creature, there must be something "behind" such a fact; the creature must somehow explain her remarkable fortune.

She does, certainly, in a great measure explain it, though it is not less to be noted that the fortune appears as yet to have been subjected to no very searching analysis. When it is a question, in other words, of what the success of our so predominant type consists of, we encounter, I think, a certain looseness of answer, mitigated by some glittering mention of the ladies who have married European nobles and diplomatists. The looseness, however, is for many reasons inevitable, and, beyond contradiction, the general postulate does represent a reality. Only the reality, I think, is a much more interesting matter than any pretended record of the exercise of charms and the carrying off of prizes. Of the conditions in which these numerous exploits have been performed there would be much to say—including the fact that they are not so numerous as not to have been, in a hundred quarters, made the very most of. But grant them all, and everything they are supposed to represent, the reality I speak of is still the key to the true sense of the case. The more we look at American life the more we see that any social aspect takes its main sense from its democratic connections. The star of the most organized and most active of Democracies that ever was shines upon it; that is the light in which we read it clearest. It is therefore what her social climate and air have done, and have failed to do, for the American woman that tells us most about her, and we really approach her nearest in studying her full-blown ubiquity as that of the most confidently "grown" and most freely encouraged plant in our democratic garden. The conditions of American life in general, and our great scheme of social equality in particular, have done many things for her, and left many others undone; but they have above all secured her this primary benefit that she is the woman in the world who is least "afraid." There is no doubt that, as a foundation, this has been an excellent thing for her; it has had at any rate more to do with her "success" than all the rest of her attributes together.

There have been fewer things about her for her to fear than about her sisters languishing under other laws; and this partly because there have been fewer things of any sort—because she has grown up in an emptier, a less settled and crowded world. Her surrounding medium has not pressed upon her, as it is of the nature of the different parts of old and dense civilizations to press—and to press especially where weakness and sensibility prevail. She was not, from the first, to be put on her guard, as feeling herself too often and too possibly an object of prey and of patronage; conscious, from the cradle, of being, in her family circle and on her social ground, as "good" as any one, as good as the best, doubts, anxieties, terrors, were far from her thought, which provided her as little, even in its wildest flights, with any generic terms for comparison, any vision of "superior" classes, persons, or things. One of the forms of fear is diffidence, not to say respect; and in what presence was a being of a consciousness so restricted not to feel at her ease? The product of an order in which no presence was really so taken for granted as her own, her view of relations was thereby inordinately simplified. All this was to be, as I say, of happy effect for herself, no doubt, and even for those dealing with her, so long as the general case for her remained that of her immediate habitat, her native conditions. She was for a long time indeed to know none others, and her type, in so favoring an air, under this large simplicity of state, was gradually, but quite definitely, to establish itself. It was to do more than this; it was to reveal itself, with the inevitable growth of opportunity, the spread of intercourse over the world, to communities that, in different conditions, had evolved quite other types, and was to take these communities altogether by surprise. It was to affect them as a new thing under the sun, a remarkable variety of a species of which they had supposed themselves to have exhausted the forms. They had known, they had produced women of many kinds, but they had produced nothing that resembled the American.

It all came back, absolutely to her one great sign; it was by that they knew her, and it was by that she made her way. She wasn't afraid, they couldn't at first get over it—this was to take them a long time. They have not wholly got over it yet, even—though a beginning clearly has been made; and the reason is partly, no doubt, in the great number of relations, all absolutely new to her and all serenely faced on the spot, as to which, time after time, they were to see her courage tested. It was to show itself moreover not as a grim and gloomy, but, very considerably, as a light and lively courage, and was to represent, to observation, an extraordinary sum of exemptions. These exemptions were to call attention, on the other hand, we may take it, to all those attitudes of fear that had been immemorially considered, in "Europe," to grace the feminine character; so that their influence might practically have been, on foreign ground, toward a complete revision of it. It is not too much to say that the revision has to a certain extent taken place; it is not for nothing, at least, that the daughters of other climes have become acquainted with the American idiosyncrasy. It is not for nothing that they have been allowed to see what it is to go in fear neither as matrons nor as maidens, neither as sweethearts nor as wives, neither as mothers nor as daughters nor as sisters, neither as members of society, nor as "leaders" of it, nor as free and independent conversers in it. The bearings of this impression upon the sex elsewhere is not, however, what concerns us; but only the fact of the prompt and prolonged flush of recognition by the world at large of a creature on whose head so many immunities had accumulated. It concerns us scarcely more to go into the history of these immunities and inquire how they have come so to gather and cluster—though that investigation too, at our leisure, would, I feel, much beckon me on. It is not important even to trace the process by which the early amazements I glance at have rather noticeably passed into the phase of reaction. Much more pertinent than any question of what it has meant in strange countries that our women should be as they are, is the question of what it has meant, here at home, for themselves and for their companions.

It has not meant, to begin with, at all the same thing. The *advantage* of their dauntless confidence is inevitably less striking in a world in which dangers have continued, on the whole, not to assault them. There are embarrassments to which we really seem never to see them exposed, so that their serenity affects us as, at the least, quite proportionate to any need. No one dreams of unduly or irrelevantly making love to them, of challenging, snubbing, bullying them; no one ever summons them for an account of themselves in the light of their remarkable position; neither does any one desire, on any ground, too upliftedly to consider them. They have, thanks to our particular social order, neither stages, probations, nor any form of discipline to pass through; they have none of the hierarchical complications of the older societies to reckon with. They constitute, as a result of all this, a product easily, freely, and inexpensively grown; and one speaks of them with small fairness, I hasten to affirm, without granting that, for such a product, they are, on a wide view and taking one with another, remarkable enough. It would perhaps even be possible to argue that, so considered, they testify more directly and vividly to the success of our civilization than any other mass of evidence we have to show. In what other world would the fact that so little trouble is taken about them—that is about some of them at the cost of others— leave them, all together, roughly speaking, so presentable? The "presentability" of the most pleasing specimens of the sex in more mature societies is expensively arrived at, we must assuredly always remember; arrived at by a sufficiently ruthless process of selection: it is at the cost of certain others, at the best, of certain obscured, hindered, sacrificed growths, that the happiest examples of any rich human efflorescence have hitherto managed to bask in the light. It comes back to that old observation in respect to the "European" social order bequeathed even to our modern view by antecedent conditions, that almost the main clue in the great complexity is the number of common figures and common lives required always and everywhere to fertilize the ground for the single type of the gentleman. This truth has been as unmistakable for the type of the lady, and it is what we refer to when we speak, as I just now spoke, of "trouble," in any such interest, taken or not taken. The fertilization of the social ground represents the sum of that penalty for those who bear it; and the case is therefore simpler when, far and wide, over the scene, there has (save in one quarter, of which I shall presently speak) been no penalty to be paid. The soil has undergone, for the plant of the fine individual life, none of the preparation of the grinding, the trampling, the packing into it of other lives, lives resigned to a mere subsidiary and contributive function.

The world about the American woman has not asked of her anything of that sort—that she shall have definite conceptions of duty, activity, influence; of a possible grace, of a possible sweetness, a possible power to soothe, to please, and above all to exemplify. It has simply, in its ignorance, its inexperience, its fatal good-nature, which has let so many precious opportunities, socially speaking, slip, taken her for granted as a free, inspired, supreme thing, nobly exempt, as I began by saying, from any sort of fear. What is being complete but a fear of the consequences of not being so? What is sacrificing to grace and charm, to the idea of a tone and of manners, but a fear of the penalty for indifference and neglect? Who, on the practically so perfect mistress of the situation (of ours,) is to impose such a penalty? and who, even, for that matter, is to be gratified by observances as regards which a measure, a social register, exists only in conditions quite other than ours? There are violations which, from the moment she is taken as civilized, as educated, as capable of a social part, the "European" woman is made to pay for; and first among these, it may be said, is that of the unwritten law that a lady shall speak as a lady. She may *talk* as she likes—and in proportion as society is "good" it grants her on that point more and more license; but her speech must be to the liking of those whose ear has been cultivated and has thus become sensitive. She affronts this sensibility at her peril; so that here immediately, as we see, she finds something to be afraid of. There are in fact whole constituted circles in which she is really perhaps more afraid of it than of anything else in the world; and if that degree of dread may strike us as, in strictness, disproportionate, we yet note on occasion that it often accompanies, in these same circles, high civility, true urbanity, of feminine type, and that it indeed appears more or less directly to guarantee such felicities.

That successful submission to law—unless we call it that crouching bondage to form—represents the opposite pole from the state, for a lady, of speaking as she "likes," and still more from the state of being able to give no account whatever, in such a matter, of any preference or any light. We might accept this labial and lingual and vocal independence as a high sign of the glorious courage of our women if it contained but a spark of the guiding reason that separates audacity from madness; but where do we find them prepared to answer the simplest of questions? "You speak, you claim, as you like: well, *how* is it then that, individually, you do like?—which, as the basis of your taste, it would be interesting to know. Even the cows in the field, the lambs on the moor, the asses on the green, low and bleat and bray with a certain consistency and harmony. It is true that they conform to the definite usage of their various circles; and there are many things of which they are, poor dears, mortally 'afraid'!" The great truth, for our purpose, no doubt, is that common courage is no more reasoned than common fear— unless it be a still greater one that taste, without opportunities for selection and comparison, without liability to criticism or control, is wofully apt to wander wild. That is at any rate the state of this sovereign principle among ourselves and amid that half of us in particular to whom we most look for it—the state of it on all this ground of the pleasure of the ear: which is as much as to say that practically we have no taste at all. It is a connection, accordingly, in which the predicament of our women is dire, or so grave at least as to suggest the possible profit of some free inquiry. What is the strange history of the case, and how has it become so bad? What is the prospect, if any, of its generally and gradually improving? I stand before it, I confess, with a sense of cause within cause and depth below depth; I look into it, deep down, as into the obscure, the abysmal. But an interest, a great interest, somewhere lurks and, as we fix it, seems, in huge dimness, to shape itself; so that we must at least try, with another effort or two, to let in the light.

PART TWO

There could be no better sign of the social success, as I have called it, of our women, than the fact that it is of *them* we find ourselves primarily speaking, and all irresistibly and inevitably, as soon as the question of American speech comes up. We take it, immediately, as most conspicuously lighted, over the social scene at large, by their example and attitude; for we are conscious, I think, if we reflect a little, that, for strange and portentous reasons, we all the while assume the speech of the men, and in the very same conditions, to be scarce so much as discussable. I need hardly observe, of course, that in any discussion of such a matter our reference is wholly to the "walks of life" in which a care for it and an attention to it are conceivable and presumable, and to the classes so conditioned as to recognize all that depends, for intercourse, on the way in which we address and communicate with each other. There are in the halting civilization even of the most "advanced" peoples large populations whose speech has remained as instinctive and irreflective, as untutored and unformed, and sometimes indeed as blindly felicitous, as the utterance of furred or feathered animals; but it is not to them we allude when we talk of the responsibilities and refinements of speech. We take for granted an existing or a possible *consciousness*—we at least appeal to that; and we impute no such luxury either to Georgia crackers or to Dorsetshire hinds; people endowed doubtless with a standard in regard to many of their interests, but helplessly destitute as regards this one. It is not the helpless, in short, that we consider, but those who are helpful, precisely, because their consciousness has been roused and their intelligence schooled, so that the supersession of instinct and the acquisition and application of acuteness are their especial boast. Their culture and their manners rest essentially upon the schooled state, and it is in connection with the schooled state that we observe and estimate them.

It is therefore vain for the delinquents of such societies to plead, in extenuation, the example and countenance of Dorsetshire hinds or Whitechapel hooligans—even when they plead them not only on behalf of Georgia crackers and Bowery toughs, but on behalf of the best society of Oshkosh or of American City; the case being, essentially, that the crackers and the hinds, the hooligans and the toughs, are as yet, on the whole ground, so new and unaware, so condemned, for a while longer, to struggle with dim perceptions, that we still allow them, critically, the benefit and relief of their mere instincts. At Oshkosh and at American City we expect the game, on the other hand, to be more regularly played. We may be more charmed or less charmed, as we approach these localities—which I take, I need scarce say, quite at hazard and as loosely typical—with portends, promises, aspects; but we are at any rate instantly reminded of the supreme claim of Education. It is written as large, against the sky, as towering brick-and-mortar can write it; the locality may bristle, to the wondering eye, with a thousand forms of raggedness; but, all in strange consonance with these, the very temple of the American ideal, overarching the sacred fount of human converse, the massive State schoolhouse, in short, dominates the scene and strikes the note of a new scale in the relations of objects. You may miss the church, the bank, the principal drug-store and even the hotel; you can never miss the academy. *That* fact at least is trim and square and solid; that fact, with its lines and edges and corners sharp against the sky, represents gregarious neatness where many others would appear rather desperately to fail of the indication: it seems, indeed, fairly to raise aloft the standard of the compact and the clear-cut. So much we may say for this delimitation of our field. It is the vast field of the general life of the most schoolhoused of peoples—in other words of the society supposititiously the most reclaimed from witless intellectual ways. It is the field over which the voice of the American woman resounds.

How comes it then, I am much moved to ask, that, were it not for the high-shouldered structures I have named, we might cross this vast area from sea to sea without a suggestion that the blessing of articulate speech is in the least appreciated? The voice of the American woman, enjoying immense exercise, is lifted in many causes, but the last it anywhere pleads is that of its own casual interest or charm. It pleads in a thousand places the cause of culture—which its possessors have so much at heart that they have organized, East and West and North and South, an unprecedented system of clubs and congresses for the promotion of it; yet all with a serenity of indifference to the very key of the *effect* of the cultivated feminine consciousness, a serenity which is perhaps the most bewildering incongruity in a world of incongruities. It is not certainly the only one, for the particular world we are considering contains plenty of others, at some of which I may still hope to glance; but none is so calculated to arrest and confound the observer. He finds himself, to put it simply and strongly, in presence of an anomaly which leaves him, even after much experience, still rubbing his eyes—if I may not indeed much more properly say still inveterately, and almost undisguisedly, stopping his ears. This consists, on the part of the votaries in question, of the pretension, marked by the stupendous serenity aforesaid, simply to *dispense* with that attribute which is accounted in other civilizations the sovereign stamp of the well-conditioned woman. Such a fruit of evolution as this last is, at her happiest, on her domestic and social side, perhaps *the* most precious conquest of the struggle for a better life; and the consensus of taste, the last word of enlightenment, about her, has been, ever so wisely, as it may well seem to us, that she shall be known, at her happiest, by a clearly unmistakable mark. This conviction, in mature and fortunate communities, has never been displaced or superseded, and we may neglect, critically, any trivial symptom that it is ever likely to be. For the expressional tone of a well-bred, and much more of a duly charming, person is, when we consider, the most universal of her resources and the least precarious of her supports—being the thing in the world, in this matter of the amenities, to which conscience and good-will have it most in their power to contribute.

Such has been, as I say, the social wisdom of the ages—which we immediately recognize as having made so, in the long run, for the humane effect. It has never pretended that all women can, even by taking thought—or, as who should say, by taking trouble—be either beautiful or witty; but it has distinctly kept account of a source of influence, for them, or of "success," as the critic of a vulgar age may be free to call it, closed not even to the least brilliant. It has in fact but registered its adhesion to a precious primary truth—the truth that the vocal sounds with which a woman affects the ear of man may almost at any time save her situation. It has decreed thus that no situation is practically desperate for her, that in fine the "plainness" of her other attributes is never necessarily fatal. And it rests this enlightened piety on the fact of the fundamental sensibility of the male; no substitute for his companion's intimate and irrepressible relation to him, as nature has cunningly constituted him—nature working so subtly for women, as men have tried so clumsily to work for themselves—having yet been invented. It is easy to see therefore to what possibilities of personal and social action our women are, contentedly, cynically, deplorably, blind. And it is vain for them to urge, as one can imagine their doing, that their pains would be wasted, that this particular sacrifice to the agreeable in life is the last for which they may, in the nature of the case, hope to receive credit. It is vain for them to contend that, however it may be with the man, the "educated" man, of other countries, the American male, in *his* conditions, is incapable of caring for a moment what sounds his women emit: incapable of caring because incapable of knowing—of knowing, that is, what sounds *are*, what they may be, what they should or what they shouldn't be. Of what sounds other than the yell of the stock-exchange or the football-field does he himself, we on these lines hear it asked, give the cheering example? Of what sensibility, on this score, has he really ever shown the first sign, and how, with the rudiments of sensibility, could he bear to listen, on so many occasions and in so many connections, to himself and his comrades? Isn't it everywhere written that the women, in any society, are what the men make them? And isn't it exactly visible, by that law, that the women, in societies where they do speak, have taken their cue in the first place from the men? Isn't it unmistakable in England, say, and in France, that the men have invented the standard and set the tune, and that they constitute, in the whole matter, the authority?

Inevitable, yes, some such contention as this; but constituting among us, really, as I say, a mere hollow defence, and that in view of a much more pertinent truth. That truth is simply that the women, on our side of the world, actually enjoy and *use* the authority, pleading in no other connection whatever the least unfitness for it. They have taken it over without blinking, they are encamped on every inch of the social area that the stock-exchange and the football-field leave free; the whole of the social initiative is in other words theirs, having been abandoned to them without a struggle. Their position, entrenched behind their myriad culture-clubs, could therefore not well be worse for pleading either helplessness or the fear of responsibility. The second fiddle, in any concert, plays certainly the tune of the first; but there is nothing the American woman socially less resembles than a second fiddle. It is before her, and her only, that the score is open, while, without any hesitation, and with a play of elbow all her own, she brandishes the bow. The ladies' culture-club is the most publicly taken engagement, surely, that ever was. It engages for those things which in the ancient world, as it survives around us, are held to come *after* the habit of harmonious speech, and assumed, by the same stroke, to be discussable only in its terms and with its aid; an air of grotesqueness attaching inevitably to their preceding it or dispensing with it. What it comes to then is that if our heroine's abdication, on this delicate ground, may be described (and I have so described it) as the tradition of not taking thought, so her refusal to take thought amounts really to her refusal to take trouble. This simple expression gives really the picture of her case as any general observation of our life shows it. Nothing is more apparent, in presence of any positive tradition of speech, any felt consensus on the vocal, the lingual, the labial question, on the producing of the sound, on the forming of the word, on the discriminating of the syllable, on the preserving of the difference, than that a great deal of trouble has been somewhere and somehow originally taken to establish such things, and that this attention, with all that it implies of vigilance and amenability, is the result of a very highly "evolved" discipline. Things are worth trouble when you stand or fall by them, and it is not too much to say that men and women alike, in "Europe," stand or fall by their degree of mastery of the habit of employing their vocal organs after the fashion of good society.

If it is women perhaps who most measurably totter or escape tottering, this is doubtless not because the intention of agreeable speech is more prescribed to them—it is prescribed to the men just as much—but because it is in their chords to give more effect to the intention. That happy condition the woman is mistress of, that there is practically no limit for her to the colloquial comfort she may so diffuse, the colloquial credit she may so enjoy. No one can doubt it who has listened to the speech of a succession of well-bred women—well bred in the sense that an incalculable amount of thought has been taken for their manners, and that their native organization and social piety, as it were, have enabled them to justify it. The vocal tone of such women, placed as it is by their code in the very forefront of manners, renders the question the inestimable service of what we may call settling it. It makes the demonstration—shows us what tone may do for intercourse and the beauty of life; what grace it may, even in the absence of other enrichment, contribute to the common colloquial act. It does this, I repeat, when the trouble involved has been immense and far-reaching; but for what if not exactly *for* this, from the moment the amenities are in question, should the plot *not* be deep laid? We scour the surface of American life in vain for the semblance or the echo of a plot; and who shall vividly enough utter the intensity of impression, piled up and rubbed in, of an innumerable sisterhood, from State to State and city to city, all bristling with the same proclamation of indifference, all engaged in reminding us how much the better sisters may, occasion favoring, speak even as the worse? Our thoughts then hark back and straggle away: we recall the different fashion in which this favor of occasion is apt to act in the fertilized communities, how it there often happens that the worse speak even as the better. The abrogation of a care for the question by those charged with it has, at any rate, for consequence, a diffused commonness, and the commonness has in turn for *its* character an inimitable union of looseness and flatness. I talk of character, but a tone without form and void, without charm or direction, is best described by negatives—which amounts indeed to saying that, like the course of a rudderless boat, heading nowhither, it can scarce *be* described. Its marks are lost in its poorness and thinness, its unnourished state; since we remain vague about it even when we speak of it as slipshod and slobbery; the difficulty of analysis being obviously great in proportion as parts and particles, shades and intentions, detail and finish, have dropped out of the case. There remain no elements for the critical process to reduce such a laxity *to*—it has already been so reduced; and to attempt to represent it by imitative signs is, besides being a waste of ingenuity, to impute to it a consistency which is really the last thing it owns. We rather avert our ears from it, on the whole, all considerately, as we avert our eyes, for the human pang within us, from any abject and total surrender.

There is, of course, no report of any received impression without a certain simplification; so it may be conceded as much as any injured innocence requires that there are degrees and differences, that, though the cause of the want of charm remains constant, the produced effects perceptibly vary and shift, encountering here and there (even when not consciously invoking it) accidental mitigation, circumstantial relief. These variations, these practical stirrings of the general conscience, exist, it may be granted once for all, and yet without their for a moment invalidating one's thesis. For it is not simply that the scale of variation, the degree of the departure from looseness and flatness, is at the best merely comparative and noticeably narrow; it is, emphatically, that the greater or smaller quantity of effect is an issue all negligible in face of the accepted ubiquity of the cause. One may as cheerfully as possible record one's awareness of several ladies in several cities who really articulate and who approximately soothe; one may even cherish the memory of several (and oh indeed that one here could gratefully name!) whose lips positively *do* confer on emitted sound the essence of urbanity and the principle of sweetness, yea almost of distinction; one may do these things—or even glance at sections of the country in which, roughly speaking, our affliction more heavily or more lightly treads—without touching for a moment the heart of one's contention. One's contention is that, under these mere cloud-shadows, the vast, desolate promoting *cause* of the affliction stretches, like a pall of ice, without a break. Attenuations are superficial and exceptions irrelevant so long as that remains the case. What is the cause then, so described— there is no difficulty in describing *it!*—but the fact that the question of its in the least mattering how people may speak, and how, in especial women may, is as absent from American education, either of the home or of the school, as if belonging but to the economy of another planet. This fundamental force, at least, knows no deflection from consistency—never deviates for an instant into shades or degrees. It lies there without a crease in its smoothness, it stares up at the observer wherever he turns—any observer who may happen not to be, for his comfort, either a simpleton or a sneak. The only thing is that, the scale of it being great, he really, to take it all in, has to proceed, with a certain patience, as well as, with all his bewilderment, from aspect to aspect and from point to point. He sees, in the exercise of this consideration, his observations multiply, but at the same time, if he be not mistaken, sees them much assist each other; so that, frankly speaking, I am struck with the wealth of those I have still to register.

PART THREE

Clear remains with me yet a particular impression received years ago—so many that I might, in the absence of fresher and corroborative ones, hesitate now to produce it. The corroborative abound, however, and them too I shall presently treat as mentionable. A quarter of a century has elapsed, but the appearance then presented to me has visibly not changed—and all the less, doubtless, that it was presented in Boston, the city, as we had then at least learned to think, of supremely conservative instincts. I was spending there three months of the springtime, and it so happened that, living in rooms ostensibly furnished, but as nearly as possible void of any enhancement of domestic service or other household ministration, I used to sally forth for my breakfast, to which convenience prescribed thus a late hour, and then walk back, to work, across the pleasant Common and down the spacious slope of Mount Vernon Street. This caused my passage almost invariably to coincide with the hour of "recess" of a seminary for young ladies flourishing hard by; the attendants at which, in the fine weather, were, for purposes of sport, in possession of the public scene. Nobody else, no doubt, during that part of the morning, was much in possession—so that the vociferous pupils (those of the "most fashionable school in Boston," as I heard their establishment described,) had the case all in their hands. My point is simply that, being fashionable, they yet *were* vociferous, and in conditions that, as they ingenuously shrieked and bawled to each other across the street and from its top to its bottom, gave the candid observer much to think of. They were freely and happily at play, they had been turned out for it to the pavements of the town, and with this large scale of space about them for intercourse they could scarce do other than hoot and howl. They romped, they conversed, at the top of their lungs, from one side of the ample avenue to the other; they sat on doorsteps and partook of scraps of luncheon, they hunted each other to and fro and indulged in innocent mirth quite as if they had been in a private garden or a play-room.

And yet the scene, alike for its implications and explanations, was of high interest; it gave one in a moment the key to so much of the surrounding speech. It was to connect itself too, I remember, with a word caught in much later years, the amusing mention on the part of an American friend, a lady who had married in Europe and was settled there, of a remark made to her during a visit that, after a long absence, she had just paid her native city. Her old friends there had mustered in force, had rejoicingly crowded about her, shrieking *à l'envi* and talking all at once, while she, naturally responsive and rising to the occasion, had mingled her own highest note with the inimitable choir. A near relation, tried perhaps, as the inhabitants of the native place *are* in general tried by indications of divergence in the reobserved absentee, had been present at two or three of these concerts and then had triumphantly spoken. "How you do, my dear, after all, still enjoy a good yell!" On which my friend had, of course, explained that any emphasis at all, or indeed any audibility, had necessarily, in such conditions, to take the form of the shout: which plea, however, it had had to be owned, was a dishonest evasion—the charge being not simply that she had yelled, but that she had yelled with gusto. "That then is what the little schoolgirls, the littler and the bigger, were doing, of old, in Mount Vernon Street," is the comment I remember making at the time. "They were getting into form for the good yell, they were acquiring the tone that was afterwards to be of social use to them." It was to be of use— that was the point—not in the gregarious life of labor, not in the rough world of the tenement, the factory, or the slum, the world unconscious of semitones, of vocal adjustments, but in the drawing-rooms and ball-rooms of the best society the country could show. The observation of my friend's critical sister had for me meanwhile the rare interest and refreshment of *being* an observation, even if but a limited one, and it was to remain, to my consciousness, even after another belated visit of my own, almost unique of its kind.

For even more striking to me, at this recent hour and under the impression of a wider view and more evidence, than the fact itself of the crudity of tone of my countrywomen in general, was the immunity from comment, from any shadow of criticism, that it serenely enjoys. This sinister circumstance of the social silence surrounding them was really what had constituted my key, as I had called it, to the license of the poor children—poor children of the rich—who, under expensive tuition, tuition of a cost often so startling to "European" ears, were vociferating over the Boston gutters. The supremely interesting thing was that, even at the fountain-head of our native culture, nobody, and least of all their remunerated instructors, seemed to doubt for a moment that these were good formative conditions. The imagination attuned to the "European" view of what is good and what is bad for growing creatures of the more sensitive sex, recoils in dismay before the conception thus involved of the duties and the standards, the general authority and quality, of such strange presiding preceptresses. The first duty laid upon a preceptress, in a society differently constituted from ours, the first accomplishment expected, for that matter, either of a competent shepherd or of a competent shepherdess of the male or of the female young, is to exemplify perfect propriety of vocal tone, perfect harmony as distinguished from perfect crudity. Yet it never befell me, that I remember, from one end of the country to the other, to hear any such personage, of either gender, challenged or checked, made, even in the mildest degree, a subject of animadversion, in presence of no matter how much displayed unfitness. Wasn't there every ground for one's wondering, right and left, by the process of shouting up and down what streets the intonations of certain apparently all-esteemed dispensers of precept and example to young sensibilities had themselves, originally and preponderantly, been formed?

Such wonderments send one back, all yearningly, to those Early-Victorian and Mid-Victorian governesses of English girlhood, daughters of country parsons and half-pay officers, heroines (while their fashion lasted) of sleepy three-volume novels, whose meagre erudition, whose melancholy music, whose painting on velvet, it was so easy and so usual to deride, but whose deep-seated sense, whose cultivated and consecrated instinct, for the speech of the gentlewoman, the product of bowery rural homes uninvaded as yet by the strident newspaper, covered a multitude of sins. This lady's "use of the globes" may have been open to revision, but she was, in a thousand cases, an exquisite, an almost unconscious instrument of influence to a special end—to that of embodying, for her young companions, a precious ripe tradition. She often embodied it, doubtless, better than she knew— even though the most distinctly recognized of her functions was to conjure away, in the schoolroom, caught or communicated vulgarities. A fiercer age, at any rate, appears even in her own country to have pretty well done with her, if not with the tradition itself; perhaps indeed after extracting and assimilating all she had so sweetly and so dimly to give. More influences had wrought upon *her*, mere inspired, purblind transmitter, than she could at all have named, and it was precisely her price that she was the closed vessel of authority, closed against sloppy leakage, and that that is one of the ways in which authority can be conveyed. It is better to be reduced, under pressure of convenience, to that way than not to be able to recognize *any* way. How, meanwhile, over the vast American distances, is authority conveyed? We smile, on behalf of our sisters and daughters, at the lean, limited governess; we even smile at the good ladies of the higher French convents, with their so arranged and restricted scheme, but who were primarily responsible, during long years, for the basis of converse in the women of the "best society" the world was to know: yet where, none the less, do we see *our* receptacles? I found it impossible not to feel, with the echo of that question in my ears, that to press it very much anywhere, in American conditions, would be to elicit the desperate declaration: "Well, we don't here, you know—in the matter of speech or anything else—*acknowledge* authority!" Which would have been, truly, for the critic, a conquest to treasure up!

I should like to insist, for further emphasis, long enough to note an uneffaceable impression, that of a large and new, a highly modern private school for boys, admirably situated, wondrously appointed in all material respects, and in none better, doubtless, than as to its scale of fees. Its architecture, its views, its command of country for sports and excursions, its hygienic conditions, its conveniences of every sort, were apparently well worth paying for; but at no hour so much as during the moments I spent in taking all this in did the greater educational interest at stake seem to wear so wan and so helpless a face. In what form was the tradition of civil speech there to be handed on? What provision for it had been dreamed of, and what intonations, in the high chambers, the halls of study, were to prevail? What influences, in a word, were to be looked to for counteracting the example of the zealous and robust young head master himself, whose vocal formation of his words, whose treatment of his syllables, whose confusion of his sounds, whose dire uncouthness of utterance, in short, testified to an absolutely unawakened conscience? What admonition, of the smallest value, on these matters, was to proceed from him? what admonition would such a speaker, in fact, under any provocation, be moved to make? I couldn't shake it off, I confess, the idea of how his admonitions in general would be tariffed, with such a "plant" as I saw about me—for indeed it was all "plant"!—and I thought many thoughts; some in particular about the state of mind of parents prepared to pay so much *not* to have their boys taught to speak as gentlemen. I recalled a different order, beyond the sea, in which the proviso that the schoolmaster shall speak as a gentleman is so absolutely vital. What most beset me, however, perhaps, was the wonder of how the dignity, how the *general* authority, of the pedagogic character, the pastoral allocution reduced even to its simplest sounds, could operate, could be preserved at all, in such conditions.

But I must not linger on this haunting reminiscence—which I might yet match with several others; even though, if we be not specifically talking of the way the boys are neglected, the fact that they *are* so has its bearing on the state of the girls. The finer interest of both facts really lies deep; lies where the explanation of so many American social appearances lies, in that universal non-existence of any criticism, worthy of the name, at which I have already glanced, and to which we mainly owe (though with democracy aiding) the unlighted chaos of our manners. That criticism is nowhere, in proportion to the need of it, is the visiting observer's first and last impression—an impression so constant that it at times swallows up or elbows out every other; though further light seems indeed to break for him when, in addition to so intensely missing any play of the precious principle, he makes out that it is not only dispensed with as in no other great community, but is ingeniously forestalled, practically interdicted. Then it is that he seems really to possess his subject! For it is forestalled, to begin with, by Advertisement, on a scale that is a new thing under the sun, and that not only takes the wind out of the critic's sails but blows all there is of it straight back into his face. This feature of the unequalled potency of advertisement we must indeed reserve some other occasion for considering: what is most to the point just here is our observer's perception of the way critical control cannot *but* so be baffled. It is baffled by the enormous *scale* of the flourishing impunity—the scale an inordinate level democracy, the hugest that has yet graced the globe, was alone to be capable of establishing. The impunity defies the criticism, and the criticism, gasping at the impunity, is reduced to the impotence of the traveller, waiting, carpet-bag of notes in hand, at a by-station, for the train that whizzes past without stopping. Whence the wondrous vicious circle—the train ignorant of a goal, but never so much as slowing up, the traveller conscious of a mission, but never so much as making a dash. Whence, in other words, the rare perfection of the impunity, assured *in advance* of the non-intervention of criticism. It has its own note, among us; we know it as American impunity, just as we know air-brakes or elevators or a thousand other things as American inventions. It has the sign that, if it certainly exists elsewhere, among ourselves it essentially flourishes, that its growth has been peculiarly favored. Advertisement has been able to hold the field for it long enough to make it safe, and that has made all the difference. Every place is taken, every seat occupied, there is not even "standing-room only." Criticism but walks round outside.

These remarks may appear portentous as applied, even indirectly, to our subject, but, certainly, our women's slovenly speech has its full share of what I have called the distinctive note—the note not simply of existing but of flourishing. Let alone as it is, how should it *not* grow great, how should it not bristle with every sign of the abuse guarded and protected, almost cherished? I asked myself on fifty occasions when or where any elder person was to appear to me struck with the sounds emitted by any younger; when or where any younger was to betray a shade of diffidence in the presence of any elder. I was to catch a hint of conceived responsibility as little on one side or the other; so that the perfect comfort, all round, attested the benediction of prosperity. And one was to make, in this direction, the strangest observations; as to the manner, for instance, in which, even in good old comparatively conscious New England, the younger species were, positively, without compassion felt for them, without rebuke offered, falling straight away from the elder. The New England speech of other years had represented, indubitably, and from far back, the highest type of utterance implanted among us. It had been wanting in the finer charm, wanting in distinction, touched always with a certain Puritan rusticity, as by the echo of the ox-team driven, before the plough, over stony soil, and of the small and circumspect town-meeting; but it had its coherence, its congruity, its dignity, and, on the lips of those who used it best, it was an interesting, a really tonic form of English utterance. It offered, above all, an excellent basis for individual intelligence and virtue, the expressional effect of the few capable of taking themselves, and of keeping themselves, in hand—capable even of taking and of keeping their wives, their daughters, their sisters. I remember well, from far-away years, the recurrent impression of the whole matter on passing from Boston to New York and back again. The general speech of New York had a way of appearing, by contrast, a poor and vain and abortive, an almost unemployable thing; so much more positive, more seated and established, or, as a few persons put it even then, more "finished," was that of the banks of the Charles, dignified as these were by the Boston Latin School and by Harvard College. High and fine to this hour one's recall of the local tone of distinguished men—speaking indeed, as they did, from a sense into which, by fortunate opportunity in each case, the light had been well admitted. And I am perhaps still more piously aware of the continued existence of two eminent ladies (to confine the number to those it's convenient to mention), who recently were to strike me afresh as supremely perpetuating, for an all but thankless age, the interesting tradition: one of them, in the New England capital itself, rarely beautiful of voice, full of years and honors, and devoted, with every enhancement of wit and ardor, to great causes; the other, of illustrious name, guarding the good idiom, and the good use and the pleasant sound of it, in the particular elm-shaded air in which it was perhaps most at home, and with a fidelity that fairly makes of her admirable continued presence a lesson and a reward for the pilgrim curious of history, of poetry, of linguistics.

One's stupefaction then was in one's watching the modern process with a mind full of such facts as those—the modern process of the apparently bland acceptance of the rising tide of barbarism by those who had so many reasons to "know," and who would have had so many rights to protest. There it was, while a whole group of Boston maidens slobbered unchecked, that the restless critic, lonely outlaw, could yet supremely feel that, in spite of the dire discredit attaching to criticism, something still might, as the phrase is, be "done." What this effective thing may hope to be he doesn't just now pretend to say: all he does is to see a possible first dawn of it in some indication, however limited, of the presence and intention of criticism. What will come after it will certainly be of profit to see; but without that beginning, still more certainly, nothing whatever will come. Everything, on the contrary, will go; so far, that is, as there is anything left to go in an order from which—and among "such pleasant people," such animated, bright-eyed young women, all articulating as from sore mouths, all mumbling and whining and vocally limping and shuffling, as it were, together—a small significant occurrence comes back to me. I had happened, had perhaps even sought to mention, occasion favoring, that it was of a fortunate effect, as in the enunciation of such a word as "due," to keep it quite distinct from such a thoroughly other word as "do"; and I had ventured to follow this up by the hint that, in like manner, we get a value in the articulation of "suit" that we quite lose when we make its two vowels operate like those in "boot"; whereupon I was promptly to find that I had challenged a deep-seated scepticism, not to say an appreciable resentment. But I must wait to tell what came of that.

PART FOUR

I have mentioned that several of my young friends had clearly not at all liked my plea for the mild effort of differentiation; and, wondering why, after all, they should dislike it so much, I had afterwards, as befell, a chance all earnestly to ask for some hint of their grounds; which was given me by a candid and charming person who had herself "sympathized," as she professed, with her injured sisters. She had the merit of proving, in her way, capable of reflection—which had not, for all their bright eyes, been the case with the others; and her defence of their common position testified to the precious fact that the vice of my appeal for the varied articulation which recognizes, among noted sounds, variations of identity, had struck them all as residing in my very conception of its virtue. Its virtue, by my contention, had been exactly *in* the truth that to have to render this sort of justice, and to render it so as a matter of course that the habit becomes a second nature, is to have had sooner or later to take thought. Now this truth, it was interesting to learn, positively represented, to those eyeing it askance and for the first time in their lives, a new (or, as my interlocutress would have it, a "noo") and oppressive obligation. It was not in the nature or the position of the American woman, I was given to understand, to put up with oppression; and when it came to our threshing out a little the bearings of the question—for it did, admirably, come to that!—I derived really a light of high significance.

I was for urging that so small and easy an application of taste made really not for servitude of situation, but for interest of intercourse; yet it was only from the moment I was able to put forward the bribe of this pretended interest, this possible occult charm, that I could feel myself make the least headway. Intelligibly expressed, my young lady's attitude was that discriminated sounds, indicated forms, were at the best such a vocal burden that any multiplication of them was to be viewed with disfavor: I had indeed to express this *for* her, but she grunted (her grunt had, clearly, always passed for charming) an acceptance of my formula.

Dimly she appeared to have made out for herself, on behalf of her vocal muddle, that convenience, not to say luxury, lay in the smallest number of discriminations, of tonic differences, that she could stumble along with—the smallest number from which a rough meaning might, by persons habituated, be extracted. She would have been willing to admit, I inferred, that this economy could be carried but to a certain point, and that expression and comprehension might, beyond that point, alike break down. But the right tendency, for her, really, was that of never discriminating, or detaching, or presenting, of never really sounding, a tone unless the sacrifice of it should give away *all* sense. Syllables and consonants, for instance—it had practically appeared to her and to her friends quite inspiring to discover—might be almost unlimitedly sacrificed without absolute ruin to a rough sense.

The ideal therefore would be, wouldn't it? to carry this sacrificial spirit as far as possible and apply it as frequently—since it would so, for the most part, still leave speech to consist of a certain number of rude signs for words. Anything that would sufficiently stand for the word, and that might thereby be uttered with the minimum of articulation, would sufficiently do, wouldn't it?—since the emancipation of the American woman would thereby be attested, and the superstition of syllables, of semitones, of the beginning of a sound, of the middle of it, and of the end of it, the superstition of vain forms and superfluous efforts, receive its quietus. The word, stripped for action (if "action" its drop into the mere muddle of sense can be called) would thus become an inexpensive generalized mumble or jumble, a tongueless slobber or snarl or whine, which every one else would be free, and but too glad, to answer in kind; as under a debased coinage you get a tin shilling back for the tin shilling you pass. This statement of the case for simplification—if I may call it a statement when I had so to help it out—left me for a moment, but for scarce more than a moment I can frankly declare, considering.

"Yes, I see all that's so done for you—in conditions in which, all round, so much is being done. But what becomes, all the same, of the interest—?"

My young lady seemed to wonder. "The interest of talk—?"

"Ah, of 'talk,' no—the interest of talk, and the matters that make for it, are a big question, involving many things, such as even you and I, I fear, can't pretend just now and here to settle. But the interest of speech, the prime *agrément* of intercourse, and the most immediate and common and general opportunity for taste that we know. What becomes of that?"

"The opportunity for taste?" She looked at me with a sinister eye. "How does that come in?"

"Why, taste isn't *all* concerned in the form of your hat and the choice of your fiction. Some of it has to be free for other purposes."

But she brooded still. "The *agrément* of intercourse? Does that depend on the number of our syllables?"

"For the vast majority of our occasions of intercourse, yes. These depend, for diminishing the friction of life, and for keeping up the sense of life instead of letting it drop, on the quality of our speech; which depends again on the quality of our sounds; which depends in its turn on the integrity of our syllables: seeing that we have to divide our speech, for articulation, into parts, and that we so denominate, for convenience, the most important of those parts. It is open to us, of course, to sink as many parts as possible, to sink them all, if need be, and go in only for large, loose, easy, yet perhaps, for the total effect, majestic or incisive wholes. That is the character arrived at by the moo of the cow, the bray of the ass, and the bark of the dog. It would leave you certainly *all* your taste for the selection of your shirt-waists and of your novels. But still, as I say, the human interest—!"

At this, for the first time, she appeared a little to give ground. "Yes, in the novel it *is* syllabled, it *is* spelled out. The 'parts,' as you call them, *are* retained."

I quickly followed up my advantage. "Depend upon it, dear young lady, these parts are there, theoretically, *all* sounded. The integrity of romance requires them without exception. And what are novels but the lesson of life? The retention of the covenanted parts is their absolute basis, without which they wouldn't for a moment hang together. The coherency of speech is the narrow end of the wedge they insert into our consciousness: the rest of their appeal comes only *after* that. They so take for granted, therefore, and they by the same stroke consecrate, what I call its interest. This isn't, and can never be, in the effect of a sordid cheapness, the effect of our offering tin shillings for silver ones. When you have made a single rude semblance serve as many different purposes as possible, you will still have left aside everything that, as we feel, ought to make our medium amusing."

At this, indeed, she looked bewildered. "I thought your contention was quite that we do so make it funny."

"Ah, by amusing I don't mean grotesque! I use the term in that higher, that charmingly modern sense that represents the something more than merely 'answering,' merely sufficing to its ordinary function, that we ask of almost any implement we employ. A table would still in strictness serve, would suffer an object or two to be placed on it, if it were only a lumpish block, a knife still serve without an ivory handle, the spread of our dinner pass muster without a bowl of flowers. But everything that makes in us against a gross monotony would be put on starvation diet; the result of which would be that we should soon become, to express it summarily, poor and mean and stupid creatures. I figure by these opprobrious epithets the unhappy being whose sensibility has lost an edge, who has parted with an intimate perception, and to whom thereby half of life is closed. Don't let us have women like that," I couldn't help quite piteously and all sincerely breaking out; "in the name of our homes, of our children, of our future, of our national honor, don't let us have women like that! The parts of our speech," I after an instant more calmly went on, "the syllables of our words, the tones of our voice, the shades of our articulation, are among the most precious of our familiar tools. An occasional picnic, with chopsticks, the level surface of a rock, the splash of the rustic runnel, may do for an hour of childish fun; but let us, so far as possible, for properly and habitually entertaining each other, have ivory and silver, smooth clean damask and the bowl of flowers. It's only with *them*," I weightily wound up, "that we know where we are. And that good knowledge is necessary for interest."

This insistence on interest, all "noo" to her, evidently affected her as open to suspicion, as half uncanny; but I was aware at the same time that I had made an impression she couldn't quite brush away, though she tried, poor dear, her best. "Are you sure you don't make too much of the interest?"

"Are you sure *you* don't make too much of the unimportance and of the trouble? The trouble, I mean, of cultivating a sense that it's such a poverty to lack; the unimportance, I mean, of missing half the beauty of life. Yes," I persisted, "that's exactly what I mean—that's exactly what you do miss. For everything hangs together, and there are certain perceptions and sensibilities that are a *key*— a key to the inner treasury of consciousness, where all sorts of priceless things abide. Access to these is through those perceptions; so don't hope that you can just rudely and crudely force the lock. Everything hangs together, I say, and there's no isolated question of speech, no isolated application of taste, no isolated damnation of delicacy. The interest of tone is the interest of manners, and the interest of manners is the interest of morals, and the interest of morals is the interest of civilization: to which you all (I still allude to our young friends) are really so far from being indifferent that, if you'll kindly remember, there's nothing you so little like as being pronounced in any particular barbarous. You see I could be eloquent," I went on; "but I don't want to bore you—I only want to answer you still a little more pertinently on that point of my perhaps exaggerating what we have agreed to call the interest."

"Oh, I beg your pardon," said my companion; "I haven't agreed to call it anything!"

"You've surely agreed to connect with it at least—with this matter of attention and discrimination—the idea of importance, or of unimportance, the idea of trouble accepted or shirked. That, as I have already noted for you, represents in you the first faint stir of a tribute to the question. But one answers you better than in any other way by asking you if you've ever happened to listen to any such speech as is really pleasing in itself, as has the right, complete felicity."

My young lady, on this, with eyes that were a little strange, looked at me long. "I don't understand you."

She had spoken with some majesty, but I couldn't repress a groan. "Oh, I was afraid you wouldn't, that you (if you'll allow me to say so) *couldn't*; and so comes in, precisely, your terrible attestation. Here you are, the pretended heiress of all the ages, and don't so much as know what, on the part of those taking thought for it, a happy tone *is*. You do, miserable child, sufficiently meet my inquiry. Your state is so desolate that you've been literally deprived of what should have figured for you as a common opportunity. In other words you've been starved."

Oh this, of course, my young friend—and flushing all proudly—wouldn't in the least have. "I've *not* been starved!"

"You've been fed on cheap, innutritive food—and on that only; it comes to the same thing. Your condition's of the worst possible. You contest the interest of an appreciable variety as against a vulgar monotony, of noted and developed intonation as against no intonation at all; and you've all the while no conception— having had no experience—of what the pleasant speech may be. Such are the abysmal traps your condition sets for you. One doesn't know where to begin with you."

That was at this stage, for her, a matter of marked indifference. "I like the way my friends talk—I like them as they are. I should be ashamed to desert them."

"My dear young lady," I returned, "I'm only appealing to you to rally to them. They're incapable themselves—they're incapable of anything. We must work *for* them; we must take them in hand. Yet, for yourself, there you are again with your 'talk'! I'm not touching on their talk—that must wait for another time; though I *may* remark that they do appear to talk prodigiously, and that I've often thought it a pity any class of persons *should* so give way to that impulse before they've learned to speak. Babyhood once past, it appears but to make their speech worse."

She seemed to think a moment, and I could do justice, after all, to her effort of patience. "Don't you contradict yourself when, stating that we're reduced to signs so rude that they limit our expression, you yet grant that our talk is remarkable for its rich abundance?"

"I quite admit that if you did speak you'd perhaps charm the world: so much would this do—would the art of speech I mean, do—for that possibly high value in you which is not as yet disengaged or presented. The values your inarticulate state perhaps leaves buried in you, leaves buried even in the rich abundance, as you say, of your talk—well, represent at the worst a dismal little waste." And I remember that I was on the point here of breaking out: "Did you ever listen to the speech of a small child so favorably placed as to have heard from the first, from those nearest him and most appealing to him, nothing but real, but true utterance, nothing but the achieved as distinguished from the abortive tone, nothing but pleasant and competent and civilized sound—with the consequence of your noting how positively sweet, how thoroughly interesting, the effect may be even in so simple a form? Haven't you felt it interesting *in itself*, independently of the scant childish sense or wit?—interesting as I urge that your own and your companions' speech would become for you under revision. Haven't you so observed the action, even for artless infant utterance, of a good surrounding tradition, once it surrounds closely enough? Haven't you recognized what a lesson that is in itself?" These questions, I say, had risen to my lips, but I checked them in time to avoid the appearance of indicating wantonly, as eatable and nutritive, the remote inaccessible fruit that might pass for the mere golden apples of fable. Where and how *should* my luckless maids have been prompted to such inductions? There was something, none the less, as to which this particular young woman had meanwhile taken a hint, for as soon as she spoke I saw she had been moved by the tribute wrested from me (scant as I myself felt it) to the verbal gush, at least, of the sisterhood.

"It has been remarked, you know, that American girls have a larger vocabulary—"

"Than any other girls on earth?"—I took her up without difficulty. "Yes, it's of course notorious; the comparative statistic enjoys the publicity that everything that concerns you enjoys. But just that fact has perhaps more than anything else to do with the very eminence of your misfortune. I've known in 'Europe' little persons whose speech ranged delightfully through a vocabulary of fifty words, and I've known quite big ones here who managed to render distressing—by extending their ravage through it—a vocabulary of five thousand. The number of sounds you don't form doesn't soothe the sensitive ear, believe me, by merely becoming immense. I had rather you were dreadful on a smaller scale—just as I find any scale of secure sweetness and harmony large enough. There it is. It isn't every woman who has use for a million words—if you look at the matter in the light of a happy economy; but there is none surely so bereft of the occasional right chance that she may not turn a few to the utmost account. Now there's only one way to do that—which is, if you please, to utter them."

My victim had at last gathered herself—I saw the end of our passage. But there were two points too she wished still to make, and even while she made the first the second loomed behind it. "You can't make out, at any rate, that we don't say everything we want."

It gave me pause but an instant. "You force me to distinguish, in the matter, between your intention, which is your own affair, and your effect, which is the affair of your hearer—the two things being, it strikes me, desperately different.

How can your hearer—from the moment he's in the least your critic (and it's only then he's worth speaking of) possibly suppose you to 'want' to get only *such* value of your sounds?—no more than half the value of human intercourse, no more than half the value of clear communication. If you limit yourselves to that, your reasons are your strange secret, with which he has nothing to do: he would never guess it for himself. His one impulse, in respect to your intention, is to pity you for having so to fall below your need."

I think that already, however, she scarce caught my sense; she had had her great card, all the while, up her sleeve, and was full of the necessity of playing it. "Why is it, then, that, all the world over, people so admire us just as we are?"

It was as if, from the very first, I had felt this coming; and now that it was there I knew I couldn't even have borne to miss it. My answer had, therefore, a perfect preparedness. "Because, designated as I admit you all to have been for a remarkable fate, it was needful you should see certain things apparently done, you should feel certain illusions created, you should be blind to the baiting of certain traps, that are all part and parcel of the fulfilment of your destiny. This destiny you *are* carrying out, to the joy of the ironic gods—who have locked you up, as an infatuated, innumerable body, a warning to the rest of the race, in perhaps the very best-appointed of all the fools' paradises they have ever insidiously prepared for humanity."

My friend gave me, for this, one of her longest stares, and I am not sure that, under the effect of my words, she had not really turned pale. "Locked us up—?"

"Yes, for I doubt if, within any measurable time, you'll be able, as an imprisoned mass, to get out; the gods having their own times and ideas, their wonderful ways, their mysterious ends. Still," I continued, "I won't answer for it that there may not be here and there hope of escape for individuals."

I had spoken in such evident good faith that I made her out at last as touched with dismay. But she could only echo: "Hope—?"

"Yes, of your perhaps quietly slipping out one by one." And then as, distinctly, alarm had stirred in her at the chill of my breath, "You want to know how that may be managed?" I asked. "Well, by letting me just hover here at the gate and have speech of you when you can steal away. Only look out for the gleam of my lantern, and meet me by this low postern. I'll take care of the rest."

The Manners of American Women

IX

PART I

It was a scant impression, no doubt, yet a prompt and a suggestive, that I gathered, of a bright fresh afternoon early in October, in the course of a run from Boston down to the further South Shore. It had, at any rate, I remember, its own small intensity—it took light from so many others I had already received and it helped to light so many that were still to come. The train, all of ordinary cars, stopped at each station, and there entered it together, from one of these, a bevy of four young, very young girls (I have never quite taken the numerical measure of the "bevy") on their way home from a morning at some considerable school. They were soon established, as confronted couples, on a pair of adjusted benches, but even before this they had had for me the effect of taking vociferous possession of the car. Having at first to place themselves a little provisionally, till other seats had been quitted, they carried on their interests up and down the peopled perspective, calling, giggling, changing, treating the great dusty public place, from the point of view of tone and manner, quite as their playground or maiden-bower, void of all other presences and subject to no other convenience. These charming invaders may have numbered from fourteen to sixteen years; they had ceased to be little girls, but were not yet "young ladies"—as indeed it would have been hard to say when, at such a rate, they would ever take on that more and more archaic character; a character that was to strike me, over the land, as remaining in general, and whether for the better or the worse, now almost completely in abeyance.

From *Harper's Bazar* 41.4 (Apr. 1907): 355–59; 41.5 (May 1907): 453–58; 41.6 (June 1907): 537–41; 41.7 (July 1907): 646–51.

Nothing in America perhaps more easily defies assurance or more frequently conduces to interest, for the taker of social notes, than the question of the presumable "social standing" of the flourishing female young as the occasion may happen to present it. Every critical measure that has served him in other societies here quite gives way. His immediate appeals in other societies, is to the question of tone; but that makes him, for the most part, in American air, no coherent answer. What was to be said, I found myself asking at the end of ten minutes, of the tone of these blooming, healthy, happy children of nature, wearing neither hats nor gloves, carrying each in her hand a text-book or two and a note-book, but sufficiently pretty and perfectly "turned out," with their fair braids gathered in by their big fresh bows of ribbon, with nothing of the vulgar or the sordid either in their facial type or their equipment, and nothing of the educated, of the "formed," or even of the formable, in any act or attitude? They couldn't be daughters of the people—they would have had in this case coarser clothes and coarser features, and would not, probably, have enjoyed the expensive habit of travel. Yet how, on the other hand, could they, shouting, flouncing, romping, uproariously jesting, be products of any guarded or tended condition, of any sphere tainted in any degree with the tradition of taste, the subtle vice of discrimination? This was freedom for the family circle—when the family circle is represented by the village street or by the snug, sociable slum of the great town; but what could one say of it all with the crowded indifferent car playing that part? and playing it all the more that my incident appeared to excite, amid the indifference, no shade of remark.

It was, of course, after the charming creatures had placed themselves together that they abounded most in the spirit, in the perfect good faith, of their indescribable, their altogether innocent immodesty. We all sat silent and solemn, though doubtless only one of us awestruck, while the voices, the fresh repartee, the restless gayety, of our young companions rose above the rumble of the train. They got out after three or four stations, having really, I felt, enriched my notes with the worth of a volume; and it so befell that even while I pondered their case, which but lost itself, for the time, in the wonderful, the unanswerable, another small circumstance—small as being all of the common and immediate order—cast its weight into the scale. As our stops were to be many the station precedent to my place of descent had been mentioned to me, and, though I had remained a trifle vague about its name, I bethought myself at a given moment, with the brakeman's call in my ears, that we must have just passed it. The conductor making his way, however, a minute later, through the aisle, I put him my little question from my pew: would my station (which I named) be our next arrest? He desired apparently to show that this weak overture deserved as little notice as possible, but had to wait a moment to decide how he should best express that minimum. He decided, justly, I afterwards could see, that the measure of sound (speech it could scarce be called) expressed it better than the measure of silence, and he put me in my place with a grunted, stinted, unsupplemented "No" that made an effectual end, for the time, of the brief relation with him that I had rashly attempted to form and that yet, by my own fond conception, might have been, for all its brevity, so agreeable. He would consent, clearly, to no relation whatever; and he was no exception, in this respect, to any car-conductor save only one, enshrined for me on tablets of finest ivory, whom I was afterwards to encounter.

The essence of a relation, I thus more than ever perceived, is that it involves, at the worst, some slight margin; which margin is occupied, for the most part, in communities where the general question of manners has an importance, by the *form*, so to speak, that clothes the naked fact. The margin here, for instance, would have left room, on the one side, for my friend's recognition—recognition other than undisguisedly grudging—of my appeal, and on the other for my own acknowledgment of his recognition. So the margin would just have housed the small structure of civility; and so, as the case stood, it showed the mere ugly waste that we know as want of finish. A relation is complete, so far as need be, when it has begun, has continued, and has ended—begun, say, with courtesy of interrogation, the "I beg your pardon," the "Will you be so good?" that are thrown in, so to speak, for the auspicious start, and ended, say, the business once transacted, with the "Much obliged" or "I see, thanks!" that are thrown in for the happy conclusion. In strictness, no doubt, the relation may operate, to a given end, without these vain graces, and the general American habit, as I was after a long absence immediately to reobserve, is contentedly to accept it as so operating. It operates, however, at this rate, *unattestedly*, and there are numbers of relations in life, especially of the casual and superficial order, as to which the attestation may easily affect us as the best part of the business. It may sometimes, in fact, be the sole pleasant part—the only point at which anything is really saved for precious civility. Therefore, as intercourse is harsh without the relation, so the harshness practically abides in the relation unattested.

My contention is not, of course, that my conductor might conveniently have been *less* negative, and was not within his strict right in drying me up with the curtness of his No when that monosyllable represented the particular truth I was concerned to receive. It is, on the contrary, that he might really have been much more positive, and that three or four words more, rightly placed, would have largely amplified and enriched his position. They might have been taken as coming afterwards, these three or four words—as I mentioned to a friend with whom, a little later on, with experience gained, I found myself discussing the general forms of conductors. He passed me in the aisle, eventually, with a "This is the place you want"—though with his back immediately presented not only to my acknowledgment of his information, but to the business of my disengaging, from my contracted pew, and dragging to the end of the car, the few *impedimenta* with which I had doubtless too inexpertly charged myself. "Ah, then, he *was* civil!" my friend triumphantly exclaimed on this; as if my reflection on the curtness characteristic of his class had thereby collapsed. He had not let me ride on and miss my connection without notifying me—it appearing to be implied that he would have had a perfect right to do this if so disposed. So, by the same token, he had not knocked me down, nor prevented my alighting. He had conformed to every grace expected of a conductor. I had not, however, waited for that comment to be aware of the peril mostly attending any discussion of the question of manners—attending it at least in conditions in which the question has not happened to undergo a good deal of practical and fortunate settling. Terms and meanings, one may then perceive, have to be defined; people may differ from each other so fundamentally, for instance, as to what the disputed interest *is*, what manners "amount to anyway"—and even quite, that is, as to the degree in which importance or urgency, or anything but affectation and futility, may be claimed for them.

I am afraid I have no better warrant for the tenuity of my anecdote than the fact that while I sat in my car on the very commonplace occasion I refer to I felt myself treated to as vivid a revelation as I could have desired of that easy view of any such issue as virtually *no* issue. The bright frank autumn light, the "larking," giggling girls, all ignorance yet all predominance, the silent shoving people, all security yet all vagueness, the revolving official, all detachment save as modified by nudges and nods—these things somehow filled my impression with meaning, if only I could arrive at a measure of the meaning. All the elements for so doing were naturally not present just at that hour; but what was present, essentially, was the sharp presentiment that they would come, and that the more I should see the more the connection of my actual scant, yet after all so appreciable, *data* would be clear. The question of manners in a general medium as to which this small special medium was exemplary would in other words make a surpassing appeal—that of the inquiry as to how, in a society other than just rudimentary, it had been, to every appearance, so effectually and so successfully relegated. "We propose," the whole carful might have been saying to me straight, "to get on virtually without the confounded things, and if the demonstration of what comes of that, first and last, happens to interest you—why, you're welcome to get what you can out of it. You can't say we're not strictly decent, can you? You can't say those pretty girls over there, bless their innocent hearts, are doing any *harm*, can you? You can't say the conductor isn't a portly freeborn American man and that he doesn't take the tickets all right—why, he takes 'em about every three minutes, and you don't want him to keep passing you any *more*, do you?—and that it isn't a good deal your own fault (since that's the way we fix things here) if you haven't grasped the location of South Braintree, or whatever your plaguey place may have been. Isn't that so? Well, then, what more do you want?"

I wanted, as I thus mystically listened, so much more that the quickened consciousness became verily a delight; I wanted to miss no further impression that would enable me to do honor to the revelation, as I have called it, in course of being made me. I wanted, that is, not to miss a single connection of the phenomena to which my sensibility had already responded; and I wanted supremely to grasp betimes the most striking connection of all. What would this be but the very obvious truth that if the general scheme (as lighted by the microcosm of my cheerful little car) involved the neglect of manners, the neglect would be most registered, and thereby most appreciable, in the sex for whose evidential value our pretty girls, so salubrious, so obstreperous and so innocuous, most testified? They had begun indeed to testify, by my reckoning, as soon as they entered the place; but it was perhaps only after a little that I saw just why they became still more important, as it were, as soon as I had made my small second observation. The so evident impunity, the so felt adequacy of the conductor's curtness, his so easy enjoyment of his right only to nudge and nod, to thrust out an unaccompanied hand, to thrust back an unacknowledged response, to leave the burden of all procedure involved, all ascertaining, producing, unfolding, refolding, understanding, on the patient passenger alone—these things were in the highest degree contributive. It was already a familiar truth that there is no *isolated* question of manners, that any particular aspect of them is part and parcel of fifty other aspects, indeed of a thousand other matters altogether; but this truth could from time to time take on a freshness. When had it not been that once we begin to follow the connections of any significant and typical case of good taste or of bad, of civility or of its opposite, they seem to spread as far as we can see? Certainly just then, however, it appeared to come home to me as not before that if one inevitably asked what sense for the forms of intercourse on the part of the matron was implied, and would be guaranteed, by the constant absence of any sense on the part of the maiden, and if in that fashion one's speculation took for subject the general conditions of "polite intercourse" among one's countrywomen, so this special issue would in turn almost lose itself in any whole view of the state, of the visible cultivation or the visible neglect, of the amenities.

The terms of civil intercourse, in any community, are really a single great matter and not any particular number of separate ones: which was precisely exemplified by the incident of my having got full in the face that little whiff of a common male conception of them at the very moment I was trying to distinguish, as I might say, for the benefit, or at least for a comprehension, of the feminine position. Little reflection is in fact required to see that, as neither sex can very well have all the manners, or enjoy all the absence of them, those of each must have much to say to those of the other: there should be a relation quite traceable, for instance, between those of my quartette of schoolgirls, those of the proud "homes" to which, with so good a conscience, they were returning, and those of the society, in general, to which, though inordinately addicted to rushing about by rail, it had never occurred to extort from the agents of that process, and whether by precept or by example, any comfort of decorum. Again and again, in other words, it had been written clear that the habits of address of one set of persons largely determines and shapes the habits of address of another; and on the American scene nothing could well be more striking than the intensification of this effect by the fact that there immeasurably more than elsewhere sets of persons are intermixed and confounded. There might for a particular set, no doubt, be an appreciably predominant, preclusive action; this would of course depend on its success in getting the start—though, indeed, I may add that, as the case stands in America (by which I mean in presence of some of the phenomena of manners) it is difficult, after the fact, to apportion the energies.

I had often wondered, say, if the address of so many of the persons of either sex serving in so many of the shops had originally come after or come before the address of so many of their customers of both sexes. I had held my breath on certain occasions to hear these parties all imperturbably stand and bark at each other (since that affected me, inveterately, as the nearest image for their intercourse); and would have given worlds to be able to make out, in the spirit of the historian, which, in the bright morning of our national life, could possibly have begun it. One of them *must*, the hearer could but helplessly suppose; a consensus, a coincidence more precipitate and instinctive was too difficult to imagine. No, one of them *had* to be responsible for the other, since what social order with any self-respect would consent to be responsible for both? There were times when I inclined, on certain showings, to lay the burden on the shop-people; but then again, as sundry accents from the other side of the counter smote my ear, who would be so bold? There was to remain with me, it was yet true—for so I earnestly balanced—the sense and sound of a person employed in an immense establishment at Philadelphia, an elderly, grizzled, truculent woman, presiding, with a certain incongruity, over various items of men's "underwear," against whose practical defiance of approach and whose long impunity, as one felt, of insolence, it was inconceivable that any social body coerced to communication with her should *not* have organized for reprisals, for some desperate game of repaying her, horribly, in kind. She pushed so to the extreme, I recollect, on the ground in question, the displeasing effect of her general type, that she immediately took her place, for me, with all importance—the importance expressed by this commem-oration—as a monument to the strange patience of the public. One would have primarily asked oneself how a place of business organized to carry transactions through could have afforded to employ her, had one not rather more wondered if a public patient enough to endure her could ever conceivably have "begun" anything.

Such a case, in fine, for my general meditation, but confounded the question; but meanwhile, none the less, I had not ceased to have it before me that the apparent disconnectedness of classes and groups is but a matter of suppressed transitions—quite as much in the generalization of bad manners as in that of good. The reasons for such an absence of sweet shyness in my romping maidens might decline to have anything superficially in common with the reasons for such a repudiation of the human opportunity by the railway servant whom I have cited but for his illustrative value. This didn't prevent, however, their being, for further research, and certainly for further interest, flowers of the same great democratic garden, with roots more intermingled than might on one side or the other be suspected. The sole difficulty was, therefore, not that, for consideration of the subject, any link would be missing, but that, on the contrary, links would be only too numerous and the subject—the manners of the American people at large—defy consideration by its extent. That would never do; there were aspects that, for any clearness, one would have to *keep*, in a fashion, distinct.

The women's having certain manners, in a particular society, is doubtless partly a cause and partly a consequence of the men's participation in the same; just as the exhibition on the men's side affects and is affected by that made on the women's. It would be one vast body of phenomena before which, in short, the rapt student might easily lose himself, were it not that, as I have already hinted, he promptly enough felt his consciousness lightened, and saw his field cleared, by an apt reflection. The favoring air for social forms, or for their lapse and disuse, was practically the same, in the great Republic, from sea to sea, but the value and the bearing of the demonstration were not everywhere the same—and for a sufficiently obvious reason. The aspects have everything in common but the degree of interest they present. It is in the manners of the women that the social record writes itself, if not largest, then at least finest; since, by an ineradicable instinct, it is of them we expect most. Say what we will, moreover, as to their community of origin with those of the men, we feel that the latter have not equality of influence—which expresses precisely, for the women's case, the wider reach and the heavier weight. It matters most, otherwise stated, whether the mothers and wives and daughters and sisters—let alone the large and apparently growing class of not specially occupied single women as such—cultivate, with a feeling for them, the forms of civil intercourse, or whether, without a feeling for them, they let them, as the phrase is, take care of themselves.

I seemed (to revert an instant) to have been seeing them take care of themselves in the indifferent little sphere of my car-haunting quartette; and this it was that above all put a price for me on that other corroborative hint of a continuity in things. It would be enough for the moment, at the same time, if I should confine my pursuit of more light to certain fixed relations. These would clearly be of such interest just as they were and wherever they stopped. One was conscious of one's impression, indubitably: the terms of intercourse here were not, from place to place and from scene to scene, where the women were concerned, as the terms of intercourse in the other great human aggregations in which one had been able to observe them. Here, accordingly, too, was a fine flaming light in which the presumption of continuity became intense and vivid. How could they be the same when the independence and indifference so advertised by our rampant maidens had to be taken as for the show and proof of a budding conception of them? Blest would be the continuity—for one's further attention—when it could so bristle with implications! If the general manners of the women were what one had from far back begun to note, how they were explained, for the time—though with a certain indirectness, I recognized, that but made the explanation richer— by this view of the general manners of the girls! If the general manners of the girls were indeed no less familiar a fact, how inevitably they must lead on to something connected and consequent in the general manners of the women! How could the mothers of such daughters be as the mothers of daughters who were different, how could the daughters of such mothers not betray their affiliation, how could the general conception or misconception of forms, in such "homes" as so abounded in the documentary, not be a matter very much by itself? To ask these questions was to feel how the subject tempted one to explore. I explored them to the best of my light, and shall endeavor to tell my readers how far I went.

PART II

There was always of course on the threshold, for admonition, that familiar little truth about "the people one knows," the truth that *their* manners, when once knowledge had gone far enough, seemed, as one might say, all right; and that the question had somehow been practically superseded—superseded by that of their morals, as a general thing so extraordinarily good, by that of their almost inveterate and quite explicit good intentions, their amiability, their vivacity, their veracity: conditions as to which one could scarce say if they consisted of forms, if they even altogether consorted with forms, or not. One had known, in one's native air, so many charming women—as who had not? and how could they have come so to rank themselves if they had not had some law and rule of grace? They might give one pause indeed—might easily give it, that is, about themselves; and I recognize clearly that they do. But I recognize at the same time the *whole* effect of my profiting by this challenge. It makes one, when asked if *they* then hadn't as good manners as one could have desired, avail oneself, after a minute's reflection, of the freedom of a mixed answer.

What that reflection conveys is that the case must very much have depended, and that they had them in proportion as it was governed by one or other of three conditions, at the foremost of which alone I may for the moment glance. They had them, incontestably—manners definitely and completely good—when they were virtually daughters of another age, products, so to speak, of the antique world, or of the period that has already begun to wear for us that blander face; early and comparatively uncompromised participants in our harsh modernity. They were growing old, alas, while the order about them was growing new, and is it not their perceptibly bewildered maturity that one remembers, and that recedes, more and more, to our melancholy vision, hand in hand with their disconcerted urbanity? The privilege of a memory that can go back and back is a qualified joy, so far as implying a "time of life"; but, that qualification apart, it may be, in presence of the actual, a great help to understanding and to knowing. It casts a chill, in other words, to feel how old one must be to recall the American time when manners had an importance, and the definite and frequent testimony of one's shocked and critical elders to the decline of that importance; but at least one is so more at one's ease about the connections of things.

With a sense still vivid, at any rate, of every impression of my younger years, I might, with more space, almost reproduce the detail of that view of the new, or at least of the more and more allowed, violations of a due decorum that these witnesses of the preceding order inevitably entertained and expressed. I might enumerate the different "forms" of which, to their explicit dismay, they saw the generations rising before them uncorrectedly careless, just as I quite recollect the interest of being able to feel that these were on their part inherited sensibilities and measures and to reflect on the virtue and force that the general canon would have had, *a fortiori*, in the world in which they had grown up. When parents and uncles and aunts—and I think especially of aunts and mothers—uttered for the benefit of their juniors their disapproval, for instance, of the unchallenged practice, by the visitor or the chance acquaintance, of a free and familiar egotism, of that sign of the want of breeding that consisted in an immediate and continuous descant on the speaker's own affairs and concerns, without reference or deference to those of others and with an unlimited assumption of the interest and curiosity at the listener's disposal, the indication was clear of a comparatively ruled and ordered past, a past with another conception of the considerate, the discreet, and the decorous.

Distinctly it had been a past on its guard, so far as might be, against the taking of liberties and the non-observance of forms, and its voice lingered on, precisely, in this frequency of the word "forms," and in another refrain, that of the "want of consideration," to which the ear of my adolescent time appears to have been much attuned. Constant and explicit the plea for this last-named virtue. Consideration comes back to me as the great educative idea of those times domestically speaking—in face of the fact, I mean, that it already seemed to be passing away. When it befell me accordingly, after long years—for it was but a short time since—to move over the American scene more freely than ever before, to travel further across it and to get a nearer view of those peopling it, without my happening once, so far as I now recall, to gather from the lips of any woman, young or old, encountered in the hazard of travel, any acknowledgment of any civility offered or demanded, or any preface, however perfunctory, to any such demand, I seemed to make out as never yet what the old extinct voice had meant, and what extent of deviation the old closed eyes had begun to foresee. There had been, in fine, for a number of persons, the definite, the informed and quickened vision of what it particularly *was* to be considerate; and was I not finally reaping the fruit of the gradual and at last complete failure of that vision?

Pursue your pilgrimage long enough, by rail and road, and accidental contacts with your fellow pilgrims (as distinguished from those persons to whom you have been, more intimately, "introduced," those acquaintances you have more formally made), naturally ensue: people make inquiries of you, invite assistance, approach or appeal to you, momentarily, on this or that or the other ground. Small incidents and accidents in short occur—of which the main or the only interest may be that they throw a certain light on social conditions. The light thrown then, to my own apprehension, from this general source, during a considerable tour, was *all* a confirmation of the truth looming so portentously up from the first hour of repatriation, the great truth of the non-existence of any approach to manners on the part of the nation at large. It was more nearly the nation at large that one was thus seeing, as one felt—one's situation being for the time the nearest approach to it one had made and perhaps would ever make; and to the nation at large, in railway-trains and hotels, in shops and in city streets, in all centres of the particular life the most gregarious that the "principal countries" have to exhibit, women contributed a vast and conspicuous contingent.

The suggestive fact was accordingly that, on noting the consistency with which these ladies, asking, for their convenience, some question, or receiving, to a like effect, some information, never either introduced the one or by any equivalent of "I beg your pardon," or accepted the other with any audible articulation of thanks, I recognized the consummation that my cherished prophets had foretold, and, with the vast scale of it, the rate at which, above all, it had come to pass. I am far from saying that such an observation was not, after a fashion, a more interesting one than any mere impression of settled amenities; since this latter would somehow have raised no questions, would have seemed rather to lull a good many to sleep. It is the great characteristic of the American scene, for the visitor, that it does raise questions; and the wonderment that came up, in particular, under the whole impression so made, was as to how, in so immense a gregarious life, a life of perpetual contacts and personal, material concussions, the forms, the graces, the civilities, the significations of address and response, were successfully dispensed with.

"Successfully" was of course, all the while, one was well aware, a large term to take for granted: the success might be sufficient, for instance, to avert complete social disintegration, yet might fall so measurably short of representing social felicity. It might just fail to draw down ferocious reprisals—which was ground for wonderment enough—without contributing the element of positive security, without ministering in any degree to one's sense of an equilibrium really achieved. A practical decency, none the less, prevailed, and one asked oneself repeatedly how, with so few forms, it did assert itself, or why the logic of rudeness should have broken down at all. It did break down, one seemed to recognize, from the moment one was not taken by the throat or hurled out of the elevator, from the moment one was supplied across the counter or answered in words at all; and the odd law that lurked in this would be surely worth one's seeking. I was to obtain perhaps ultimately, with effort and labor, some glimpse of it; but what beset me meanwhile was this easy triumph of chaos.

The approach and the interrogation descended, in trains and stations, inveterately, out of the blue, without the aid of an intonation or a hint of its being an appeal; it seemed to me indeed, round about me, that when I heard an inquiry spring from a woman's lips, whether directed to a stranger of her own sex or to some adjacent man, the fine free "Say!" as a demand for attention, ushered it in; though if my own participation was for some reason, by my remembrance, less invoked by the "Say," there yet comes back to me no case in which the slightest adjustment of tone, or any betrayed consciousness either of asking a favor or of receiving one, mitigated the crudity of the incident. The general condition was apparently one in which, even when neither reluctance nor resentment was supposable, interchanges were reduced (and, on the trains, as though the grim example set by the conductors themselves) to the barest utterance of meaning that would serve. It was a social air, in fine, in which the *explicit* of civility, and with it in particular the habit of certain acknowledgments, had never flowered at all: so that, little by little, the great truth stood out that it was an order in which, among a hundred things that had never been formulated, the idea of manners as the law of social life was the one that most recorded this omission.

With the final complete distinctness of that truth almost everything began to show as a consequence or a cause: things not intrinsically pleasing, not intrinsically interesting, took on a value from their relation to it; became, as the observer might say, implications and explanations. One of these illustrative phenomena does come back to me, for that matter, as positively touching—it was an observation I had occasion so often to make. The "boys" at hotels, the agile youths who answer bells and, at any pressure of any spring, precipitate themselves, as a matter of course, with the tinkle of ice against crockery, this useful little band struck me as, in general, a much more uniformed and disciplined phalanx than in earlier days, and as imposing on the hapless traveller much less of the burden, with any given member of it, of beginning the young unfortunate's education again at the root. But it repeatedly, it in fact inveterately, befell that when, having summoned one of them, I uttered thanks for any service performed or information given, I was treated to the positive little pathos of the ingenuous lad's "How?" or "What?" Touching, as I say, its note of vagueness; almost, as I sometimes felt, of bewilderment: the betrayal of a state so unacquainted with articulate recognitions as to be moved to vain speculation over one's words.

My own general wonderment—as to any one's ever thanking them—was reinforced accordingly by the question whether the women in particular didn't, the innumerable members of that everywhere so vast and so visible presence. The men mightn't, if it was conceivable the men had too many other things to do; but where was the best opportunity of the gentler sex, under conditions so fostering its ubiquity, if not, precisely, in some such solicitude for the graces and urbanities that might well strike women, at times, as *all* left to them? To begin so to spin conjectures, anywhere, was inevitably, however, to go further still, and to note that, as the urbanities and the graces, in any community, perceptibly hang together, there might be light upon them from many sources. How favorable to them was the general air, and from what range of habit and practice other than that of articulate speech might one gather evidence about them? There were two admonitions that, I confess, never failed, as I circulated; the sight of the newspapers American women were reading, and the sight of the food they were engulfing.

The aspect of the newspapers had volumes to say on this point of the suggestion and encouragement of good manners, and the fashions of feeding of one's fellow travellers, always so conspicuous, were a constant attestation of the absence of the same principle. This absence, one soon enough perceived, was simply that of taste, that of a sense even for the primary forms of civilization. What *would* be the civilization, what in other words would be the manners, of a lady who, surrounded at breakfast, at luncheon, at dinner, by a couple of dozen or so of small saucers of the most violently heterogeneous food, should proceed to exhaust the contents by a process of incoherent and indiscriminate spooning? Of what elementary power or disposition to discriminate, of what confused invocation of the light of taste, would her practice of slobbering up a dab of hot and a dab of cold, a dab of sweet and a dab of sour, of mixing salads with ices, fish with flesh, hot cakes with mutton chops, pickles with pastry, and maple syrup with everything, appear to be, in general, the symptom and pledge?

What a *picture* of manners, what an evocation of chaos, the dazed observer could but inwardly exclaim as, from across the table, he followed, under a baleful fascination, the strange sequences and the wild wanderings of the fond alimentary utensil. Irresistibly moved to reckon up, so far as calculable, the number of little oviform dishes barricading for the time their consumer, he saw the dauntless ladle plunge into the sherbet without prejudice to its familiarity with the squash, and straggle toward the custard while still enriched with the stuffing of the turkey. What law and what logic prevailed, he asked himself, at such a conception of a meal, and what presumption for felt congruities, for desired or perceived delicacies, in the other reaches of life, would it rouse in the mind of a visitor introduced for the first time to the spectacle? It was inevitable to feel, after a little, that speech and tone and the terms of intercourse were, on the part of these daughters of freedom, notions exactly as loose and crude as such notions of the nature of a repast.

But things certainly hung most together when one happened to perceive one's companion, sated with her strange commixtures, seek to combat digestive drowsiness with one of the horrific printed and figured sheets that succeed in darkening, to the traveller's eye, so much of the large American air. Where or how, he asks himself, do these unmitigated ugly things fit into a feminine sensibility that has begun to confess, at any point, to cultivation? It is not my concern here to attempt a sketch of the common, the ubiquitous newspaper face, with its mere monstrosity and deformity of feature and the vast open mouth, adjusted as to the chatter of Bedlam, that flings the flood-gates of vulgarity further back than anywhere else on earth; it speaks—if we may talk of speaking—for itself, and the evil case for it may dispense at this time of day, and after a single glance at the field, with presentation. What measure of social grace might you suppose yourself invited to attribute to a lady living contentedly in the daily air it exhaled? What would be the natural effect on articulation and utterance themselves—so I found myself put the case—of all the unashamed grossness and blatancy and illiteracy and impudence, what that of the perpetual vision of head-lines elongated as to the scream of the locomotive, what the consequence of such a scattering to the winds, as by the flight of a terrified nymph before riotous satyrs, of the precious saving salt of a felt proportion in things?

The consequence—this was all one could say—would be quite what one measured it; for such, again and again, was one's recognition of the immediate connection, over the scene, of all the *parts* of the exhibited life. What was plainer than that, as civility begets civility and appeal begets response, so rudeness communicates rudeness and indifference to every grace makes everything *but* indifference impossible? Never perhaps did I read this moral clearer than on an occasion when, journeying at some length in the State of Illinois, I had before me for a couple of hours in the Pullman an animated family whom I found myself regarding after a little with an intensity of interest. They were numerous and yet actively united—parents, mature sons and daughters, a presumable son-in-law, a possible daughter-in-law; which, to begin with, was highly pleasing, and they absolutely, in their generous cluster, conversed with each other: a fact that I found, I confess, a delight, after the sterility of silence I had noted on such a scale between associated persons in general; these latter so destitute, for the most part, apparently, of the forms and traditions of interchange that one was reduced to explaining it by some supposition of the conscious lack of a lingual medium, of any possible range of articulation or of allusion.

My interesting family—for one found one's imagination, starved for human color, quite bask in any such vision and give it the benefit of perhaps even absurd possibilities—*had* a range of allusion; which happened to play for the time over the field of music; where they appeared, and almost equally, actively and confidently at home. They had gone up to Chicago from their town of residence, at which in due time they were to alight again, for a course of opera, and were returning with all their impressions and with the happiest disposition to discuss them. This it was that struck me as making them, on the general scene, a windfall; this it was that gave them, in my experience of "car life," an inordinate value. Yet they were to deal me such a blow—the point, exactly, of my small story—as was to come from no other directed hand, and of which, in their company, it took me some little time to be fully aware. When I became aware indeed it was to see *them* all disfigured by their use of their weapon; aware, I mean, that each member of the group, while he or she talked or listened, was primarily occupied after the manner of a ruminant animal. They were discussing Wagner in short under the inspiration of chewing-gum, and, though "Parsifal" might be their secondary care the independent action of their jaws was the first.

Slow, resolute, inexorable, eternal, it had yet managed for a little, amid their talk, to beguile suspicion; but once detected it spoiled for me, I confess, not only the quality of that exhibition but the very fact of it, which had been dearer to me still; since, obviously, I could now, indifferent to this value, do nothing but ask myself if a sense for manners were the more likely to be rooted in a gentleman rolling his bolus about while he talked to a lady, or in a lady who rolled hers about while he was so engaged. Where, definitely, were the civilities, as one expects women to embody them, when such practices and such patiences as those were part of the training for them? What address, what response, what pleasantness of propriety in general, might be held to consort, for a woman of whatever age, with her having not to "mind" that her interlocutor, of whatever condition, should chew in her face for sweet freedom or with his having not to mind that she should chew in his?

It was the way my good friends who got out at a station that nothing on earth would induce me to name didn't mind, strictly decent as they seemed to be—it was this that promoted depth of meditation, and the vast daubed signboards by which, on the highways of travel, the land is dishonored, grew to resemble more than ever the *disjecta membra* of murdered Taste, pike-paraded in some September Massacre. The vulgar compound had proclaimed itself to high heaven in rude and monstrous characters, wherever the prospect opened, wherever the side of a shanty or the back of a fence or the breast of nature, free from other disfigurement, could be made to suffer; but whereas its connection with manners, as manners might come home to one, had previously seemed remote, the revelation of that melancholy hour made it direct and immediate, and was in fact the beginning of a generalization that grew as I moved westward. The bedaubed hoardings, so omnipresent and so hideous, constituted thus, clearly, a real reference to the habit of millions of ruminant persons, and my great light was, in consequence, that, as one felt oneself always *with* the millions, always in the crowd and the stream and the huge continuity, there came to be no doubt either about the quantity of public rumination or about the quantity of public acceptance of it. The publicity was, by my generalization, the great note, for manners, as also the way in which my Illinois pilgrims were not asking or taking one from the other more than each was ready to receive and to give. These were manners of a sort, but how far did they lend themselves to any idea of "formulation"? I mayn't deny that, even after the little observation here recorded had been made, I still found myself subject to puzzlements and doubts. The question couldn't be settled at a stroke and in the sense of "There is absolutely, for the relation of address and response, the 'considerate' relation, no ideal; there is only the instinct, immensely diffused and of course on the whole very salutary, of keeping the air clear and the ground firm for business transactions." There were cases—that was the disturbance—in which one caught distinctly the gleam of a conception.

I was to remember for instance how in the course of a walk taken in Chicago with a gentleman in whose society I had been lunching, my companion, describing to me the wonders of a monstrous shop, the pride of the city and the biggest

organization of its sort (of course) in the world, kindly offered to lead me
through the place, at the end of which we should come out as near our objective
point as in proceeding by the street. The establishment had indeed all the
appearance of vastness so easily brought about by the conditions of modern
traffic, and, spying a small article of which I had been in want, I stopped to
purchase it. A prompt young person, waiting on me, made the transaction, and
that of the acquisition of another object or two, rapid; and, pocketing my scant
spoil, I went my way with my friend. But he pulled me up at the distance of a
few yards by the elated emphasis of his demand: "Did you notice how polite
she was?" I allowed that I had in fact not felt her to be uncivil; so that,
commemorating the rare occasion by the longest stretch I could make of my
impression, I replied that it had indeed struck me as a case of good manners.
"Well," he exultantly said, "it's the same in the whole place!" "Ah then," I granted,
"it's a triumph;" but the interesting and significant thing remained the freshness
of his boast. I noted the pathos of his relief and cherished the memory of his
pride. It was a conquest for civilization that I hadn't paid, save in coin, for my
rashness; it had been "polite" of the posted saleswoman to render my purchase
rather feasible than impossible.

PART III

It would still have been easy to be challenged meanwhile, on that ground of the
relation borne by one's emphatic pronouncement—that we have, as a people,
no sense of manners at all—as to the state of the civilities among one's personal
acquaintance; especially as I have spoken of the existence of more than one group
to which some cultivation of the sense in question may be more or less imputable.
I have already named the scattered cluster of those among whom the example
and the precept of the earlier time are not wholly spent; and I recognize as
neighboring with it, indeed as more or less merged in it, that perhaps still larger
body of Americans exposed to the influence of various parts of the social order
across the sea. Confines here are vague and separations equivocal, inasmuch as
any set of persons for whom the civilities exist tend more to "march with"
societies of similar conscience—however uncertain the conscience may sometimes
be—than with populations of no conscience at all. Of this class who have had,
whether from afar or from nearer, some revelation of light there is easily more
to say than I may here embark on; suffice it for the moment that they represent
my second class.

   After which, since I have mentioned a third, I distinguish the company the
most interesting of my trio, the sacred band of good Americans whose development
has been happy and has yet been, as one may say, sufficiently homogeneous. I

see it, this development, as watered at the roots by the antique, the lingering tradition of finer discriminations, and I see it, on occasion, as warmed by the sun of civilizations riper than our own; but I feel at the same time—or try to think I feel!—the particular American sense and quality of it, our own especial note of responsibility. The pleasant persons, not strikingly numerous, whom I thus focus, are those of the conscience the most acute; but they are also those who have most of a struggle for their ideal. My first-named contingent has, I make out, ceased to struggle; its torch of tradition, a little more neglected by each generation, burns dim and smoky—so that frankly there are moments when the smoke, to my eyes, hides everything. As for my Europeanized examples, the principle of conscience has had among them not much to say to the matter; the instinct of imitation and conformity, rather, has acted—all inevitably and on the whole beneficently: the effect of acquaintance with *trained* populations being not only perceptible, but being favorable, in proportion as the contact has been close.

It has never been without profit to the individual American, I think, to have taken in the truth, as societies other than his own put it before him, that in a difficult and complicated world it is well to have had as many things as possible discriminated and thought out and tried and tested for us, well to remember that the art of meeting life finely is, what the art of the dramatist has been described as being, the art of preparations. There is always a thrill for us at home in the observed operation of our law that any one may become among us, at two minutes' notice, anything possible or impossible, even a gentleman, even a lady; but the deeper impression attaches, none the less, to the exhibited effects of being tutored, which correct usefully our too habitual, too national belief in the sweet sanctity of free impulse. By which I am far from hinting that every adventurous compatriot either comes back from the more lessoned and disciplined world charged with its richer spoil or stays on in it for pure love of the same; that personage being often unsurpassed, I fear, in the knack of faring far to gather little—when not in that of extracting from alien sources, by a strange and perverse chemistry, elements of which he is apt to have already enough and to spare.

The unmistakable thing is, at any rate, that the conception of manners is at the very best, among us, a struggle more or less fierce: which circumstance effectually disposes of any effective protest against my generalization. What it comes to, no doubt, is that those who struggle comparatively alone have to struggle hardest—while those fortified by some real experience of the boon acquired and established, those who are able in some degree to band together and create for themselves thereby a working illusion and an optimism possibly fallacious, have less of the heat and burden. The condition of all alike remains

yet the same—since one makes it out as the state of never appreciably ceasing
to be menaced with submersion. The question rises, at every turn, acute: are the
forces that make for the good old idea of the finer "forms" sufficient to withstand
the tremendous forces—and in particular the most insidious of all, of which I
shall presently speak—that make against them? (To speak of the "finer" forms
is meanwhile, obviously enough, to excite suspicion: millions among us regard
them as the customs agents at our ports regard the new clothes and other
conveniences rummaged out of trunks in sheds constructed to that end—place
them under the ban, tax them as contraband and injurious to the home-grown
article. Which represents, precisely, one of the cold waves of the rising, extinguish-
ing tide.)

To what degree is not an ideal inevitably doomed that has to consent at every
turn to compromises and concessions?—that is so subject, when it stirs abroad,
as one may say, to solid shocks of discouragement, and that must blow with all
the patience of private piety to keep the sacred flame alight? The gravity of the
case is that a consistent care for the civilities has to contend, of all things in the
world, with that very aspect of our collective existence which has most ministered,
these forty years past, to our pride and joy. It has simply to contend with our
immense general prosperity and facility—a condition disfigured as much as we
may be willing to admit with local and partial infirmities and plague-spots, but
still finding its boast in the fact that we are the most money-making people in
the world and the one among whom the hard-pressed of other lands are most
eager to be numbered.

This general high prosperity is then our general large ease, our confidence of
being accepted on the spot for anything in life we may pretend to; whereby, as
our general large ease is in so many directions our general large looseness, so *this*
most comprehensive of all our luxuries is our school of manners, the flood in
which our few "forms" dispersedly sink or swim, *rari nantes in gurgite vasto.* Our
theory of social equality, combined with our unsurpassed disposition to accumulate
those dollars that lighten the burden of consciousness, has had the effect of
providing that the individual consciousness shall sit light, and of deprecating
with vigilance all uncanny attempts to disconcert it. Therefore as, in spite of
whatever drawbacks and complications, the prosperity has tended to fill the world
with its sound, so the side-wind of the great growth, blowing as ubiquitously as
the breath of some colossal lusty housewife, has prevented any settlement of the
gray dust of pessimism. Any enforcement of the ideas of preparation and probation,
any challenge of sweet impulse, any arrest of facility and felicity, any analysis of
"success," in fine, or any plea for discipline, is held to savor of the unholy critical
spirit; whereby it is our practical claim that our manners shall flourish in an air
from which criticism is absent. What is criticism but pessimism, and where is

sacred spontaneity, that of the younger generations in especial, rising and clamoring round us, if we pretend really to analyze or appreciate anything?

Here it is we put our finger, assuredly, on our erratic pulse; here it is that we catch at work the force that makes, to the detriment of education, for what I have called the submersion of the struggler. It is impossible for any witness of the process who has been able to watch it some time not to note the virtual inveteracy with which the "ways" of the female young, for instance, fail to strike him in any degree as an improvement on those of the women whose remembered youth comes back to him with another note; just as their speech, that of these latter, seems to him to have had a comparative sweetness at the extinction of which in their daughters they have helplessly and almost unconsciously assisted. Did *they*, pushing without a shade of trepidation and with their sense of social proportion and perspective deeply participating in the universal stupor, straight to the front of every attempted talk, of every otherwise fortunate occasion, take the words from their mothers' mouths to their interlocutors' consternation, regard themselves almost explicitly as the only objects of interest, and heart-breakingly exhibit in short the serenity of their pampered ignorance?

Decidedly not, or at least ever so much less, we unhesitatingly feel; for if the germ of that extravagance may have been visible in earlier days the plant has flowered in our time with quickened profusion, and after a fashion that shows us how the young are remaking on every side the education of their predecessors. They are educating each other as never before, and this with such a violence—by which I mean with a triumph so prompt and unchecked—that any voice from the remonstrant rear drops before it is uttered. Always, no doubt, it appears that the maidens of one's early time were milder than those of one's later; it being incontestable that the maidens of all times have a sense for the immediately aptest uses of their best mildness. The signs and portents of what I have called the compromise—the surrender of discriminations and ideals, the letting of standards go because they are simply shaken from a relaxed grasp—are too numerous and obvious, the symptoms of demoralization fall, as it were, too much together.

One of the liveliest, no doubt, is just the truth, well before me as I write, that to express one's sense of the absence of discipline is probably to invite some pitying derision of one's superannuated state: as if one were uttering some stale refrain on the value of ancient bread and water and the ancient rod of castigation. There could be no better disproof perhaps of any general large or helpful comprehension of the term. What *should* it in fact mean, the vain critic wonders, to generations among whom social, civil, conversational values have achieved the feat of getting, by most evidence, irretrievably muddled? Social, civil, conversational discipline consists in having to recognize knowledge and competence and authority, accomplishment, experience and "importance," greater than one's own; and it is in a bad way therefore, obviously, in communities in which it is so important to be a chattering little girl—before becoming, by the same token and as for the highest flight, a "social leader"—that every measure of everything gives way to it.

From the moment we feel the making of "queens" on such easy terms as flourish for the candidates in the American world to be mainly the making of almost tragic victims, from that moment our judgment of their case as favorable to the acquisition of manners would fain despoil itself of every harshness but the harshness of perfect lucidity. It may be good to have become a queen in conditions of great difficulty and danger, or even, say, when only your precursors have paid for it by their blood or their genius; but to become one as you become a *débutante* or a fiancée or a flirt or a bridge-player or a wife and mother, or even (so far do I go) a president of a Society of Dames, would be, in an air less fatally beguiling, to expose yourself to some rather straight challenge of your titles. Full of bearing on that question seemed, not long since, I remember, the inquiry made of me by a charming American daughter who, in a great European city, had been visibly puzzled by the lapse of local testimony to this fact of her natural royalty.

She had arrived a few days before in the eminent company of her father, an artist of the highest distinction and geniality, and, in presence of prompt invitations to luncheon and to dinner, had been candidly surprised at their not being addressed to herself. He had been invited with the hope that he would bring his amiable daughter; it was not she who had been invited with the hope she would bring her celebrated sire. She was beautiful and intelligent and modest and good— which made the case, for her candor, all the more exemplifying: the candor, in New York and in Boston, would have been so almost cruelly abused. She rose to the occasion, I hasten to add, and consented to lay off for the time her crown; but her question meanwhile had not been the less illuminating. She could shine in "Europe" but with a secondary light: it was she who was her father's appendage, and not—as I gathered from her that the American form would have represented the matter—her father who was hers. She could hope for no social existence without him, while he, strange to say, might hope for any amount without her.

It was "quaint" to have to explain such things; and if it happened to be in this particular instance all delightful, that was mainly by reason of the light thrown for me on the exquisitely trained state of my old friend; who, if not really unprepared for such readjustments, had at least been too long schooled by his own social medium to be rashly uplifted. He, certainly, represented the element of training, or at any rate that of concession and surrender, since he couldn't have been, after all, at bottom, unconscious of the major importance of those fine things of the mind and of the artistic experience for which his name and example were valued. All of which interpretation of the matter didn't moreover exhaust for me its significance. Meeting my friends a day or two later at dinner in a considerable company, I was again interested in the fact that my charming young lady had, as I was afterwards to learn, found it amusingly queer and picturesque (for her criticism was indulgent) to sit between a couple of men of "age"—one indeed of extreme and honored and distinguished age—instead of between a pair of merry youths expressly provided for her. "This being a situation then," I asked, "in which a girl couldn't have found herself in 'America'?" "Ah, but never! This was delightfully—as you call everything—'quaint'; but from the moment a girl is invited at all (and of course she's invited all the time) something special is done for her, which she feels she has a right to count upon." "And the something special then is always the merry youth?" "Yes, always: quite as if she were following a certain diet or drinking a prescribed wine, so that her particular dish or particular bottle is remembered and set before her." Upon which, all the while, one could but muse. "And what is done—specially—for the elder women? Are *their* 'tastes' remembered?" " 'Specially,' no. They," said my brilliantly lucid young friend, "are not pampered!" The point of which slight and simple words, if I be asked for it, was that, spoken in European air, they immediately evoked for me a social condition, an image that appeared to drag after it a whole train of light upon manners.

The picture was of the realm of the unfortunate "queens"; to whom there was seemingly no one to suggest the possible privilege and profit, even for competent queenship, that may proceed from a recognition of the *related* state. No, it appeared, women's fostered sense of themselves "over there" was as creatures absolute, with the single qualification that raw youth tended so perpetually to snatch from round ripeness the prize of domination; therefore how would it strike one, on the scene itself, that the drawback of the absent educative forces was to be met?—the drawback, that is, for the "queens," forming their manners, of their having no wholesome social rigor of any sort to reckon with. Social rigor exists and becomes wholesome from the moment social relations of a more composite order than the leaving of cards and the dancing of the cotillion are attested, established, embodied things, involving attention and deference, involving the sacrifice of easy presumptions, and the mistrust of cheap pretensions, and the cultivation of informed estimates, and the patience, generally, of the consciously comparative state—the state of suspecting that there are probably more things in a civilized world, or even in any mere decently "good" society, than are dreamt of in the philosophy of free chatter.

I was to see "over here," unquestionably—when the occasion presently came— what I saw; but inevitably, meanwhile, any wandering air charged with the message of the queenship seemed a direct contribution to my experience, just as on the spot itself I found myself desiring, for all justice, to live, in imagination, if possible, through the ordeal of those persons who might be *feeling*, tragically enough, their civil tradition slip from them. Such cases, I was soon enough to see, were but different aspects of the same chaos; and it at all events chanced that I just then found observation quickened by a succession of small other testimonies. It easily happens that, observed in alien air, American "ways" put on, for better or for worse, their intensest value—and those with which we are here concerned were precisely not such as manifest it for the better. When an English friend, a lady who had lately been in the States, remarked to me, for instance, in allusion to the most patent source of distress for American housewives, that the distress might be equal in England—domestic upheavals, that is, might be quite as frequent—if the employers of servants were often heard to address them in such tones and with such a manner as she had noted the use of in America. English servants (the moral of this was) wouldn't "stand" it: their own amenities of address—the fruit, definitely, of cultivation on their part as well as on that of their patrons—absolutely implied reciprocity, could only be met by forms *equally* cultivated: on which all smoothness of service was felt to depend.

I was subsequently to smile, on my native soil, at this idea of reciprocity really practised—so haunted was I to be, from an early moment, with the case of a gentle relative (which I have already somewhere commemorated) who, summoned to meet a representative of her laundress, found a man inquiring if she were the woman of the house—in which case he had come from the washer-lady. That, no doubt, is one view of the reasonable give and take, a view the acceptance of which by the woman of the house leaves plenty of room for discretion; but it is only an extreme illustration of the sort of "form" on the ground of which people have, right and left, to be met, to be tolerated, to be dealt with and conversed with and lived with—from the moment internecine war doesn't take place. That means, for the American woman at large—over and above the fond possession of daughters in an acute state of queenship and inflamed with the pride and power of the same—the liability to intercourse with domestics instinctively interested, though by the most pitiful of fallacies, in dragging communion down to a level of tone at which they may easily have the best of it. Our women would need, I grant, a high dose of superiority not to fall more often than not into the trap there is such a conspiracy to lay for them. That is, no doubt, their misfortune as much as their fault—the resigned acceptance of the vulgar term imposed on them, when the term not vulgar is found not to be workable without more patience and reflection than the case seems worth.

On the scene itself then, in due course, I was to find myself wondering—and again especially in the hotels and trains—what patience and reflection were imputable to the feminine type or two that most surrounded me. What conception of the "tone of home" as a treasure in their keeping did I imagine my fellow travellers capable of forming?—some of the innumerable ladies of the hotels above all; those accompanied, after dinner, as the plot thickened and the evening waned, by the terrific bedizened hotel-bred little girls, whom one somehow felt as so destined, while thus imbibing the rudiments of queenship, to put a rod in pickle for domestic use a few years later. To what vision of feminine sweetness were these small unfortunates being trained, and what example of that grace was given, for the most part, in the hard faces and harsh accents of the mothers? Fresh from the frequent statistic and accessible, all round, to the voices of the air, I couldn't, as a restless analyst, rid myself of the conviction that the majority of the mothers and wives thus met and noted were of divorced and divorcing condition and intention—to which presumption their so frequently quite unhusbanded appearance much contributed.

I had at least the interest of *this* opening, that, when speculating, in the States of cheap and easy divorce, as to the sort of "personality" that would most be engaged in it, the men and women about me became at once and alike a vivid match to the idea. This was what cheap and easy divorcers *would*, for any suggested civility, resemble: the convenience was surely one such a generation would have invented if it hadn't existed. To which I may add indeed that if asked whether I make the monstrous statement that these publicly-viewed of my countrywomen struck me as *all* unamiable, I find small difficulty as to my answer. American women offered themselves, definitely, to my enlarged view, as of three categories, of differing extent. I place in the first and smallest those for whom, by hook or by crook, some civil scheme still has contrived to exist. I place in the second, less small—fortunately, rather, of respectable dimensions—those for whom it either never has existed or has gone into eclipse, but among whom a conscientious substitute for it fairly struggles on. And I place in the third the formidable array of those innocent apparently alike of the forms and of the provisional yearning. Our general hope is doubtless where the real hope almost always is, in the precious, the smallest, minority having weight; but my particular interest is in my middle class, as it were, of which I shall next especially speak. We must certainly consider the provisional yearning, the conscientious substitute.

PART IV

If I speak of a "conscientious substitute" for forms of intercourse habitually observed I must still explain, no doubt, what I mean by it, and in particular by insisting on the element of conscience. This element, as applied to private life and personal dealings, certainly made the basis of our old social order, and we have produced nothing socially interesting in which something of that foundation may not be felt. It must always have operated to keep down vain professions and hollow compliments, too marked a disparity between attitude and conduct; but it made on the other hand for reciprocal interest and aid, for practical sympathy and anxious care. It made, for every one, against indifference to the particular conditions or predicaments of others, since it was largely inspired by a sense of what is good and salutary for us all. It is good for us all at times, for instance, to be told the strict truth about ourselves, and that duty was doubtless unflinchingly performed, and with an earnestness of spirit for which we have to-day unlearnt any such application—for which indeed we have almost no use at all. We have no use for the luminous candor which used to make neighbors say to neighbors "How dreadfully you're looking!" as soon as any reason for a failure of bloom was suspected; or to move the frequent appeal as to the conscious purity of a friend's motives.

More consideration accompanied these sincerities, in many a case, than attends for the most part either the liberties we of a later generation take or the easier overlookings we practise; for those honest austerities were, in their way, never rudenesses—they were essentially anxious and strenuous *forms*, tributes to the idea of a social relation. They have to a certain extent broken down, and many of them, no doubt, not wholly for the worse; but they still have this reality, that in the scattered patches of their native soil, where impunity, as I have called it, the impunity of ignorance and presumption, so largely riots, their discredited spirit yet helps us a little to understand why our life is virtually attended with certain alleviations. It comes back indeed to the old frequent question: "We are so humane that what does it matter if we are rough? we are so mutually helpful under stress that what does it matter if we confine our notion of help to the extreme case? So long as we take it almost for a joke that you have broken your leg by the wayside—arranging as our general good-nature and democratic give-and-take arrange for broken legs—what does it matter if among 'real people,' as you go about, you're not smeared over with butter and honey? Besides, it may be perfectly held that in 'society' you *are*—since American society notoriously isn't real."

This ingenuous claim is, oddly enough, no mere superstition; there are plenty of documents to prove the contrary—to prove the truth of the general legend of our common charity and ready-handedness in face of troubles. The "figure" of our monstrous subscriptions, which follow so close on our monstrous catastrophes, would speak much of this, should we appeal to it; which we perhaps don't do, however, lest it should appear to speak too much more of our mere monstrous wealth. The light in which the image of the great ready-handedness would most conveniently and distinctly shine for the careful student of evidence, meanwhile, would surely be that of the "short story" of American life in general, and of the New England in particular, as our charmed generation has known these compositions—extraordinary records of mere mutual accommodation, as they strike in especial the reader immersed in distant and differing conditions. I needn't specify, for recognitions here are easy, and most of all because this literature is almost solely from the hands of women, whose sense for the minor mercies and mitigations of the hard lot is always to be trusted.

The general record is certainly of the hard lot, and it is observable, I think, the world over, that the poor are kinder to the poor, in proportion, than the rich themselves are, or even than the rich are to the rich. It sticks out, none the less, that, simply expressed, people "do more" for each other in the ugly, funny, sturdy, happy, dreary order portrayed by the charming artists in question than any other such exhibition of manners anywhere represents them as doing. They "take right hold," in their own phrase, for neighbors or friends, for any fellow mortal, under the pinch of any crisis; they pop in and out of each other's houses and each other's affairs with extraordinary freedom, but almost always to comfort and serve, to help to do the work and shoulder the burden: it "occurs" to them to go over and make pies for the people across the way, or to stay all day or sit up all night with them, when these people are at all prostrate, as it appears to occur to no other class registered in history. Hence we have the picture of a society with as few persons as possible appointed to specific charges and duties, but with almost any person doing almost anything to, or for, or in the house of, almost any one, as impulse on the one side prompts or patience on the other side permits.

One hardly knows whether most to admire the patience or the impulse: the general result is so wondrous an exhibition of the equal play of these forces— of the life of communities carried on by the law that every one shall intimately and directly put up with every one and be in the same degree put up with. Manners are a help in life—a help not only to avoid certain vices, but to bear with certain virtues; yet the villagers and townspeople so depicted have not that assistance, and we wonder what it is that saves them, their nerves or their temper or their lives or their breakable objects—what it is that holds them or their hearthstones together. The explanation, when it comes, is touching; since it consists apparently in the fact of the so prolonged and so equal participation of every one in the essential hardness and grimness of the old American condition. Life was long bare and strenuous and difficult, but was so for all alike, with the fortunate exceptions, the representatives of privilege and exemption, few in number, and not so remarkably fortunate, after all, nor so armed with resources. People could thus have the sense and the imagination of each other's states in a much more unbroken way than in "Europe," where great differences of state had long since grown up, and where, accordingly, with the danger of taking liberties operating as a check to spontaneity, the reflective and calculated freedoms were much more numerous, but both the independence and the dependence much less acute.

And that this generalization does not apply solely to the populations humanized, not less than brutalized, by the common condition of poverty, is proved by the so vivid and interesting evidence contained in Mr. Howells's novels—which are surely so documentary as to a large part of American life and a whole side of the American spirit that were we not, to our humiliation and disgrace, deplorably destitute of any large and competent criticism, some study of them in the light of this documentary value would long since have been made. For it is Mr. Howells above all who helps us to recognize what has hitherto made our association possible and enabled us to hold out against the daily effect of our surrender of forms. He marks this surrender, at every point, with an infallible hand, and yet, in the oddest way in the world, a perfect gospel of optimism is to be extracted from his general picture. For here we get the exquisite *detail* of the mutual, the universal patience—with the strangest impression, as a whole, I think, of every one's, men's and women's alike, trying, all round them, by universal readiness and response, to deprecate and forestall the great peril of fatal aggravation.

Every one takes for granted everywhere an unlimited alacrity of service, sympathy, mercy, or, still more, active encouragement, and no one seems disappointed or betrayed, in a world where almost the only salient vital convenience is the ability of every one to get criticism restricted and errands obligingly, not mercenarily, done. What need for manners, any more than for any other detail of comfort, we thus seem eventually taught to wonder, in communities where nobody misses anything—by reason precisely of this merciful *pitch* of criticism? The pitch can with perfect convenience be low when passion and irritation are on their side so successfully kept down. It is as if every one feels the equilibrium too precious to be endangered; where there is so little other convenience, so little of the *margin* supplied by manners, that sole security counts double, and it is with peculiar intensity in every one's interest to be good—or in other words to be easy.

This then, this necessity of good-humor, is the great ease, the great bond and the great lubricant; so that it is as if the author's subtle sense of what the whole situation hangs by were the key to his wit and his pathos, his rare note of reality, his mastery of American truth. Such an expert study of the whole element as is supplied for instance in *The Kentons* catches in the very act the system to the working of which he all so ironically yet so incorruptibly testifies. This unsurpassed attempt to sound the grayest abysses of the average state and the middle condition projects for us the measure of how little their occupants may neglect the conviction, at least as a saving instinct, of the equal importance of all; all, that is, as a charge on the common forbearance or, to speak more nobly, the common humanity. The forbearance of Mr. Kenton in respect to his wife is only equalled by hers in respect to her husband, and the parental philosophy again only by that of the daughters, filially and fraternally. Nobody makes "short work," in a word, of any one or of anything, no matter how "impossible," and if we at moments rather fail to see how or why anybody finally either spares or is spared, we yet do see that on this strained basis the society depicted does in a manner creak along.

All of which explains my reference to that precarious principle—the active fellowship, founded on a more or less dire common experience—that works, we have seen, in considerable patches as a substitute for the finer amenity. But what interestingly happens is that, even on these floating rafts of salvage, it may often occur to the individual that the substitute is really more expensive than the prime commodity, and that our consenting to be reduced to it is perhaps the circumstance best describing a civilization addicted to nothing if not to waste. Manners are above all—and it is the best plea for them—an economy; the sacrifice of them has always in the long run to be made up, just as the breakages and dilapidations have to be paid for at the end of the tenancy of a house carelessly occupied. These changes in the mass become so large that the tenant ruefully asks if a little less smashing mightn't have been the better plan. By an excess of misuse moreover a house is fatally disfigured—rendered, that is, unfavorable to life; in which case we become liable for the total ruin: to the infinite dismay of those members of the family (and there are always such, to be cherished and grateful for) to whom the vision of such waste is a vision of barbarism.

Let me thus then, making my image comprehensive, invite it to cover the case of the whole social opportunity of women in our rough American world—that world indeed whose apparently admirable capacity for still feeding innumerable millions makes us even yet resent the application to its liberality of any invidious epithet. We have to breathe low that it *is* rough, and that the free hand we have given on all sides to our women has done much less than we might have dreamed to smooth it: we otherwise invite ourselves to taste overmuch of certain forms of the roughness. This, however, is a trifle if we only succeed in insisting, insisting with lucidity; than which there is no better way, doubtless, than to appeal with directness. Directness is achieved, accordingly, when this petition to the American woman is made, absolutely, *against* her much-misguided self, and when it is asked of her to recognize, not that her path is more lighted than that of her downtrodden sisters in other worlds, but that she literally stands in need of three times their sufficiency of admonition. It is in other words not three times easier for her to please and soothe and happily to exemplify, but three times more difficult—by reason of the false lights that have multiplied about her and that an atmosphere absolutely uncritical has done nothing to extinguish.

The appeal to her should have but one sense, a sense so important that beside it none other matters: that of her replacing the old theory of her having, in her native air, nothing to fear by the perception, so urgent now, that she has almost everything. She has, to begin with, the poison of the gross fallacy that such vast complacencies, no matter how fostered and flourishing, can ever promote any appearance of the graceful, the tender or the sweet—as if it were not true that the more things amiability and charm have to reckon with the better for them, for their very selves, so long as these things be the right ones. They are the right ones—and this is the best of all measures—when they keep the air clear of the grotesqueness so easily attaching to vain presumption and so certainly attaching to high fatuity. They are the right ones, in fine, when the men of a community have not treacherously abjured the manly part of *real* appreciation—letting, in the guise of generosity, the whole question of responsibility, of manly competence and control, example, expectation, go by the board. The spectator of such a chaos is constantly forced back to it: the fatal trap was thus originally set for the luckless assumption by our women of the most distinctive of their marks, that of their having been "grown" in conditions all preponderantly easy because preponderantly feminine; the great feminine collectivity asserting itself as against all interference and so quite effectually balancing against any discipline of friction within the herd.

The man in America may correct his wife when he can, just as the mother may correct her daughter when she dares; but no mere man may correct a mere woman in any contingency whatever, since this undermines the whole theory of queenship at which we have already glanced. He has abdicated his right to take his stand on what pleases him, and can accordingly but shift it all ruefully, in the service of his mate, to those perilous ledges which represent all the admonitory margin now left him. In societies other than ours the male privilege of correction springs, and quite logically, from the social fact that the male is the member of society primarily acting and administering and primarily listened to—whereby his education, his speech, his tone, his standards and connections, his general "competence," as I have called it, color the whole air, react upon his companion and establish for her the principal relation she recognizes. The question of her speech—as the simplest illustration—floods, for instance, my whole contention with light; just as the question of her talk follows it very close. Supreme thus in any atmosphere of the "liberal" education the law that the man claiming to be accepted as civilized shall speak as a gentleman, and vital therefore for the maintenance of that character the testimony he so renders.

It is from his maintenance of it that the woman, as a social creature, gets her lead and her cue and her best sanction for her maintenance of hers; since she is never at all thoroughly a well-bred person unless *he* has begun by having a sense for it and by showing her the way: when—oh *then* beautifully and wonderfully and in a manner all her own!—she often improves on it and carries it, in the detail of application, much further than he. The point, at any rate, is that, if she would only take this truth as revealed to her, the wisdom of the ages has everywhere quite absolved her from the formidable care of extracting a conception of the universe and a scheme of manners from her moral consciousness alone—the burden that among ourselves she has so rashly and complacently assumed. She betrays no shadow of doubt of her competence for the feat—which is precisely the strongest mark of her issuing from a society of women. No party, no inspired or alarmed minority, in the vast congregation ever cautions or undeceives the mass, and so, with their immense delusion, they collectively launch themselves upon the world.

Practically, of course, the result is that the huge hard business-world which has found no direct use for her has, by leaving her so cruelly to herself, given her away; but the apparent perfection of her state is such that the word of warning has to contend at first with the immensity of her surprise. What! *she*, of all the grouped ornaments of the human scene, laboring at a peculiar disadvantage, and thereby to be pitied and relieved and rectified and set on a better path, instead of positively enjoying (in her socially unshackled state, her celebrated queenship, her notorious success, her facility of marriage with foreign nobles, the frequent wealth of her father, the constant absence of her husband, the approved propriety of her conduct and the rare observed occasions of her embarrassment,) the highest of all advantages? "Even so" is what we must reply—with all respect to the foreign nobles and other producible trophies that we rank, on the whole, as conspiring much more against than in favor of the real felicity of so many victims of the ironic fate. Who, with any sense of the possible graces of life, has seen without compassion one of these unfortunates chatter with all the gayety of unabashed self-reference and all the confidence of perfect inanity, in a circle virtually hushed to despair by the exhibition of so good a conscience in so bad a cause, and thus in fact fostering on the part of the performer the fond error that "success," round the fire, consists in the quantity of good talk she has kept waiting at the door. Few of us surely but have been present on occasions when conversation, fairly dreading the sound of her, has refused to come in before her bright, triumphant, charming departure.

Let the appeal be made to our sisters therefore in the name of any number

of those treacherous cases that confront the sweet supremacy of their inspiration
and the sweet simplicity of their scheme with a world the very interest of which
is exactly that it is complicated. It is complicated with the idea of acquired
knowledge and with that of imbibed modesty, with that of imposed deference
and with that of a thousand differences of condition and character, of occasion
and value. For the American woman to feel herself above these things may be
one way of describing her as too often fatally outside of them—the drawback
of which is that she is so deprived of any relation to them. In *that* way it is that
the consecration of discipline falls at a stroke from all her forms; since it really
consists in the state of being related to as many good things as possible—and
of having, up to the hilt, paid for the fact. Noting lately two or three examples
of what one must again and again call, before anything else, the betrayed condition—in other words simply the unregenerate conscience—it was impossible to
me not to feel the dim dreariness of the limbo into which, even if all unwitting,
the hapless subjects had been thrust forth. I have left myself space, however, but
for a single instance. Several young persons—of whom I was one!—had achieved
together, in European air, a considerable run on bicycles, and it had befallen
that, at the start, the machine of a young lady of the party, who was not an
American, had required a small rearrangement which it promptly, even if a little
awkwardly, received at the hands of a member of the party who *was* an American.

I was struck by the charming tone of the explicit and insistent tribute of
thanks rendered to this slight service; struck even after no small observation of
the inveterate emphasis of such acknowledgments, often the prettiest intensified
emphasis in the world, on the lips of European beneficiaries. It happened an
hour later that the bicycle of another of our companions, the American girl of
the group, gave way in some weak place; whereupon a halt being called, our
handy compatriot, supremely obliging, if not supremely expert, devoted some
ten minutes and much patience to repairing its disorder. He made it over to its
owner working quite smoothly again, and she dropped him, as she remounted,
a thin, short, perfunctory "Thanks" which had the effect of making our eyes,
his and mine, the next moment, meet in wondering intelligence. The young lady,
who was in no way allied to him, had acknowledged the larger assistance, by
habit and as her fruit of fashion, as meagrely as her European sister had a short
time previous copiously acknowledged the smaller. One was reminded afresh of
the scant practice, in this direction, enjoyed by queens; yet as the American girl
rode, at her queenly rate, away, she struck me as faring, all unconscious but all
doomed, into the strangest desert of solitude and ignorance. It was the last thing
she could have dreamed of, but it was as if she had written herself, by her
renunciation of the power intimately to touch, lonely, blighted, and disinherited.
She was blind, she was deaf, to the stops of the social pipe, and its broken

fragments seemed to crunch under her as she passed. All of which sudden perception was, dimly, dawningly, in the eyes of our bewildered swain, who struck me as having for the first time, poor youth, really tasted of the tree of knowledge. He had caught a snatch of the finer music, and I have asked myself repeatedly since, what it is that restored to his native order, he must have begun to fancy he misses.

III

Metaphysical Essay,
1910

Is There a Life After Death?

X

PART I

I confess at the outset that I think it the most interesting question in the world, once it takes on all the intensity of which it is capable. It does that, insidiously but inevitably, as we live longer and longer—does it at least for many persons; I myself, in any case, find it increasingly assert its power to attach and, if I may use the word so unjustly compromised by trivial applications, to amuse. I say "assert its power" so to occupy us, because I mean to express only its most general effect. That effect on our spirit is mostly either one of two forms; the effect of making us desire death, and for reasons, absolutely *as* welcome extinction and termination; or the effect of making us desire it as a renewal of the interest, the appreciation, the passion, the large and consecrated consciousness, in a word, of which we have had so splendid a sample in this world. Either one or the other of these opposed states of feeling is bound finally to declare itself, we judge, in persons of a fine sensibility and whose innermost spirit experience has set vibrating at all; for the condition of indifference and of knowing neither is the condition of living altogether so much below the human privilege as to have little right to pass for unjustly excluded or neglected in this business of the speculative reckoning.

That an immense number of persons should not recognize the appeal of our speculation, or even be aware of the existence of our question, is a fact that

From W. D. Howells, Henry James, John Bigelow, Thomas Wentworth Higginson, Henry M. Alden, William Hanna Thomson, Guglielmo Ferrero, Julia Ward Howe, and Elizabeth Stuart Phelps, *In After Days: Thoughts on the Future Life* (New York: Harper, 1910), 199–233.

might seem to demand, in the whole connection, some particular consideration; but our anxiety, our hope, or our fear, hangs before us, after all, only because it more or less torments us, and in order to contribute in any degree to a discussion of the possibility we have to be consciously in presence of it. I can only see it, the great interrogation or the great deprecation we are ultimately driven to, as a part of our general concern with life and our general, and extremely various— because I speak of each man's general—mode of reaction under it; but to testify for an experience we must have reacted in one way or another. The weight of those who don't react may be felt, it is true, in one of the scales; for it may very well be asked on their behalf whether they are distinguishable as "living" either before or after. Only the special reaction of others, or the play of *their* speculation, however, will, in due consideration, have put it there. How *can* there be a personal and a differentiated life "after," it will then of course be asked, for those for whom there has been so little of one before?—unless indeed it be pronounced conceivable that the possibility may vary from man to man, from human case to human case, and that the quantity or the quality of our practice of consciousness may have something to say to it. If I myself am disposed to pronounce this conceivable—as verily I expect to find myself before we have done—I must glance at a few other relations of the matter first.

My point for the moment is that the more or less visibly diminishing distance which separates us at a certain age from death is, however we are affected toward the supposition of an existence beyond it, an intensifier of the feeling that most works in us, and that in the light of the lamp so held up our aggravated sense of life, as I may perhaps best call it, our impression of what we have been through, is what essentially fosters and determines, on the whole ground, our desire or our aversion. So, at any rate, the situation strikes me, and one can speak of it but for one's personal self. The subject is portentous and any individual utterance upon it, however ingenious or however grave, but comparatively a feeble pipe or a pathetic quaver; yet I hold that as we can scarce have too many visions, too many statements or pictures of the conceived social Utopia that the sincere fond dreamer, the believer in better things, may find glimmer before him, so the sincere and struggling son of earth among his fellow-strugglers reports of the positive or negative presumption in the savor of his world, that is not to be of earth, and thus drops his testimony, however scant, into the reservoir. It all depends, in other words, the weight or the force or the interest of this testimony does, on what life has predominantly said to us. And there are those—I take them for the constant and vast majority—to whom it in the way of intelligible suggestion says nothing. Possibly immortality itself—or another chance at least, as we may freely call it—will say as little; which is a fair and simple manner of disposing of the idea of a new start in relation to them. Though, indeed, I must add, the contemplative critic scarce—save under one probability—sees why the universe should be at the expense of a new start for those on whom the old start appears (though but to our purblind sight, it may, of course, be replied) so to have been wasted. The probability is, in fact, that what we dimly discern as waste the wisdom of the universe may know as a very different matter. We don't think of slugs and jellyfish as the waste, but rather as the amusement, the attestation of wealth and variety, of gardens and sea-beaches; so why should we, under stress, in respect to the human scene and its discussable sequel, think differently of dull people?

This is but an instance, or a trifle, however, among the difficulties with which the whole case bristles for those on whom the fact of the lived life has insisted on thrusting it, and which it yet leaves them tormentedly to deal with. The question is of the *personal* experience, of course, of another existence; of its being I my very self, and you, definitely, and he and she, who resume and go on, and not of unthinkable substitutes or metamorphoses. The whole interest of the matter is that it is my or your sensibility that is involved and at stake; the thing figuring to us as momentous just because that sensibility and its tasted fruits, as we owe them to life, are either remunerative enough and sweet enough or too barren and too bitter. Only because posthumous survival in some other conditions involves what we know, what we have enjoyed and suffered, as our particular personal adventure, does it appeal to us or excite our protest; only because of the *associations* of consciousness do we trouble and consult ourselves—do we wish the latter prolonged and wonder if it may not be indestructible, or decide that we have had enough of it and invoke the conclusion that we have so had it once for all. We pass, I think, through many changes of impression, many shifting estimates, as to the force and value of those associations; and there is no single, there is no decisive sense of them in which, throughout our earthly course, it is easy or needful to rest.

Whatever we may begin with we almost inevitably go on, under the discipline of life, to more or less resigned acceptance of the grim fact that "science" takes no account of the soul, the principle we worry about, and that, as however nobly thinking and feeling creatures, we are abjectly and inveterately shut up in our material organs. We flutter away from that account of ourselves, on sublime occasion, only to come back to it with the collapse of our wings, and during much of our life the grim view, as I have called it, the sense of the rigor of our physical basis, is confirmed to us by overwhelming appearances. The mere spectacle, all about us, of personal decay, and of the decay, as seems, of the whole being, adds itself formidably to that of so much bloom and assurance and energy—the things we catch in the very fact of their material identity. There are times when *all* the elements and qualities that constitute the affirmation of the personal life here affect us as making against any apprehensible other affirmation of it. And that general observation and evidence abide with us and keep us company; they reinforce the verdict of the dismal laboratories and the confident analysts as to the interconvertibility of our genius, as it comparatively is at the worst, and our brain—the poor palpable, ponderable, probeable, laboratory-brain that we ourselves see in certain inevitable conditions—become as naught.

It brings itself home to us thus in all sorts of ways that we are even at our highest flights of personality, our furthest reachings out of the mind, of the very stuff of the abject actual, and that the sublimest idea we can form and the noblest hope and affection we can cherish are but flowers sprouting in that eminently and infinitely diggable soil. It may be as favorable to them—as well as to quite other moral growths—as we are free to note; but we see its power to put them forth break down and end, and ours to receive them from it to do the same— we watch the relentless ebb of the tide on which the vessel of experience carries us, and which to our earthly eyes never flows again. It is to the personality that the idea of renewed being attaches itself, and we see nothing so much written over the personalities of the world as that they are finite and precarious and insusceptible. All the ugliness, the grossness, the stupidity, the cruelty, the vast extent to which the score in question is a record of brutality and vulgarity, the so easy non-existence of consciousness, round about us as to most of the things that make for living desirably at all, or even for living once, let alone on the enlarged chance—these things fairly rub it into us that to *have* a personality need create no presumption beyond what this remarkably mixed world is by itself amply sufficient to meet. A renewal of being, we ask, for people who understand being, even here, where renewals, of sorts, are possible, that way, and that way, apparently, alone?—leaving us vainly to wonder, in presence of such obvious and offensive matter for decay and putrescence, what there is for renewal to take hold of, or what element may be supposed fine enough to create a claim for disengagement. The mere fact in short that so much of life as we know it dishonors, or at any rate falls below, the greater part of the beauty and the opportunity even of this world, works upon us for persuasion that none other can be eager to receive it.

With which all the while there co-operates the exhibited limitation of our faculty for persistence, for not giving way, for not doing more than attest the inextinguishable or extinguishable spark in the mere minimum of time. The thinkable, the possible, we are fairly moved to say, in the way of the resistances and renewals of our conceded day, baffle us and are already beyond our command; I mean in the sense that the spirit even still in activity never shows as recovering, before our present eyes, an inch of the ground the body has once fairly taken from it. The personality, the apparently final eclipse of which by death we are discussing, fails, we remark, of any partial victory over partial eclipses, and keeps before us, once for all, the same sharp edge of blackness on the compromised disk of light. Even while "we" nominally go on those parts of us that have been overdarkened become as dead; our extinct passions and faculties and interests, that is, refuse to revive; our personality, by which I mean our "soul," declining in many a case, or in most, by inches, is aware of itself at any given moment as it is, however contracted, and not as it *was*, however magnificent; we may die piecemeal, but by no sign ever demonstrably caught does the "liberated" spirit react from death piecemeal. The answer to that may of course be that such reactions as can be "caught" are not claimed for it even by the fondest lovers of the precarious idea; the most that is claimed is that the reaction takes place *somewhere*—and the farther away from the conditions and circumstances of death the more probably. The apparently significant thing is none the less that during slow and successive stages of material extinction *some* nearness—of the personal quantity departing to the personal quantity remaining, and in the name of personal association and personal affection, and to the abatement of utter personal eclipse— might be supposable; and that this is what we miss.

Such, at least, is one of the faces, however small, that life puts on to persuade us of the utterly contingent nature of our familiar inward ease—ease of being— and that, to our comfort or our disconcertment, this familiarity is a perfectly restricted thing. And so we go on noting, through our time and amid the abundance of life, everything that makes, to our earthly senses, for the unmistakable absoluteness of death. Every hour affords us some fresh illustration of it, drawn especially from the condition of others; but one, if we really heed it, recurs and recurs as the most poignant of all. How can we not make much of the terrible fashion in which the universe takes upon itself to emphasize and multiply the disconnectedness of those who vanish from our sight?—or they perhaps not so much from ours as we from theirs; though indeed if once we lend ourselves to the hypothesis of posthumous renovation at all, the fact that our ex-fellow- mortals would appear thus to have taken up some very much better interest than the poor world they have left might pass for a positively favorable argument. On the basis of their enjoying another state of being, we have certainly to assume that this is the case, for to the probability of a quite different case the inveteracy of their neglect of the previous one, through all the ages and the spaces, the grimness of their utter refusal, so far as we know it, of a retrospective personal sign, would seem directly to point. (I can only treat here as absolutely not established the value of those personal signs that ostensibly come to us through the trance medium. These often make, I grant, for attention and wonder and interest—but for interest above all in the medium and the trance. Whether or no they may in the given case seem to savor of another state of being on the part of those from whom they profess to come, they savor intensely, to my sense, of the medium and the trance, and, with their remarkable felicities and fitnesses, their immense call for explanation, invest that personage, in that state, with an almost irresistible attraction.)

Here it is, at any rate, that we break ourselves against that conception of immortality *as* personal which is the only thing that gives it meaning or relevance. That it shall be personal and yet shall so entirely and relentlessly have yielded to dissociation, this makes us ask if such terms for it are acceptable to thought. Is to be as dissociated as that consistent with personality as we understand *our* share in the condition?—since on any contingency save *by* that understanding of it our interest in the subject drops. I practically know what I am talking about when I say, "I," hypothetically, for my full experience of another term of being, just as I know it when I say "I" for my experience of this one; but I shouldn't in the least do so were I not *able* to say "I"—had I to reckon, that is, with a failure of the signs by which I know myself. In presence of the great question I cling to these signs more than ever, and to conceive of the actual achievement of immortality by others who may have had like knowledge I have to impute to such others a clinging to similar signs. Yet with that advantage, as it were, for any friendly reparticipation, whether for our sake or for their own, in that consciousness in which they bathed themselves on earth, they yet appear to find no grain of relief to bestow on our anxiety, no dimmest spark to flash upon our ignorance. This fact, as after middle life we continue to note it, contributes to the confirmation, within us, of our seeming awareness of extinct things *as* utterly and veritably extinct, with whatever splendid intensity we may have known them to live; an awareness that settles upon us with a formidable weight as time and the world pile up around us all their affirmation of *other* things, and all importunate ones—which little by little acts upon us as so much triumphant negation of the past and the lost; the flicker of some vast sardonic, leering "Don't you see?" on the mask of Nature.

We tend so to feel *that* become for us the last word on the matter that all Nature and all life and all society and all so-called knowledge, with everything these huge, grim indifferences strive to make, and to some degree succeed in making, of ourselves, take the form and have the effect of a mass of machinery for ignoring and denying, the universe through, everything that is not of their own actuality. So it is, therefore, that we keep on and that we reflect; we begin by pitying the remembered dead, even for the very danger of our indifference to them, and we end by pitying ourselves for the final demonstration, as it were, of their indifference to us. "They must be dead, indeed," we say; "they must be as dead as 'science' affirms, for this consecration of it on such a scale, and with these tremendous rites of nullification, to take place." We think of the particular cases of those who could have been backed, as we call it, not to fail, on occasion, of somehow reaching us. We recall the forces of passion, of reason, of personality, that lived in them, and what such forces had made them, to our sight, capable of; and then we say, conclusively, "Talk of triumphant identity if *they*, wanting to triumph, haven't done it!"

Those in whom we saw consciousness, to all appearance, the consciousness of *us*, slowly *déménager*, piece by piece, so that they more or less consentingly parted with it—of *them* let us take it, under stress, if we must, that their ground for interest (in us and in other matters) "unmistakably" reached its limit. But what of those lights that went out in a single gust and those life passions that were nipped in their flower and their promise? Are these spirits thinkable as having emptied the measure the services of sense could offer them? Do we feel capable of a brutal rupture with registered promises, started curiosities, waiting initiations? The mere acquired momentum of intelligence, of perception, of vibration, of experience in a word, would have carried them on, we argue, to *something*, the something that never takes place for us, if the laboratory-brain were *not* really all. What it comes to is then that our faith or our hope may to some degree resist the fact, once accomplished, of watched and deplored death, but that they may well break down before the avidity and consistency with which everything insufferably *continues* to die.

PART II

I have said "we argue" as we take in impressions of the order of those I have glanced at and of which I have pretended to mention only a few. I am not, however, putting them forward for their direct weight in the scale; I speak of them but as the inevitable obsession of those who with the failure of the illusions of youth have had to learn more and more to reckon with reality. For if I referred previously to their bearing us increase of company I mean this to be true with the qualification that applies to our whole attitude, or that of many of us, on our question—the fact that it is subject to the very shifting admonitions of that reality, which may seem to us at times to mean one thing and at times quite another. Yet rather than attempt to speak, to this effect, even for "many of us," I had best do so simply for myself, since it is only for one's self that one can positively answer. It is a matter of individual experience, which I have seen multiply, to satiety, the obsessions I have named and then suffer them to be displaced by others—only once more to reappear again and once more to give way. I speak as one who has had time to take many notes, to be struck with many differences, and to see, a little typically perhaps, what may eventually happen; and I contribute thus, and thus only, my grain of consideration to the store.

I began, I may accordingly say, with a distinct sense that our question didn't appeal to me—as it appeals, in general, but scantly to the young—and I was content for a long time to let it alone, only asking that it should, in turn, as irrelevant and insoluble, let *me*. This it did, in abundance, for many a day— which is, however, but another way of saying that death remained for me, in a large measure, unexhibited and unaggressive. The exhibition, the aggression of life was quite ready to cover the ground and fill the bill, and to my sense of that the balance still inclined even after the opposite pressure had begun to show in the scale. Resented bereavement is all at first—and may long go on appearing more than anything else—one of the exhibitions of life; the various forms and necessities of our resentment sufficiently meet then the questions that death brings up. That aspect changes, however, as we seem to see what it is to die—and to have died—in contradistinction to suffering (which means to warmly *being*) on earth; and as we so see what it is the difficulties involved in the thought of its not being absolute tend to take possession of us and rule us. Treating my own case, again, as a "given" one, I found it long impossible not to succumb—so far as one began to yield at all to irresistible wonder—to discouragement by the mere pitiless dryness of all the appearances. This was for years quite blighting to my sensibility; and the appearances, as I have called them—and as they make, in "science" particularly, the most assured show—imposed themselves; the universe, or all of it that I could make out, kept proclaiming in a myriad voices that I and my poor form of consciousness were a quantity it could at any moment perfectly do without, even in what I might be pleased to call our very finest principle. If without me then just so without others; all the more that if it was not so dispensing with them the simply *bête* situation of one's forever and forever failing of the least whiff of a positive symptom to the contrary would not so ineffably persist.

During which period, none the less, as I was afterward to find, the question subtly took care of itself for me—waking up as I did gradually, in the event (very slowly indeed, with no sudden start of perception, no bound of enthusiasm), to its facing me with a "mild but firm" refusal to regard itself as settled. That circumstance once noted, I began to inquire—mainly, I confess, of myself— why it should be thus obstinate, what reason it could at all clearly give me; and this led me in due course to my getting, or at least framing my reply: a reply not perhaps so multitudinous as those voices of the universe that I have spoken of as discouraging, but which none the less, I find, still holds its ground for me. What had happened, in short, was that all the while I had been practically, though however dimly, trying to take the measure of my consciousness—on this appropriate and prescribed basis of its being so finite—I had learned, as I may say, to live in it more, and with the consequence of thereby not a little undermining the conclusion most unfavorable to it. I had doubtless taken thus to increased living in it by reaction against so grossly finite a world—for it at least *contained* the world, and could handle and criticise it, could play with it and deride it; it had *that* superiority: which meant, all the while, such successful living that the abode itself grew more and more interesting to me, and with this beautiful sign of its character that the more and the more one asked of it the more and the more it appeared to give. I should perhaps rather say that the more one turned it, as an easy reflector, here and there and everywhere over the immensity of things, the more it appeared to take; which is but another way of putting, for "interest," the same truth.

I recognize that the questions I have come after this fashion to ask my consciousness are questions embarrassed by the conditions of this world; but it has none the less left me at last with a sense that, beautiful and adorable thing, it is capable of sorts of action for which I have not as yet even the wit to call upon it. Of what I suggestively find in it, at any rate, I shall speak; but I must first explain the felt connection between this enlarged impression of its quality and *portée* and the improved discussibility of a life hereafter. I hope, then, I shall not seem to push the relation of that idea to the ampler enjoyment of consciousness beyond what it will bear when I say that the ground is gained by the great extension so obtained for one's precious inward "personality"—one's personality not at all in itself of course, or on its claims of general importance, but as conceivably hanging together for survival. It is not that I have found in growing older any one marked or momentous line in the life of the mind or in the play and the freedom of the imagination to be stepped over; but that a process takes place which I can only describe as the accumulation of the very treasure itself of consciousness. I won't say that "the world," as we commonly refer to it, grows more attaching, but will say that the universe increasingly does, and that this makes us present at the enormous multiplication of our possible relations with it; relations still vague, no doubt, as undefined as they are uplifting, as they are inspiring, to think of, and on a scale beyond our actual use or application, yet filling us (through the "law" in question, the law that consciousness gives us immensities and imaginabilities wherever we direct it) with the unlimited vision of being. This mere fact that so small a part of one's visionary and speculative and emotional activity has even a traceably indirect bearing on one's doings or purposes or particular desires contributes strangely to the luxury—which is the magnificent waste—of thought, and strongly reminds one that even should one cease to be in love with life it would be difficult, on such terms, not to be in love with living.

Living, or feeling one's exquisite curiosity about the universe fed and fed, rewarded and rewarded—though I of course don't say definitely answered and answered—becomes thus the highest good I can conceive of, a million times better than not living (however *that* comfort may at bad moments have solicited us); all of which illustrates what I mean by the consecrated "interest" of consciousness. It so peoples and animates and extends and transforms itself; it so gives me the chance to take, on behalf of my personality, these inordinate intellectual and irresponsible liberties with the idea of things. And, once more—speaking for myself only and keeping to the facts of my experience—it is above all as an artist that I appreciate this beautiful and enjoyable independence of thought and more especially this assault of the boundlessly multiplied personal relation (my own), which carries me beyond even any "profoundest" observation of this world whatever, and any mortal adventure, and refers me to realizations I am condemned as yet but to dream of. For the artist the sense of our luxurious "waste" of postulation and supposition is of the strongest; of him is it superlatively true that he knows the aggression as of infinite numbers of modes of being. His case, as I see it, is easily such as to make him declare that if he were not constantly, in his commonest processes, carrying the field of consciousness further and further, making it lose itself in the ineffable, he shouldn't in the least feel himself an artist. As more or less of one myself, for instance, I deal with being, I invoke and evoke, I figure and represent, I seize and fix, as many phases and aspects and conceptions of it as my infirm hand allows me strength for; and in so doing I find myself—I can't express it otherwise—in communication with *sources*; sources to which I owe the apprehension of far more and far other combinations than observation and experience, in their ordinary sense, have given me the pattern of.

The truth is that to live, to this tune, intellectually, and in order to do beautiful things, with questions of being as such questions may for the man of imagination aboundingly come up, is to find one's view of one's share in it, and above all of its appeal to *be* shared, in an infinite variety, enormously enlarged. The very provocation offered to the artist by the universe, the provocation to him to *be*— poor man who may know so little what he's in for!—an artist, and thereby supremely serve it; what do I take that for but the intense desire of being to get itself personally shared, to show itself for personally sharable, and thus foster the sublimest faith? If the artist's surrender to invasive floods is accordingly nine-tenths of the matter that makes his consciousness, that makes mine, so persuasively interesting, so I should see people of our character peculiarly victimized if the vulgar arrangement of our fate, as I have called it, imputable to the power that produced us, should prove to be the true one. For I think of myself as enjoying the very maximum reason to desire the renewal of existence—existence the forms of which I have had admirably and endlessly to *cultivate*—and as therefore embracing it in thought as a possible something that shall be better than what we have known here; only then to ask myself if it be credible that the power just mentioned is simply enjoying the unholy "treat" or brutal amusement of encouraging that conviction in us in order to say with elation: "Then you shall have it, the charming confidence (for I shall wantonly let it come to that), only so long as that it shall beautifully mature; after which, as soon as the prospect has vividly and desirably opened out to you, you shall become as naught."

"Well, you *will* have had them, the sense and the vision of existence," the rejoinder on that may be; to which I retort in turn: "Yes, I shall have them exactly for the space of time during which the question of my appetite for what they represent may clear itself up. The complete privation, as a more or less prompt sequel to that clearance, is worthy but of the wit of a sniggering little boy who makes his dog jump at a morsel only to whisk it away; a practical joke of the lowest description, with the execrable taste of which I decline to charge our prime originator."

I do not deny of course that the case may be different for those who have had another experience—there are so many different experiences of consciousness possible, and with the result of so many different positions on the matter. Those to whom such dreadful things have happened that they haven't even the refuge of the negative state of mind, but have been driven into the exasperated positive, so that they but long to lay down the burden of being and never again take it up—these unfortunates have an equal chance of expressing their attitude and of making it as eloquent and as representative as they will. Their testimony may easily be tremendous and their revelation black. Will they belong, however, to the class of those the really main condition of whose life is to work and work their inner spirit to a productive or illustrative end, and so to feel themselves find in it a general warrant for anything and everything, in the way of particular projections and adventures, that they may dream that spirit susceptible of? This comes again to asking, doubtless, whether it has been their fate to perceive themselves, in the fulness of time, and for good or for ill, living preponderantly by the imagination and having to call upon it at every turn to see them through. By which I don't mean to say that no sincere artist has ever been overwhelmed by life and found his connections with the infinite cut, so that his history may *seem* to represent for him so much evidence that this so easily awful world is the last word to us, and a horrible one at that: cases confounding me could quite too promptly be adduced. The point is, none the less, that in proportion as we (of the class I speak of) enjoy the greater number of our most characteristic inward reactions, in proportion as we do curiously and lovingly, yearningly and irrepressibly, interrogate and liberate, try and test and explore, our general productive and, as we like conveniently to say, creative awareness of things—though the individual, I grant, may pull his job off on occasion and for a while and yet never have done so at all—in that proportion does our function strike us as establishing sublime relations. It is this effect of working it that is exquisite, it is the character of the response it makes, and the merest fraction or dimmest shade of which is ever reported again in what we "have to show"; it is in a word the artistic consciousness and privilege in itself that thus shines as from immersion in the fountain of being. Into that fountain, to depths immeasurable, our spirit dips—to the effect of feeling itself, *quâ* imagination and aspiration, all scented with universal sources. What is that but an adventure of our personality, and how can we after it hold complete disconnection likely?

I do not so hold it, I profess, for my own part, and, above all, I freely concede, do not in the least want to. Consciousness has thus arrived at interesting me too much and on too great a scale—that is all my revelation or my secret; on too great a scale, that is, for me not to ask myself what she can mean by such blandishments—to the altogether normally hampered and benighted random individual that I am. Does she mean nothing more than that I shall have found life, by her enrichment, the more amusing here? But I find it, at this well-nigh final pass, mainly amusing in the light of the possibility that the idea of an exclusively present world, with all its appearances wholly dependent on our physical outfit, may represent for us but a chance for experiment in the very interest of our better and freer being and to its very honor and reinforcement; but a chance for the practice and initial confidence of our faculties and our passions, of the precious personality at stake—precious to *us* at least—which shall have been not unlike the sustaining frame on little wheels that often encases growing infants, so that, dangling and shaking about in it, they may feel their assurance of walking increase and teach their small toes to know the ground. I like to think that we here, as to soul, dangle from the infinite and shake about in the universe; that this world and this conformation and these senses are our helpful and ingenious frame, amply provided with wheels and replete with the lesson for us of how to plant, spiritually, our feet. That conception of the matter rather comes back, I recognize, to the theory of the spiritual discipline, the purification and preparation on earth for heaven, of the orthodox theology—which is a resemblance I don't object to, all the more that it is a superficial one, as well as a fact mainly showing, at any rate, how neatly extremes may sometimes meet.

My mind, however that may be, doesn't in the least resent its association with all the highly appreciable and perishable matter of which the rest of my personality is composed; nor does it fail to recognize the beautiful assistance—alternating indeed frequently with the extreme inconvenience—received from it; representing, as these latter forms do, much ministration to experience. The ministration may have sometimes affected my consciousness as clumsy, but has at other times affected it as exquisite, and it accepts and appropriates and consumes everything the universe puts in its way; matter in tons, if necessary, so long as such quantities are, in so mysterious and complicated a sphere, one of its conditions of activity. Above all, it takes kindly to that admirable philosophic view which makes of matter the mere encasement or sheath, thicker, thinner, coarser, finer, more transparent or more obstructive, of a spirit it has no more concern in producing than the baby-frame has in producing the intelligence of the baby—much as that intelligence may be so promoted.

I "like" to think, I may be held too artlessly to repeat, that this, that, and the other appearances are favorable to the idea of the independence, behind everything (*its* everything), of my individual soul; I "like" to think even at the risk of lumping myself with those shallow minds who are happily and foolishly able to believe what they would prefer. It isn't really a question of belief—which is a term I have made no use of in these remarks; it is on the other hand a question of desire, but of desire so confirmed, so thoroughly established and nourished, as to leave belief a comparatively irrelevant affair. There is one light, moreover, under which they come to the same thing—at least in presence of a question as insoluble as the one before us. If one acts from desire quite as one would from belief, it signifies little what name one gives to one's motive. By which term action I mean action of the mind, mean that I can encourage my consciousness to acquire that interest, to live in that elasticity and that affluence, which affect me as symptomatic and auspicious. I can't do less if I desire, but I shouldn't be able to do more if I believed. Just so I shouldn't be able to do more than cultivate belief; and it is exactly to cultivation that I subject my hopeful sense of the auspicious; with such success—or at least with such intensity—as to give me the splendid illusion of doing something myself for my prospect, or at all events for my own possibility, of immortality. There again, I recognize extremes "neatly meet"; one doesn't talk otherwise, doubtless, of one's working out one's salvation. But this coincidence too I am perfectly free to welcome—putting it, that is, that the theological provision happens to coincide with (or, for all I know, to have been, at bottom, insidiously built on) some such sense of appearances as my own. If I am talking, at all events, of what I "like" to think I may, in short, say all: I like to think it open to me to establish speculative and imaginative connections, to take up conceived presumptions and pledges, that have for me all the air of not being decently able to escape redeeming themselves. And when once such a mental relation to the question as that begins to hover and settle, who shall say over what fields of experience, past and current, and what immensities of perception and yearning, it shall *not* spread the protection of its wings? No, no, no—I reach beyond the laboratory-brain.

IV

Writings on World War I,
1914–1917

The American Volunteer Motor-Ambulance Corps in France

XI

Sir,

Several of us Americans in London are so interested in the excellent work of this body, lately organised by Mr. Richard Norton and now in active operation at the rear of a considerable part of the longest line of battle known to history, that I have undertaken to express to you our common conviction that our countrymen at home will share our interest and respond to such particulars as we are by this time able to give. The idea of the admirable enterprise was suggested to Mr. Norton when, early in the course of the War, he saw at the American Hospital at Neuilly scores of cases of French and British wounded whose lives were lost, or who would have incurred lifelong disability and suffering, through the long delay of their removal from the field of battle. To help energetically to remedy this dire fact struck him at once as possible, and his application of energy was so immediate and effective that in just three weeks after his return to London to take the work in hand he had been joined by a number of his countrymen and of others possessed of cars, who had offered them as ambulances already fitted or easily convertible, and had not less promptly offered themselves as capable chauffeurs. To this promptly gathered equipment, the recruiting of which no red tape had hampered and no postponement to committee-meetings had delayed, were at once added certain other Cars of purchase—these made possible by funds rapidly received from many known and

From Henry James, *The American Volunteer Motor-Ambulance Corps in France: A Letter to the Editor of an American Journal* (London: Macmillan, 1914).

unknown friends in America. The fleet so collected amounted to some fifteen Cars. To the service of the British Red Cross and that of the St. John Ambulance it then addressed itself, gratefully welcomed, and enjoying from that moment the valuable association of Colonel A. J. Barry, of the British Army, who was already employed in part on behalf of the Red Cross. I have within a few days had the opportunity to learn from this zealous and accomplished coadjutor, as well as from Mr. Norton himself, some of the particulars of their comprehensive activity, they each having been able to dash over to London for a visit of the briefest duration. It has thus been brought home to me how much the success of the good work depends on American generosity both in the personal and the pecuniary way—exercised, that is, by the contribution of Cars, to which personal service, that of their contributors, attaches itself, and of course by such gifts of money as shall make the Corps more and more worthy of its function and of the American name.

Its function is primarily that of gathering in the wounded, and those disabled by illness (though the question is almost always of the former), from the *postes de secours* and the field hospitals, the various nearest points to the Front, bestrewn with patient victims, to which a motor-car can workably penetrate, and conveying them to the base hospitals, and when necessary the railway stations, from which they may be further directed upon places of care, centres of those possibilities of recovery which the splendid recent extension of surgical and medical science causes more and more to preponderate. The great and blessed fact is that conditions of recovery are largely secured by the promptitude and celerity that motor-transport offers, as compared with railway services at the mercy of constant interruption and arrest, in the case of bad and already neglected wounds, those aggravated by exposure and delay, the long lying on the poisonous field before the blest regimental *brancardiers* or stretcher-bearers, waiting for the shelter of night, but full also of their own strain of pluck, can come and remove them. Carried mostly by rude arts, a mercy much hindered at the best, to the shelter, often hastily improvised, at which first aid becomes possible for them, they are there, as immediately and tenderly as possible, stowed in our waiting or arriving Cars, each of which receives as large a number as may be consistent with the particular suffering state of the stricken individual. Some of these are able to sit, at whatever cost from the inevitable shake over rough country roads; for others the lying posture only is thinkable, and the ideal Car is the one which may humanely accommodate three men outstretched and four or five seated. Three outstretched is sometimes a tight fit, but when this is impossible the gain in poor *blessés assis* is the greater—wedged together though broken shoulder or smashed arm may have to be with a like shrinking and shuddering neighbour. The moral of these rigours is of course that the more numerous the rescuing vehicles the less inevitable the sore crowding. I find it difficult to express to you the sense of practical human pity, as well as the image of general helpful energy, applied in innumerable chance ways, that we get from the report of what the Corps has done, and holds itself in readiness to do, thanks to the admirable spirit of devotion without stint, of really passionate work, animating its individual members. These have been found beneficently and inexhaustibly active, it is interesting to be able to note, in proportion as they possess the general *educated* intelligence, the cultivated tradition of tact, and I may perhaps be allowed to confess that, for myself, I find a positive added beauty in the fact that the unpaid chauffeur, the wise amateur driver and ready lifter, helper, healer, and, so far as may be, consoler, is apt to be an University man and acquainted with other pursuits. One gets the sense that the labour, with its multiplied incidents and opportunities, is just unlimitedly inspiring to the keen spirit or the sympathetic soul, the recruit with energies and resources on hand that plead with him for the beauty of the vivid and palpable social result.

Not the least of the good offices open to our helpers are the odds and ends of aid determined by wayside encounters in a ravaged country, where distracted women and children flee from threatened or invaded villages, to be taken up, to be given the invaluable lift, if possible, in all the incoherence of their alarm and misery; sometimes with the elder men mixed in the tragic procession, tragi-comic even, very nearly, when the domestic or household objects they have snatched up in their headlong exodus, and are solemnly encumbered with, bear the oddest misproportion to the gravity of the case. They are hurried in, if the Car be happily free, and carried on to comparative safety, but with the admirable cleverness and courage of the Frenchwoman of whatever class essentially in evidence in whatever contact; never more so, for instance, than when a rude field hospital has had of a sudden to be knocked together in the poor schoolhouse of a village, and the mangled and lacerated brought into it on stretchers, or on any rough handcart or trundled barrow that has been impressed into the service, have found the *villageoises*, bereft of their men, full of the bravest instinctive alertness, not wincing at sights of horror fit to try even trained sensibilities, handling shattered remnants of humanity with an art as extemporised as the refuge itself, and having each precarious charge ready for the expert transfer by the time the Car has hurried up. Emphasised enough by the ceaseless thunder of the Front the quality of the French and the British resistance and the pitch of their spirit; but one feels what is meant none the less when one hears the variety of heroism and the brightness of devotion in the women over all the region of battle described from observation as unsurpassable. Do we take too much for granted in imagining that this offered intimacy of appreciation of such finest aspects of the admirable, immortal France, and of a relation with them almost as illuminating to ourselves as beneficent to them, may itself rank as something of an appeal where the seeds of response to her magnificent struggle in the eye of our free longings and liberal impulses already exist?

I should mention that a particular great Army Corps, on the arrival of our first Cars on the scene, appealed to them for all the service they could render, and that to this Corps they have been as yet uninterruptedly attached, on the condition of a reserve of freedom to respond at once to any British invitation to a transfer of activity. Such an assurance had already been given the Commissioner for the British Red Cross, on the part of Mr. Norton and Colonel Barry, with their arrival at Boulogne, where that body cordially welcomed them, and whence in fact, on its request, a four-stretcher Car, with its American owner and another of our Volunteers in charge, proceeded to work for a fortnight, night and day, along the firing line on the Belgian frontier. Otherwise we have continuously enjoyed, in large, defined limits, up to the present writing, an association with one of the most tremendously engaged French Armies. The length of its line alone, were I to state it here in kilometres, would give some measure of the prodigious fighting stretch across what is practically the whole breadth of France, and it is in relation to a fraction of the former Front that we have worked. Very quickly, I may mention, we found one of our liveliest opportunities, Mr. Norton and Colonel Barry proceeding together to ascertain what had become of one of the field hospitals known to have served in a small assaulted town a few days before, when, during a bombardment, Colonel Barry had saved many lives. Just as our Volunteers arrived a fresh bombardment began, and though assured by the fleeing inhabitants, including the mayor of the place, who was perhaps a trifle over-responsibly in advance of them, that there were no wounded left behind— as in fact proved to be the case—we nevertheless pushed on for full assurance. There were then no wounded to bring out, but it was our first happy chance of bearing away all the hopeless and helpless women and children we could carry. This was a less complicated matter, however, than that of one of Colonel Barry's particular reminiscences, an occasion when the Germans were advancing on a small place that it was clear they would take, and when pressing news came to him of 400 wounded in it, who were to be got out if humanly possible. They were got out and motored away—though it took the rescuing party thus three days, in the face of their difficulties and dangers, to effect the blest clearance. It may be imagined how precious in such conditions the power of the chauffeur-driven vehicle becomes, though indeed I believe the more special moral of this transaction, as given, was in the happy fact that the squad had blessedly been able to bring and keep with it four doctors, whose immediate service on the spot and during transport was the means of saving very many lives. The moral of that in turn would seem to be that the very ideal for the general case is the not so quite inconceivable volunteer who should be an ardent and gallant and not otherwise too much preoccupied young doctor with the possession of a Car and the ability to drive it, above all the ability to offer it, as his crowning attribute. Perhaps I sketch in such terms a slightly fantastic figure, but there is so much of strenuous suggestion, which withal manages at the same time to be romantic, in the information before me, that it simply multiplies, for the hopeful mind, the possibilities and felicities of equipped good-will. An association of the grimmest reality clings at the same time, I am obliged to add, to the record of success I have just cited—the very last word of which seems to have been that in one of the houses of the little distracted town were two French Sisters of Mercy who were in charge of an old bedridden lady and whom, with the object of their care, every effort was made in vain to remove. They absolutely declined all such interference with the fate God had appointed them to meet as nuns—if it was His will to make them martyrs. The curtain drops upon what became of them, but they too illustrate in their way the range of the Frenchwoman's power to face the situation.

Still another form of high usefulness comes to our Corps, I should finally mention, in its opportunities for tracing the whereabouts and recovering the identity of the dead, the English dead, named in those grim lists, supplied to them by the military authorities, which their intercourse with the people in a given area where fighting has occurred enables them often blessedly to clear up. Their pervasiveness, their ubiquity, keeps them in touch with the people, witnesses of what happens on the battle-swept area when, after the storm has moved on, certain of the lifeless sweepings are gathered up. Old villagers, searched out and questioned, testify and give a clue through which the whereabouts of the committal to thin earth of the last mortality of this, that or the other of the obscurely fallen comes as a kind of irony of relief to those waiting in suspense. This uncertainty had attached itself for weeks to the fate in particular of many of the men concerned in the already so historic retreat of the Allies from Mons— ground still considerably in the hands of the Germans, but also gradually accessible and where, as quickly as it becomes so, Colonel Barry pushes out into it in search of information. Sternly touching are such notes of general indication, information from the Curé, the village carpenter, the grave-digger of the place, a man called so-and-so and a gentleman called something else, as to the burial of 45 dead English in the public cemetery of such and such a small locality, as to the interment somewhere else of "an Englishman believed to be an officer," as to a hundred English surprised in a certain church and killed all but 40, and buried, as is not always their fortune for their kindred, without removal of their discs of identification. Among such like data we move when not among those of a more immediate violence, and all to be in their way scarce less considerately handled. Mixed with such gleanings one comes upon other matters of testimony of which one hopes equal note is made—testimony as to ferocities perpetrated upon the civil population which I may not here specify. Every form of assistance and enquiry takes place of course in conditions of some danger, thanks to the risk of stray bullets and shells, not infrequently met when Cars operate, as they neither avoid doing nor wastefully seek to do, in proximity to the lines. The Germans, moreover, are noted as taking the view that the insignia of the Red Cross, with the implication of the precarious freight it covers, are in all circumstances a good mark for their shots; a view characteristic of their belligerent system at large, but not more deterrent for the ministers of the adversary in this connection than in any other, when the admirable end is in question.

I have doubtless said enough, however, in illustration of the interest attaching to all this service, a service in which not one of the forces of social energy and devotion, not one of the true social qualities, sympathy, ingenuity, tact and taste, fail to come into play. Such an exercise of them, as all the incidental possibilities are taken advantage of, represents for us all, who are happily not engaged in the huge destructive work, the play not simply of a reparatory or consolatory, but a positively productive and creative virtue in which there is a peculiar honour. We Americans are as little neutrals as possible where any aptitude for any action, of whatever kind, that affirms life and freshly and inventively exemplifies it, instead of overwhelming and undermining it, is concerned. Great is the chance in fact for exhibiting this as our entirely elastic, our supremely characteristic, social aptitude. We cannot do so cheaply indeed, any more than the opposite course is found, under whatever fatuity of presumption, inexpensive and ready-made. What I therefore invite all those whom this notice may reach to understand, as for that matter they easily will, is that the expenses of our enlightened enterprise have to be continuously met, and that if it has confidence in such support it may go on in all the alert pride and pity that need be desired. I am assured that the only criticism the members of the Corps make of it is that they wish more of their friends would come and support it either personally or financially—or, best of all, of course, both. At the moment I write I learn this invocation to have been met to the extent of Mr. Norton's having within two or three days annexed five fresh Cars, with their owners to work them—and all, as I hear it put with elation, "excellent University men." As an extremely helpful factor on the part of Volunteers is some facility in French and the good-will to stay on for whatever reasonable length of time, I assume the excellence of these gentlemen to include those signal merits. Most members of the Staff of 34 in all (as the number till lately at least has stood) have been glad to pay their own living expenses; but it is taken for granted that in cases where individuals are unable to meet that outlay indefinitely the subscribers to the Fund will not grudge its undertaking to find any valuable man in food and lodging. Such charges amount at the outside to 1 dollar 75 per day. The expenses of petrol and tyres are paid by the French Government or the British Red Cross, so that the contributor of the Car is at costs only for the maintenance of his chauffeur, if he brings one, or for necessary repairs. Mr. Eliot Norton, of 2, Rector Street, New York, is our recipient of donations on your side of the sea, Mr. George F. Read, Hon. Treas., care of Messrs. Brown Shipley & Co., 123, Pall Mall, S.W., kindly performs this office in London, and I am faithfully yours,

Henry James.
London, *November 25th,* 1914.

Henry James's First Interview

XII

Noted Critic and Novelist Breaks His Rule of Years to Tell of the
Good Work of the American Ambulance Corps

One of the compensations of the war, which we ought to take advantage
of, is the chance given the general public to approach on the personal
side some of the distinguished men who have not hitherto lived much
in the glare of the footlights. Henry James has probably done this as little as
any one; he has enjoyed for upward of forty years a reputation not confined to
his own country, has published a long succession of novels, tales, and critical
papers, and yet has apparently so delighted in reticence as well as in expression
that he has passed his seventieth year without having responsibly "talked" for
publication or figured for it otherwise than pen in hand.

Shortly after the outbreak of the war Mr. James found himself, to his professed
great surprise, Chairman of the American Volunteer Motor Ambulance Corps,
now at work in France, and today, at the end of three months of bringing himself
to the point, has granted me, as a representative of THE NEW YORK TIMES,
an interview. What this departure from the habit of a lifetime means to him he
expressed at the outset:

"I can't put," Mr. James said, speaking with much consideration and asking
that his punctuation as well as his words should be noted, "my devotion and
sympathy for the cause of our corps more strongly than in permitting it thus to
overcome my dread of the assault of the interviewer, whom I have deprecated,
all these years, with all the force of my preference for saying myself and without

From an interview by Preston Lockwood, *New York Times* 21 Mar. 1915: magazine section (sec. 5), pp. 3–4.

superfluous aid, without interference in the guise of encouragement and cheer, anything I may think worth my saying. Nothing is worth my saying that I cannot help myself out with better, I hold, than even the most suggestive young gentleman with a notebook can help me. It may be fatuous of me, but, believing myself possessed of some means of expression, I feel as if I were sadly giving it away when, with the use of it urgent, I don't gratefully employ it, but appeal instead to the art of somebody else."

It was impossible to be that "somebody else," or, in other words, the person privileged to talk with Mr. James, to sit in presence of his fine courtesy and earnestness, without understanding the sacrifice he was making, and making only because he had finally consented to believe that it would help the noble work of relief which a group of young Americans, mostly graduates of Harvard, Yale, and Princeton, are carrying on along their stretch of the fighting line in Northern France.

Mr. James frankly desired his remarks to bear only on the merits of the American Volunteer Motor Ambulance Corps. It enjoys today the fullest measure of his appreciation and attention; it appeals deeply to his benevolent instincts, and he gives it sympathy and support as one who has long believed, and believes more than ever, in spite of everything, at this international crisis, in the possible development of "closer communities and finer intimacies" between America and Great Britain, between the country of his birth and the country, as he puts it, of his "shameless frequentation."

There are many people who are eloquent about the war, who are authorities on the part played in it by the motor ambulance and who take an interest in the good relations of Great Britain and the United States; but there is nobody who can tell us, as Mr. James can, about style and the structure of sentences, and all that appertains to the aspect and value of words. Now and then in what here follows he speaks familiarly of these things for the first time in his life, not by any means because he jumped at the chance, but because his native kindness, whether consciously or unconsciously, seemed so ready to humor the insisting inquirer.

"It is very difficult," he said, seeking to diminish the tension so often felt by a journalist, even at the moment of a highly appreciated occasion, "to break in to graceful license after so long a life of decorum; therefore you must excuse me if my egotism doesn't run very free or my complacency find quite the right turns."

He had received me in the offices of the corps, businesslike rooms, modern for London, low-ceiled and sparely furnished. It was not by any means the sort of setting in which as a reader of Henry James I had expected to run to earth the author of "The Golden Bowl," but the place is, nevertheless, today, in the tension of war time, one of the few approaches to a social resort outside his

Chelsea home where he can be counted on. Even that delightful Old World retreat, Lamb House, Rye, now claims little of his time.

The interviewer spoke of the waterside Chelsea and Mr. James's long knowledge of it, but, sitting not overmuch at his ease and laying a friendly hand on the shoulder of his tormentor, he spoke, instead, of motor ambulances, making the point, in the interest of clearness, that the American Ambulance Corps of Neuilly, though an organization with which Richard Norton's corps is in the fullest sympathy, does not come within the scope of his remarks.

"I find myself Chairman of our Corps Committee for no great reason that I can discover save my being the oldest American resident here interested in its work; at the same time that if I render a scrap of help by putting on record my joy even in the rather ineffectual connection so far as 'doing' anything is concerned, I needn't say how welcome you are to my testimony. What I mainly seem to grasp, I should say, is that in regard to testifying at all unlimitedly by the aid of the newspapers, I have to reckon with a certain awkwardness in our position. Here comes up, you see, the question of our reconciling a rather indispensable degree of reserve as to the detail of our activity with the general American demand for publicity at any price. There are ways in which the close presence of war challenges the whole claim for publicity; and I need hardly say that this general claim has been challenged, practically, by the present horrific complexity of things at the front, as neither the Allies themselves nor watching neutrals have ever seen it challenged before. The American public is, of course, little used to not being able to hear, and hear as an absolute right, about anything that the press may suggest that it ought to hear about; so that nothing may be said ever to happen anywhere that it doesn't count on having reported to it, hot and hot, as the phrase is, several times a day. We were the first American ambulance corps in the field, and we have a record of more than four months' continuous service with one of the French armies, but the rigor of the objection to our taking the world into our intimate confidence is not only shown by our still unbroken inability to report in lively installments, but receives also a sidelight from the fact that numerous like private corps maintained by donations on this side of the sea are working at the front without the least commemoration of their deeds—that is, without a word of journalistic notice.

"I hope that by the time these possibly too futile remarks of mine come to such light as may await them Mr. Norton's report of our general case may have been published, and nothing would give the committee greater pleasure than that some such controlled statement on our behalf, best proceeding from the scene of action itself, should occasionally appear. The ideal would, of course, be that exactly the right man, at exactly the right moment, should report exactly the right facts, in exactly the right manner, and when that happy consummation becomes possible we shall doubtless revel in funds."

Mr. James had expressed himself with such deliberation and hesitation that I was reminded of what I had heard of all the verbal alterations made by him in novels and tales long since published; to the point, we are perhaps incorrectly told of replacing a "she answered" by a "she indefinitely responded."

I should, indeed, mention that on my venturing to put to Mr. James a question or two about his theory of such changes he replied that no theory could be stated, at any rate in the off-hand manner that I seemed to invite, without childish injustice to the various considerations by which a writer is moved. These determinant reasons differ with the context and the relations of parts to parts and to the total sense in a way of which no a priori account can be given.

"I dare say I strike you," he went on, "as rather bewilderedly weighing my words; but I may perhaps explain my so doing very much as I the other day heard a more interesting fact explained. A distinguished English naval expert happened to say to me that the comparative non-production of airships in this country indicated, in addition to other causes, a possible limitation of the British genius in that direction, and then on my asking him why that class of craft shouldn't be within the compass of the greatest makers of sea-ships, replied, after brief reflection: 'Because the airship is essentially a bad ship, and we English can't make a bad ship well enough.' Can you pardon," Mr. James asked, "my making an application of this to the question of one's amenability or plasticity to the interview? The airship of the interview is for me a bad ship, and I can't make a bad ship well enough."

Catching Mr. James's words as they came was not very difficult; but there was that in the manner of his speech that cannot be put on paper, the delicate difference between the word recalled and the word allowed to stand, the earnestness of the massive face and alert eye, tempered by the genial "comment of the body," as R. L. Stevenson has it.

Henry James does not look his seventy years. He has a finely shaped head, and a face, at once strong and serene, which the painter and the sculptor may well have liked to interpret. Indeed, in fine appreciation they have so wrought. Derwent Wood's admirable bust, purchased from last years's Royal Academy, shown by the Chantrey Fund, will be permanently placed in the Tate Gallery, and those who fortunately know Sargent's fine portrait, to be exhibited in the Sargent room at the San Francisco Exhibition, will recall its having been slashed into last year by the militant suffragettes, though now happily restored to such effect that no trace of the outrage remains.

Mr. James has a mobile mouth, a straight nose, a forehead which has thrust back the hair from the top of his commanding head, although it is thick at the sides over the ears, and repeats in its soft gray the color of his kindly eyes. Before taking in these physical facts one receives an impression of benignity and amenity not often conveyed, even by the most distinguished. And, taking advantage of this amiability, I asked if certain words just used should be followed by a dash, and even boldly added: "Are you not famous, Mr. James, for the use of dashes?"

"Dash my fame!" he impatiently replied. "And remember, please, that dogmatizing about punctuation is exactly as foolish as dogmatizing about any other form of communication with the reader. All such forms depend on the kind of thing one is doing and the kind of effect one intends to produce. Dashes, it seems almost platitudinous to say, have their particular representative virtue, their quickening force, and, to put it roughly, strike both the familiar and the emphatic note, when those are the notes required, with a felicity beyond either the comma or the semicolon; though indeed a fine sense for the semicolon, like any sort of sense at all for the pluperfect tense and the subjunctive mood, on which the whole perspective in a sentence may depend, seems anything but common. Does nobody ever notice the calculated use by French writers of a short series of suggestive points in the current of their prose? I confess to a certain shame for my not employing frankly that shade of indication, a finer shade still than the dash. * * * But what on earth are we talking about?" And the Chairman of the Corps Committee pulled himself up in deprecation of our frivolity, which I recognized by acknowledging that we might indeed hear more about the work done and doing at the front by Richard Norton and his energetic and devoted co-workers. Then I plunged recklessly to draw my victim.

"May not a large part of the spirit which animates these young men be a healthy love of adventure?" I asked.

The question seemed to open up such depths that Mr. James considered a moment and began:

"I, of course, don't personally know many of our active associates, who naturally waste very little time in London. But, since you ask me, I prefer to think of them as moved, first and foremost, not by the idea of the fun or the sport they may have, or of the good thing they may make of the job for themselves, but by that of the altogether exceptional chance opened to them of acting blessedly and savingly for others, though indeed if we come to that there is no such sport in the world as so acting when anything in the nature of risk or exposure is attached. The horrors, the miseries, the monstrosities they are in presence of are so great surely as not to leave much of any other attitude over when intelligent sympathy has done its best.

"Personally I feel so strongly on everything that the war has brought into question for the Anglo-Saxon peoples that humorous detachment or any other thinness or tepidity of mind on the subject affects me as vulgar impiety, not to say as rank blasphemy; our whole race tension became for me a sublimely conscious thing from the moment Germany flung at us all her explanation of her pounce upon Belgium for massacre and ravage in the form of the most insolent, 'Because I choose to, damn you all!' recorded in history.

"The pretension to smashing world rule by a single people, in virtue of a monopoly of every title, every gift and every right, ought perhaps to confound us more by its grotesqueness than to alarm us by its energy; but never do cherished possessions, whether of the hand or of the spirit, become so dear to us as when overshadowed by vociferous aggression. How can one help seeing that such aggression, if hideously successful in Europe, would, with as little loss of time as possible, proceed to apply itself to the American side of the world, and how can one, therefore, not feel that the Allies are fighting to the death for the soul and the purpose and the future that are in *us*, for the defense of every ideal that has most guided our growth and that most assures our unity?

"Of course, since you ask me, my many years of exhibited attachment to the conditions of French and of English life, with whatever fond play of reflection and reaction may have been involved in it, make it inevitable that these countries should peculiarly appeal to me at the hour of their peril, their need and their heroism, and I am glad to declare that though I had supposed I knew what that attachment was, I find I have any number of things more to learn about it. English life, wound up to the heroic pitch, is at present most immediately before me, and I can scarcely tell you what a privilege I feel it to share the inspiration and see further revealed the character of this decent and dauntless people.

"However, I am indeed as far as you may suppose from assuming that what you speak to me of as the 'political' bias is the only ground on which the work of our corps for the Allies should appeal to the American public. Political, I confess, has become for me in all this a loose and question-begging term, but if we must resign ourselves to it as explaining some people's indifference, let us use a much better one for inviting their confidence. It will do beautifully well if givers and workers and helpers are moved by intelligent human pity, and they are with us abundantly enough if they feel themselves simply roused by, and respond to, the most awful exhibition of physical and moral anguish the world has ever faced, and which it is the strange fate of our actual generations to see unrolled before them. We welcome any lapse of logic that may connect inward vagueness with outward zeal, if it be the zeal of subscribers, presenters or drivers of cars, or both at once, stretcher-bearers, lifters, healers, consolers, handy Anglo-French interpreters, (these extremely precious,) smoothers of the way; in short, after whatever fashion. We ask of nobody any waste of moral or of theoretic energy, nor any conviction of any sort, but that the job is inspiring and the honest, educated man a match for it.

"If I seem to cast doubt on any very driving intelligence of the great issue as a source of sympathy with us, I think this is because I have been struck, whenever I have returned to my native land, by the indifference of Americans at large to the concerns and preoccupations of Europe. This indifference has again and again seemed to me quite beyond measure or description, though it may be in a degree suggested by the absence throughout the many-paged American newspaper of the least mention of a European circumstance unless some not-to-be-blinked war or revolution, or earthquake or other cataclysm has happened to apply the lash to curiosity. The most comprehensive journalistic formula that I have found myself, under that observation, reading into the general case is the principle that the first duty of the truly appealing sheet in a given community is to teach every individual reached by it—every man, woman and child—to count on appearing there, in their habit as they live, if they will only wait for their turn.

"However," he continued, "my point is simply my plea for patience with our enterprise even at the times when we can't send home sensational figures. 'They also serve who only stand and wait,' and the essence of our utility, as of that of any ambulance corps, is just to be there, on any and every contingency, including the blessed contingency of a temporary drop in the supply of the wounded turned out and taken on—since such comparative intermissions occur. Ask our friends, I beg you, to rid themselves of the image of our working on schedule time or on guarantee of a maximum delivery; we are dependent on the humors of battle, on incalculable rushes and lapses, on violent outbreaks of energy which rage and pass and are expressly designed to bewilder. It is not for the poor wounded to oblige us by making us showy, but for us to let them count on our open arms and open lap as troubled children count on those of their mother. It is now to be said, moreover, that our opportunity of service threatens inordinately to grow; such things may any day begin to occur at the front as will make what we have up to now been able to do mere child's play, though some of our help has been rendered when casualties were occurring at the rate, say, of 5,000 in twenty minutes, which ought, on the whole, to satisfy us. In face of such enormous facts of destruction—"

Here Mr. James broke off as if these facts were, in their horror, too many and too much for him. But after another moment he explained his pause.

"One finds it in the midst of all this as hard to apply one's words as to endure one's thoughts. The war has used up words; they have weakened, they have deteriorated like motor car tires; they have, like millions of other things, been more overstrained and knocked about and voided of the happy semblance during the last six months than in all the long ages before, and we are now confronted with a depreciation of all our terms, or, otherwise speaking, with a loss of expression through increase of limpness, that may well make us wonder what ghosts will be left to walk."

This sounded rather desperate, yet the incorrigible interviewer, conscious of the wane of his only chance, ventured to glance at the possibility of a word or two on the subject of Mr. James's present literary intentions. But the kindly hand here again was raised, and the mild voice became impatient.

"Pardon my not touching on any such irrelevance. All I want is to invite the public, as unblushingly as possible, to take all the interest in us it can; which may be helped by knowing that our bankers are Messrs. Brown Brothers & Co., 59 Wall Street, New York City, and that checks should be made payable to the American Volunteer Motor Ambulance Corps."

France

XIII

I think that if there is a general ground in the world, on which an appeal might be made, in a civilised circle, with a sense of its being uttered only to meet at once and beyond the need of insistence a certain supreme recognition and response, the idea of what France and the French mean to the educated spirit of man would be the nameable thing. It would be the cause uniting us most quickly in an act of glad intelligence, uniting us with the least need of any wondering why. We should understand and answer together just by the magic of the mention, the touch of the two or three words, and this in proportion to our feeling ourselves social and communicating creatures—to the point in fact of a sort of shame at any imputation of our not liberally understanding, of our waiting in any degree to be nudged or hustled. The case of France, as one may hold it, where the perceptive social mind is concerned and set in motion, is thus only to be called exquisite—so far as we don't seem so to qualify things *down*. We certainly all feel, in the beautiful connection, in two general ways; one of these being that the spring pressed with such happy effect lifts the sense by its mere vibration into the lightest and brightest air in which, taking our world all round, it is given to our finer interest about things to breathe and move; and the other being that just having our intelligence, our experience at its freest and bravest, taken for granted, is a compliment to us, as not purely instinctive persons, which we should miss, if it were not paid, rather to the degree of finding the omission an insult.

From *The Book of France in Aid of the French Parliamentary Committee's Fund for the Relief of the Invaded Departments*, ed. Winifred Stephens (London: Macmillan, 1915), 1–8. The original included the following footnote on the first page: "Remarks at the Meeting of the Committee held on June 9, 1915."

Such, I say, is our easy relation to the sound of a voice raised, even however allusively and casually, on behalf of that great national and social presence which has always most oppositely, most sensibly, most obsessively, as I surely may put it, and above all most dazzlingly, neighboured and admonished us here: after such a fashion as really to have made the felt breath of its life, across an interval constantly narrowing, a part of our education as distinguished from our luck. Our luck in all our past has been enormous, the greatest luck on the whole, assuredly, that any race has ever had; but it has never been a conscious reaction or a gathered fruition, as one may say; it has just been a singular felicity of position and of temperament, and this felicity has made us observe and perceive and reflect much less than it has made us directly act and profit and enjoy: enjoy of course by attending tremendously to all the business involved in our position. So far as we have had reactions, therefore, they have not sprung, when they have been at all intensified, from the extraordinary good fortune of our state. Unless indeed I may put it that what they *have* very considerably sprung from has been exactly a part of our general prodigy—the good fortune itself of our being neighboured by a native genius so different from our own, so suggestive of wondrous and attaching comparisons, as to keep us chronically aware of the difference and the contrast and yet all the while help us to see into them and through them.

We were not, to all appearance, appointed by fate for the most perceptive and penetrative offices conceivable; so that to have over against us and within range a proposition, as we nowadays say, that could only grow more and more vivid, more and more engaging and inspiring, in the measure of our growth of criticism and curiosity, or, in other words, of the capacity just to pay attention, pay attention otherwise than by either sticking very fast at home or inquiring of the Antipodes, the Antipodes almost exclusively—what has that practically been for us but one of the very choicest phases of our luck aforesaid, one of the most appraisable of our felicities? the very one, doubtless, that our dissimilarity of temperament and taste would have most contradictiously and most correctively prescribed from the moment we were not to be left simply to stew in our juice! If the advantage I so characterise was to be in its own way thoroughly affirmative, there was yet nothing about it to do real or injurious violence to that abysmal good nature which sometimes strikes me as our most effective contribution to human history. The vision of France, at any rate, so close and so clear at propitious hours, was to grow happily illustrational for us as nothing else in any like relation to us could possibly have become. Other families have a way, on good opportunity, of interesting us more than our own, and here was this immense acquaintance extraordinarily mattering for us and at the same time not irritating us by a single claim of cousinship or a single liberty taken on any such score. Any liberties taken were much rather liberties, I think, of ours—always abounding as we did in quite free, and perhaps slightly rough, and on the whole rather superficial, movement beyond our island circle and toward whatever lay in our path. France lay very much in our path, our path to almost everything that could beckon us forth from our base—and there were very few things in the world or places on the globe that didn't so beckon us; according to which she helped us along on our expansive course a good deal more, doubtless, than either she or we always knew.

All of which, you see, is but a manner of making my point that her name means more than anything in the world to us but just our own. Only at present it means ever so much more, almost unspeakably more, than it has ever done in the past, and I can't help inviting you to feel with me, for a very few moments, what the real force of this association to which we now throb consists of, and why it so moves us. We enjoy generous emotions *because* they are generous, because generosity is a noble passion and a glow, because we spring with it for the time above our common pedestrian pace—and this just in proportion as all questions and doubts about it drop to the ground. But great reasons never spoil a great sympathy, and to see an inspiring object in a strong light never made any such a shade less inspiring. So, therefore, in these days when our great neighbour and Ally is before us in a beauty that is tragic, tragic because menaced and overdarkened, the closest possible appreciation of what it is that is thereby in peril for ourselves and for the world makes the image shine with its highest brightness at the same time that the cloud upon it is made more black. When I sound the depth of my own affection so fondly excited, I take the like measure for all of us and feel the glad recognition I meet in thus putting it to you, for our full illumination, that what happens to France happens to all that part of ourselves which we are most proud, and most finely advised, to enlarge and cultivate and consecrate.

Our heroic friend sums up for us, in other words, and has always summed up, the life of the mind and the life of the senses alike, taken together, in the most irrepressible freedom of either—and, after that fashion, positively lives *for* us, carries on experience for us; does it under our tacit and our at present utterly ungrudging view of her being formed and endowed and constantly prompted, toward such doing, on all sorts of sides that are simply so many reasons for our standing off, standing off in a sort of awed intellectual hush or social suspense, and watching and admiring and thanking her. She is sole and single in this, that she takes charge of those of the interests of man which most dispose him to fraternise with himself, to pervade all his possibilities and to taste all his faculties, and in consequence to find and to make the earth a friendlier, an easier, and especially a more various sojourn; and the great thing is the amiability and the authority, intimately combined, with which she has induced us all to trust her on this ground. There are matters as to which every set of people has of course most to trust itself, most to feel its own genius and its own stoutness—as we are here and all round about us knowing and abiding by that now as we have never done. But I verily think there has never been anything in the world—since the most golden aspect of antiquity at least—like the way in which France has been trusted to gather the rarest and fairest and sweetest fruits of our so tremendously and so mercilessly turned-up garden of life. She has gardened where the soil of humanity has been most grateful and the aspect, so to call it, most toward the sun, and there, at the high and yet mild and fortunate centre, she has grown the precious, intimate, the nourishing, finishing things that she has inexhaustibly scattered abroad. And if we have all so taken them from her, so expected them from her as our right, to the point that she would have seemed positively to fail of a passed pledge to help us to happiness if she had disappointed us, this has been because of her treating us to the impression of genius as no nation since the Greeks has treated the watching world, and because of our feeling that genius at that intensity is infallible.

What it has all amounted to, as I say, is that we have never known otherwise an agent so beautifully organised, organised from within, for a mission, and that such an organisation at free play has made us really want never to lift a finger to break the charm. We catch at every turn of our present long-drawn crisis indeed that portentous name: it's displayed to us on a measureless scale that our Enemy is organised, organised possibly to the effect of binding us with a spell if anything *could* keep us passive. The term has been in a manner, by that association, compromised and vulgarised: I say vulgarised because any history of organisation from without and for intended aggression and self-imposition, however elaborate the thing may be, shows for merely mechanical and bristling compared with the condition of being naturally and functionally endowed and appointed. This last is the only fair account of the complete and perfect case that France has shown us and that civilisation has depended on for half its assurances. Well, now, we have before us this boundless extension of the case, that, as we have always known what it was to see the wonderful character I speak of range through its variety and keep shining with another and still another light, so in these days we assist at what we may verily call the supreme evidence of its incomparable gift for vivid exhibition. It takes our great Ally, and her only, to be as vivid for concentration, for reflection, for intelligent, inspired contraction of life toward an end all but smothered in sacrifice, as she has ever been for the most splendidly wasteful diffusion and communication; and to give us a view of her nature and her mind in which, laying down almost every advantage, every art and every appeal that we have generally known her by, she takes on energies, forms of collective sincerity, silent eloquence and selected example that are fresh revelations—and so, bleeding at every pore, while at no time in all her history so completely erect, makes us feel her perhaps as never before our incalculable, immortal France.

Henry James.

The Question of the Mind

XIV

Great public convulsions are an upheaval of many things, and are only too apt to destroy more treasure than they collect, to agitate, even fatally to deform, more questions than they settle; so that among the elements let loose and the bewilderments multiplied confusion overtakes inward values no less than outward, matters of knowledge and experience, appreciation, conviction, faith, as one has held them and as one has more or less comfortably lived by so doing. To take a thousand things for granted is to live comfortably, but the very first effect of great world-shocks is to blight that condition by laying bare all our grounds and our supposed roots. We had been believing them very deep down, but of a sudden they are tossed about on the surface, when not tossed high in the air. They are thus exposed to view at least; which, I hasten to add, is a very good thing for many of them, or may become so, and not a bad thing for any.

The difference made, however, meanwhile, by our having to face them as comparative strangers, to introduce ourselves to them afresh and then introduce them afresh to others, dealing with them on new terms and picking them over as people are sometimes figured to pick over their visiting lists with a rise in the world, this difference is perhaps like nothing so much as the obligation, under some strange and violent law, to perform in public and the garish light of day those rites of the toilet or whatever, those common preparations of personal state and appearance, which usually go on behind our most closed doors. Thus springs up a condition still more perturbed than that either of not knowing what to do

From *England at War: An Essay* (London: Central Committee for National Patriotic Organisations, 1915) 3–12.

or of having to do the impossible; predicaments these that may often depend but on indications from without and be relieved by such indications.

The recovery of a straight current of feeling has to come of itself; scattered abroad and so dislodged from the conduit of experience, it affects us with the possibility and the sharp fear of its losing itself before it re-enters a channel. Such an accident may mean waste at the very time when our yearning is most for force; but the difficulty is not that we ourselves are wasteful: that may come much rather while presumption remains unchecked and may in fact often have occurred through the absence of an account to be rendered.

What has perhaps at the very first stage come upon us in such a shaken world as the present is the sense of the huge break in experience, our most intimate and as who should say our most secret; which accordingly leaves us to stare at the separating chasm before we somehow get over to that other side on which we may, or possibly alas, may not, again find life. The dreadful thing seems that experience of so fine an order, the heart's and the soul's experience, the deepest-striking we are capable of, *should* suddenly split after such a fashion and make us feel that we must, by some art never yet practised, tinker it up, patch it together, bridge it over, in order to go on at all.

Happy then if we have not to descend into the abyss, implements in hand, and climb out again to where the opposite ground will bear us, happy if some flight of the imagination, some boldly applied hypothesis, some blest even if casual refreshment of sense, carries us across into air once more breathable; for that does mean experience again, and if the new flows into the vessel that has long contained and been scented by the old, who will say that after all we shall not recognise the savour and the tang?

All of which may perhaps figure too obscurely the fact that the social characteristics, the elements of race and history, the native and acquired values, the whole "psychological" mystery marking the people of Great Britain, were so abruptly thrust into the critical smelting-pot for a citizen of another country, a country up to the present speaking formally neutral, who had spent long years of his life on English soil and in English air, that he at first saw the case in the light in which he has just generalised it. He to-day feels no image too extravagant, none the less, for report of the drama that began so sharply, even if all subjectively, to enact itself on the stage of his anxious spirit; a drama in which the protagonist was to be simply the question of the true worth of his forty years of observation and interest, and the dénouement to crown it, through whatever ups and downs, those quite proper to the stage, with the happy critical climax. I say "simply" because the decision in suspense mattered to this fond observer himself, thrown back upon half his spiritual history, so much more than it could possibly matter to persons either not agitated at all or agitated to more demonstrable and more immediate purpose.

Yet complications really and thrillingly attended, since where would have been the suspense, which I think I must have positively cultivated in the interest of the rapture of final relief, if the fortune of my exposed and imperilled, and hence so ideally recoverable, or in other words positively ponderable, stake didn't seem at moments to sway this way and that? What did one after all, oh what *did* one, as the upshot of experience, "think of the English mind"? I should perhaps blush to translate my figure of the wavering issue, launched on scenic and heroic adventures, into such a pale and lean abstraction; blush, that is, so to translate it for others. To my own view it at once invested itself with every appearance and attribute of life; to that degree in fact as to make dependent upon it my personal consciousness, my own life and reality, all my care for what might happen to anything. I must have intimately known thus that if the action exhibited, the entanglement of my question in its dangers, with the retarded issue, was not, as we say at the play, to end happily, I should feel that I myself had declined into misery.

The great thing, however, was not to let that apprehension interfere; I was no *deus ex machina*, and would have been ashamed to be one; the question was just of the impassioned critic, impassioned because surmounting of a sudden old habits of detachment and ease and springing to his freshly-wiped fieldglass much as the summoned soldier might spring to his rifle, yet of the critic incorruptible withal and prepared to bow to fate even if fate should demolish his subject. My state became, to the exclusion of every other, since none was of comparable *portée*, the state of sought certitude, a certitude difficult but not impossible, and carrying everything with it if it should come.

The situation was of course that what you had supposed or presumed you thought was not now of the smallest consequence: to sleep at night, to hold up your head, or, otherwise expressed, your heart, to go and come save as one of the merely mechanic and bewildered, you had to *know*, and to know with that competence which would rest on your having again and more thoroughly learnt. It was true that to learn was to study, and that the pitch of the public agitation left no spacious air for *that*; every impression one had ever suffered, all impatiences and all submissions, stupefactions and recognitions alike, stale perplexities and sublime conclusions, trooped together into view and, claiming in a vague mixed manner some of them justice and some generosity, still insisted that each represented a truth and had thereby its point to make.

Great the responsibility, surely, when the British intelligence was to be on exhibition on that scale and under such a strain; the eyes of the world having now more attention for it, and of a more searching kind, than at any moment in the whole course of the appeal it had ever made to them. They had indeed, these eyes, an immense call to their different, their very own vast masses of interest; but wouldn't the effect of that be at the same time to quicken rather than restrict for them their awareness of the English affirmation, whether as hostile or as helpful, and so to make the degree and the mode of our display of genius signify, that is count all round, as it had not in all the ages had to?

Well, prodigiously to one's help, at a given moment, and quite simultaneously, turned up these two ideas of our "genius"—for it would, of course, be impossible to doubt that we *had* one—and of our being unprecedentedly in evidence and in peril; by which one meant in peril more particularly of the uncertainties of appreciation. These last would inevitably, and probably very soon, strain themselves clear; so far as to care so much meant to be so much in suspense, this clutch of the formula, this idea of a genius only waiting to be identified, gave relief to the tension and saw me as by a sudden jump ever so much further on the way.

I recognised that what I began these remarks by calling the spirit of experience had yet left undestroyed its main acquisition; which was neither more nor less than that our very genius was what made us—made our intelligence, as I have termed it, our contributive, our exhibitable, virtue, our capacity in fine for *being* on our best behaviour—so consistently worth worrying about. Our best behaviour on every face and in every relation of course—*that* was the impending need; but again, as I say, vagueness waned, or at least began to, from the moment one saw, or at any rate reasoned, that with genius there couldn't not be a light.

So what, when it came to this, had been the former, the ancient light? that of the time, too prolonged perhaps, when for the attached and familiarised individual mind to which I impute these refinements of ponderation almost any behaviour had seemed good enough on the part of so goodnatured, so incorrigibly goodnatured, a people? One thought of tests, the suddenly swarming, the unparalleled, those with which the air fairly darkened, till it struck one that after all one had done little else during the long years that represented experience but apply one's own most intimate of tests. There was the genius, in other words the nature (the good nature, and the incorrigible, again!) of the people, and if one wasn't possessed of it, if one didn't know what to think of it, after living with it on such terms, where could the fault be but in one's own infirmity of wit?

Vaguely recurred in this connection the old anecdote of the member of the *comité de lecture* of the Théâtre Français and his reply to the author of a disapproved play who had remarked to him that as he was asleep while the thing was read he had no right to an opinion. "My dear sir, what was my sleep but an opinion?" were the classic words in consonance with which I asked what a relation so established could be but an affection, and what an affection so successfully tried but an estimate. And yet if it was the collective mind withal that (exactly as in the case of the other belligerents) was to be supremely on exhibition, with the fierce light of history beating on it to the unspeakable pitch, it helped little to call that resource the English genius unless one could express to one's private satisfaction one's resultant measure of the same. What did the article supremely consist of, what had one found it in long converse to consist more of on the whole than of anything else?

The British intellect—how extraordinarily one had passed from the facetious to the earnest use of that prior term!—had done in its out-in-the-world way all the splendid things we knew, which were there, piled up behind, and yet the tradition of which didn't in familiar intercourse testify so directly, so intensely, so measurably or so showily, one might almost say, as one's previous, and indeed one's constant, profit of the general achievement would have led one to expect. There was I in presence of the curious fact that while the actual acute demand for display had pounced on the nation's understanding, had challenged its "mentality," clamouring for attestations, the great note of one's observational experience might really be described as that of the completest incapacity for show, for the current and casual play of the imagination to the impressive or attractive end, that had perhaps ever been seen on earth.

Hadn't it been much like a presentation of the mind, of the intellect, from *behind*, so to speak, and with its face turned precisely the other way from the way at present required? Hadn't the impression been as of an averted or muffled or even reluctant exercise of the faculty, exercise of free energy, free fancy, free curiosity, free wit, however one might name the blest thing—the blest thing that had at the same time been so tremendously recorded, and that was more or less continuing to be, in the documentary evidence of libraries and courts? How could one have lived in the society of so many such matters, in the presence verily of all of them, with those consequences of interest and affection, those visions of illumination and education, if, in spite of the fact that one had so almost inveterately to walk for satisfaction of curiosity, for extraction of value, round from the presented face to the quarter of the averted, the total result of acquaintance hadn't been a peculiar faith?

The answer to all of which, I saw, would meanwhile be no answer if it didn't properly provide for that truth of the genius—the genius that had somehow kept acting and impressing just in proportion as so few pains were taken about it. What was happening, accordingly, that the critic could wonder about the "display"—by which he meant about the absence of it—and yet not wonder in the least about the apparently all so sufficing force? The puzzle might have lasted goodness knows how long hadn't it been for that consciousness of the good nature, incorrigibility and all, felt as fundamental from far back, which one had been looking to right and left of, and to top and bottom of, without discovering that in the very centre of it sat one's sublime solution.

To grasp even in so absurdly delayed a manner the perception that *there* was one's golden key made the whole certitude come on with a rush. It was incredible and impossible that a people should be so incorrigible unless they were strong— no people without a great margin could for any period at all afford to be; and with that *constatation* everything was clear. It didn't matter if they were strong because good-natured, or good-natured because strong: the point was to that extraordinary tune in what they could afford.

This affording became then, to one's infinite recreation, the drama, the picture, and, to repeat the term that was the actual essence of the case, the exhibition, of their life. They were at their ease (there it was!) for their favourite amusement of putting the cart before the horse and the idea out of sight—that is behind, miles behind, everything else. They *kept* the idea in that situation, where one would find it, with one's mistrust fairly unlearnt, if one walked far enough round outside to—well, I won't say its prison, but, by way of a better image, its secret garden. Here it grew with a stoutness that spoke doubtless not so much of cultivation as of the happy patches of parent earth, and here it could be gathered, after the fashion of the savoury seasoning herb, "as required."

If such then was the case for the background by what art did the foreground not only hold together but form to the extent I have noted the place of frequentation the most attaching, not to say even the most edifying, one could have desired? By the art not anywhere else in the world so subtly practised, assuredly—that of so mixing up character, personal or, as who should say, moral, yes, positively, the dear old moral, the instinctively individual, with every other sign of understanding and every other reward of intercourse, in fact with every other condition of it. What it came to in the last fine analysis thus seemed to be that whereas in association with other people you for the most part knew by their conversability what you had got hold of, or whether this were at a given moment their reflective or their active, their cerebral or their practical part, so in the association I had happened most to enjoy there was no such clear and perhaps I should say convenient distinction, convenient in especial for the demonstration of one's grounds. This might certainly represent in regard to the others that conversability worked better, but could it represent that association did?

To put this last question, I quickly recognised, was to find it answered, and with other attendant ones disposed of really by the same stroke; not least that one of the drawback of the usual confusion. Not knowing what one had got hold of might certainly appear at the best and in no matter what connection but a muddled form of appreciation—which appearance was doubtless directly signified by your comfort in the fact that when a Frenchman or an Italian talked he really told you so much about his mind that there seemed little left to tell you about anything else.

Only, if that was satisfactory, so far as it went, and was, so far as the Frenchman and the Italian were concerned, exhaustive, there was then nevertheless no mystery more, nothing of the unexplored and, as you could put it, more eventually and shyly, call it even rather proudly, producible.

The part you had got hold of left you comparatively incurious about the other part. This exhibited, most exhibited part informed you about itself entirely, and tasted of itself, yielding by this reason whatever sharpest or sweetest savour; so that it was upon that luxury one threw one's self and fed, to the full appeasement of one's critical impulse.

If on the other hand you went by the information the Englishman gave you about his mind—the Scotsman's and the Irishman's information about *his* remains, I confess, a matter apart—you didn't by any means go such lengths; if you depended on the taste of that article alone for your sense of his power to nourish or beguile you would find a vast tract of the recorded history of your relation with him unaccounted for; you would have yourself to account for the circumstance, superficially inscrutable but nevertheless so substantial, that in no general inter-course whatever could you as a final result be left less consciously starved. You might be left hungry, beyond doubt; yet wasn't this only that you were left curious, in other words unsatisfied, but because your meal, copious though it should keep on proving, was never all served at one sitting? The reason of that might well be, no doubt, that it wasn't ready, hadn't been prepared with the punctuality and presentability of those other, those exotic repasts, those from which one got up with the wondrous sense of appetite, properly the sense of curiosity, gratified or gorged.

Such, I made out, was my inevitable figure for that dissipation of mystery in these connections which I had been feeling as an interest and even as a sensation the less at the very time of feeling it as a happy convenience and a lively social exercise the more. This pointed with the last sharpness, you were at any rate all the while conscious, that noted moral of your knowing what you had hold of. But were you then on the side of your experience of the British, roughly taken together, simply to resign yourself to the correspondingly baffled state? Well, yes, verily yes, at last, and for the very best of reasons, a reason quite magnificent, as it could only appear to me, when once I had at least got hold of that affirmative. *There* was the savour, the desideratum, the force and quantity, that we have been talking of—a savour immense and extraordinary, in relation to which the muddlement that I have called subjective came directly from the fact that it is not, like the savours to which I just paid tribute, "dished," served, administered after the fashion of precious things in general, isn't perhaps in any degree the result of what passes in other societies for preparation. It grows wild, and I had doubtless partaken of it crude—with the marvellous effect of its not disagreeing with me. Crude things, we know, mostly do disagree: there accordingly and exactly was the mystery that kept imagination on the stretch. Why hadn't it disagreed, why didn't it, why doesn't it? Why above all does it not only at last purge bewilderment of any shade of impatience, but make it a condition, not to say an adventure, romantic and agreeable? If the reply to this just at first hangs fire it floods the subject when it does come with the clearest light in the world.

The wildness, the crudity, the undressed and uneconomised state are themselves the unidentified force, or the force to the identification of which we come nearest when we catch it in its supreme act of good-nature. What a blessing to work round again to the consciousness of *that* clue, the clue of the incorrigibility, in the hand! For the good-nature was the light—the light, ever so vividly, on the character; just as the character was the light, ever so richly and blurringly, but none the less ever so extensively and perspectively, on the mind. So then I stood with my feet on the ground: the case was sole and single, and quite as splendid, yes, as one could have wished it to be. The mind was so drenched with the character, in opposition to the examples in which the character was drenched with the mind, that all one could at the very best feel (though goodness knew indeed it quite sufficed!) was that the value finally run to earth was a value which would do for everything.

Henry James

Allen D. Loney—In Memoriam

XV

I am strongly moved to offer a few words of tribute, official and personal, to the signally gallant friend of our American Volunteer Motor Ambulance Corps, Allen D. Loney, who perished with so vast a number of his innocent and victimized countrymen and countrywomen in the sinking of the Lusitania. He had been from the first one of the most ardent and active of our volunteers, friendly and devoted in every way, and sparing least of all his own splendid personal energy. That complete friendliness, where his interest was enlisted, was his great characteristic and operated round about him to the most attaching effect.

We are indebted to him for two valuable cars and their drivers, with the constant and liberal support of these elements, to which he himself was, with slight interruption, the most capable and genial of accessory forces. He put at our disposal the passion of the born sportsman, but still beyond that an active human sympathy which rejoiced in helpful service and fellowship. His life was that of a strong man happy in his strength and having always, on less agitated fields, pluckily played with it, but nothing appeared ever so to have appealed to him as the application of it, and of all his resources, to our admirable cause.

A recruit to the wonderful modern band of those who swing from America to Europe and back, as the liveliest of matters of course, on any suggestion of the hunting field or the regatta, the polo ground, the salmon river, or the grouse moor, his fondest exercise was the chase, toward which pursuit he maintained in Northamptonshire one of the best-known heavyweight stables in England. With him were happily associated in these ways his wife and his daughter, his

From *New York Times* 12 Sept. 1915: sec. 1, p. 4 (col. 2).

only child, both of whom constantly hunted with him and would have completely shared his fate had not the latter almost as tragically survived. Her father had made, under urgency, a rapid dash to his American home from the front, and was in the act of eager return to duty when he admirably met his doom, the manner of his facing which his daughter enjoys the heroic privilege at putting on record as a witness.

He had in those supreme moments insisted that his two companions, in the lifebelts he had hastily secured for them, should descend into a boat that swung from the deck below them, but which in the inevitable confusion and overloading was swamped on reaching the water. The elder lady sank in those dreadful moments, while the younger, a brave swimmer, got herself clear, to catch sight from the vast welter, all but washing then over the deck she had just quitted, of two quiet gentlemen together with a single lifebelt between them, each evidently unmoved by the other's plea that he should use it.

One of these companions was Alfred Vanderbilt, the other was our friend, and this image of them will abide for honest and remembering men. The note of everything that Mr. Loney was best loved for, and of so much that the comrades of his activity in France recognized in his gallant good will, surely shines out of that friendliest, as we may again call it, of all his attitudes.

Refugees in England

XVI

This is not a report on our so interesting and inspiring Chelsea work since November last, in aid of the Belgians driven hither from their country by a violence of unprovoked invasion and ravage more appalling than has ever before overtaken a peaceful and industrious people; it is the simple statement of a neighbor and an observer deeply affected by the most tragic exhibition of national and civil prosperity and felicity suddenly subjected to bewildering outrage that it would have been possible to conceive. The case, as the generous American communities have shown they well understand, has had no analogue in the experience of our modern generations, no matter how far back we go; it has been recognized, in surpassing practical ways, as virtually the greatest public horror of our age, or of all the preceding, and one gratefully feels, in presence of so much done in direct mitigation of it, that its appeal to the pity and the indignation of the civilized world anticipated and transcended from the first all superfluity of argument. We live into, that is we learn to cultivate, possibilities of sympathy and reaches of beneficence very much as the stricken and the suffering themselves live into their dreadful history and explore and reveal its extent; and this admirable truth it is that unceasingly pleads with the intelligent, the fortunate, and the exempt not to consent in advance to any dull limitation of the helpful idea. The American people have surely a genius, of the most eminent kind, for withholding any such consent and despising all such limits; and there is doubtless no remarked connection in which they have so shown the sympathetic imagination in free and fearless activity, that is, in high originality, as under the suggestion of the tragedy of Belgium.

From *New York Times* 17 Oct. 1915: magazine section (sec. 4), pp. 1–2.

The happy fact in this order is that the genius commits itself, always does so, by the mere act of self-betrayal; so that just to assume its infinite exercise is but to see how it must live above all on happy terms with itself. That is the impulse and the need which operate most fully, to our recognition, in any form of the American overflow of the excited social instinct; which circumstance, as I make these remarks, seems to place under my feet a great firmness of confidence. That confidence rests on this clear suggestibility, to the American apprehension of any and every aspect of the particular moving truth; when these aspects are really presented, the response becomes but a matter of calculable spiritual health. Very wonderful, I think, that with a real presentation, as I call it, inevitably affected by the obstructive element of distance, of so considerable a social and personal disconnection, of the very violence done, for that matter, to credibility as well, the sense of relatedness to the awful story should so have emerged and so lucidly insisted on its rights. To make that reflection indeed might well be to feel even here on our most congested ground no great apparatus of demonstration or evocation called for; in spite of which, however, I remind myself that as Reports and Tables are of the essence of our anxious duty, so they are rather more than less efficient when not altogether denuded of the atmosphere and the human motive that have conduced to their birth.

I have small warrant perhaps to say that atmospheres are communicable, but I can testify at least that they are breathable on the spot, to whatever effect of depression or of cheer, and I should go far, I feel, were I to attempt to register the full bittersweet taste, by our Chelsea waterside, all these months, of the refugee element in our vital medium. (The sweet, as I strain a point perhaps to call it, inheres, to whatever distinguishability, in our hope of having really done something, verily done much: the bitter ineradicably seasons the consciousness, hopes and demonstrations and fond presumptions and all.) I need go no further, none the less, than the makeshift provisional gates of Crosby Hall, marvelous monument transplanted a few years since from the Bishopsgate quarter of the city to a part of the ancient suburban site of the garden of Sir Thomas More, and now serving with extraordinary beneficence as the most splendid of shelters for the homeless. This great private structure, though of the grandest civic character, dating from the fifteenth century and one of the noblest relics of the past that London could show, was held a few years back so to cumber the precious acre or more on which it stood that it was taken to pieces in the candid commercial interest and in order that the site it had so long sanctified should be converted to such uses as would stuff out still further the ideal number of private pockets. Dismay and disgust were unable to save it: the most that could be done was to gather in with tenderness of care its innumerable constituent parts and convey them into safer conditions, where a sad defeated piety has been able to re-edify them into some semblance of the original majesty.

Strange withal some of the turns of the whirligig of time; the priceless structure came down to the sound of lamentation, not to say of execration, and of the gnashing of teeth, and went up again before cold and disbelieving, quite despairing eyes; in spite of which history appears to have decided once more to cherish it and give a new consecration. It is in truth still magnificent; it lives again for our gratitude in its noblest particulars; and the almost incomparable roof has arched all this Winter and Spring over a scene probably more interesting and certainly more pathetic than any that have ever drawn down its ancient far-off blessing.

The place has formed then the headquarters of the Chelsea circle of hospitality to the exiled, the broken and the bewildered, and if I may speak of having taken home the lesson of their state and the sense of their story it is by meeting them in the finest club conditions conceivable that I have been able to do so. Hither, month after month and day after day the unfortunates have flocked, each afternoon, and here the comparatively exempt, almost ashamed of their exemption in presence of so much woe, have made them welcome to every form of succor and reassurance. Certain afternoons, each week, have worn the character of the huge comprehensive tea party, a fresh well-wisher discharging the social and financial cost of the fresh occasion—which has always festally profited, in addition, by the extraordinary command of musical accomplishment, the high standard of execution, that is the mark of the Belgian people. This exhibition of our splendid local resource has rested, of course, on a multitude of other resources, still local, but of a more intimate hospitality, little by little worked out and applied, and into the detail of which I may not here pretend to go beyond noting that they have been accountable for the large housed and fed and clothed and generally protected and administered numbers, all provided for in Chelsea and its outer fringe, on which our scheme of sociability at Crosby Hall itself has up to now been able to draw. To have seen this scheme so long in operation has been to find it suggest many reflections, all of the most poignant and moving order; the foremost of which has, perhaps, had for its subject that never before can the wanton hand of history have descended upon a group of communities less expectant of public violence from without or less prepared for it and attuned to it.

The bewildered and amazed passivity of the Flemish civil population, the state as of people surprised by sudden ruffians, murderers, and thieves in the dead of night and hurled out, terrified and half clad, snatching at the few scant household goods nearest at hand, into a darkness mitigated but by flaring incendiary torches, this has been the experience stamped on our scores and scores of thousands, whose testimony to suffer dismay and despoilment, silence alone, the silence of vain uncontributive wonderment, has for the most part been able to express.

Never was such a revelation of a deeply domestic, a rootedly domiciled and instinctively and separately clustered people, a mass of communities for which the sight of the home violated, the objects helping to form it profaned and the cohesive family, the Belgian ideal of the constituted life, dismembered, disembowelled and shattered, had so supremely to represent the crack of doom and the end of everything. There have been days and days when under this particular impression the mere aspect and manner of our serried recipients of relief, something vague and inarticulate as in persons who have given up everything but patience and are living, from hour to hour, but in the immediate and the unexplained, has put on such a pathos as to make the heart sick. One has had just to translate any seated row of figures, thankful for warmth and light and covering, for sustenance and human words and human looks, into terms that would exemplify some like exiled and huddled and charity-fed predicament for our superior selves, to feel our exposure to such a fate, our submission to it, our holding in the least together under it, darkly unthinkable.

Dim imaginations would at such moments interpose, a confused theory that even at the worst our adventurous habits, our imperial traditions, our general defiance of the superstition of domesticity would dash from our lips the cup of bitterness; from these it was at all events impossible not to come back to the consciousness that almost every creature there collected was indebted to our good offices for the means to come at all. I thought of our parents and children, our brothers and sisters, aligned in borrowed garments and settled to an as yet undetermined future of eleemosynary tea and buns, and I ask myself, doubtless to little purpose, either what grace of resignation or what clamor of protest we should, beneath the same star, be noted as substituting for the inveterate Belgian decency.

I can only profess at once that the sense of this last, round about one, was at certain hours, when the music and the chant of consolation rose in the stillness from our improvised stage at the end of the great hall, a thing to cloud with tears any pair of eyes lifted to our sublime saved roof in thanks for its vast comprehension. Questions of exhibited type, questions as to a range of form and tradition, a measure of sensibility and activity, not our own, dwindled and died before the gross fact of our having here an example of such a world tragedy as we supposed Europe had outlived, and that nothing at all therefore mattered but that we should bravely and handsomely hold up our quite heavy enough end of it.

It is because we have responded in this degree to the call unprecedented that we are, in common with a vast number of organizations scattered through these islands, qualified to claim that no small part of the inspiration to our enormous act of welcome resides in the moral interest it yields. One can indeed be certain of such a source of profit but in the degree in which one has found one's self personally drawing upon it; yet it is obvious that we are not treated every day to the disclosure of a national character, a national temperament and type, confined for the time to their plainest and stoutest features and set, on a prodigious scale, in all the relief that the strongest alien air and alien conditions can give them. Great salience, in such a case, do all collective idiosyncrasies acquire—upon the fullest enumeration of which, however, as the Belgian instance and the British atmosphere combine to represent them, I may not now embark, prepossessed wholly as I am with the more generally significant social stamp and human aspect so revealed, and with the quality derived from these things by the multiplied examples that help us to take them in. This feeling that our visitors illustrate above all the close and comfortable household life, with every implication of a seated and saturated practice of it, practice of the intimate and private and personal, the securely sensual and genial arts that flow from it, has been by itself the key to a plenitude of observation and in particular to as much friendly searching insight as one could desire to enjoy.

The moving, the lacerating thing is the fashion after which such a reading of the native elements, once adopted, has been as a light flaring into every obscurest retreat, as well as upon any puzzling ambiguity, of the state of shock of the rational character under the infamy of the outrage put upon it. That they of all people the most given over to local and patriarchal beatitude among the admirable and the cherished objects handed down to them by their so interesting history on every spot where its action has been thickest—that is on every inch, so to speak, of their teeming territory—should find themselves identified with the most shamelessly cynical public act of which the civilized world at this hour retains the memory, is a fact truly representing the exquisite in the horrible; so peculiarly addressed has been their fate to the desecration of ideals that had fairly become breath of their lungs and flesh of their flesh. Oh! The installed and ensconced, the immemorially edified and arranged, the thoroughly furnished and provided and nourished people!—not in the least besotted or relaxed in their security and density, like the self smothered society of the ancient world upon which the earlier Huns and Vandals poured down, but candidly complacent and admirably intelligent in their care for their living tradition, and only so off their guard as to have consciously set the example of this care to all such as had once smoked with them their wondrous pipe of peace. Almost any posture of stupefaction would have been conceivable in the shaken victims of this delusion; I can speak best, however, but of what I have already glanced at, that temperamental weight of their fall which has again and again, at sight of many of them gathered together, made the considering heart as heavy for them as if it too had for the time been worsted.

However, it would take me far to tell of half the penetrating admonitions, whether of the dazed or of the roused appearance, that have for so long almost in like degree made our attention ache; I think of particular faces, in the whole connection, when I want most to remember—since to remember always, and never, never to forget, is a prescription shining before us like a possible light of dawn; faces saying such things in their silence, or in their speech of quite different matters, as to make the only thinkable comment or response some word or some gesture of reprieve to dumb or to dissimulated anguish. Blessed be the power that has given to civilized men the appreciation of the face—such an immeasurable sphere of exercise—for it has this monstrous trial of the peoples come to supply. Such histories, such a record of moral experience, of emotion convulsively suppressed, as one meets in some of them, and this even if on the whole one has been able to think of these special allies, all sustainingly, much rather as the sturdiest than as the most demonstrative of sufferers. I have in these rapid remarks to reduce my many impressions to the fewest, but must even thus spare one of them for commemoration of the admirable cast of working countenance we are rewarded by the sight of wherever we turn amid the quantity of helpful service and all the fruitful industries that we have been able to start and that keep themselves going.

These are the lights in the picture, and who indeed would wish that the lights themselves should be anything less than tragic? The strong young men (no young men are familiarly stronger), mutilated, amputated, dismembered in penalty for their defense of their soil against the horde and now engaged at Crosby Hall in the making of handloom socks, to whom I pay an occasional visit much more for my own cheer, I apprehend, than for theirs, express so in their honest concentration under difficulties the actual and general value of their people that just to be in their presence is a blest renewal of faith. Excellent, exemplary, is this manly, homely, handy type, grave in its somewhat strained attention, but at once lighted to the briefest, sincerest humor of protest by any direct reference to the general cruelty of its misfortune. Anything but unsuggestive, the range of the "quiet" physiognomy when one feels the consciousness behind it not to have run thin. Thick and strong is the good Flemish sense of life and all its functions— which fact is responsible for no empty and really unmodelled "mug."

I am afraid at the same time that if the various ways of being bad are beyond our reckoning, the condition and the action of exemplary goodness tend rather to reduce to a certain rich unity of appearance those marked by them, however dissociated from each other such persons may have been by race and education. Otherwise what tribute shouldn't I be moved to pay to the gentleman of Flanders to whom the specially improvised craftsmen I have just mentioned owe their training and their inspiration?—through *his* having, in his proscribed and denuded state, mastered the craft in order to recruit them to it and, in fine, so far as my observation has been concerned, exhibit clear human virtue, courage and patience and the humility of sought fellowship in privation, with an unconscious beauty that I should be ashamed in this connection not to have noted publicly. I scarce know what such a "personality" as his suggests to me if not that we had all, on our good Chelsea ground, best take up and cherish as directly and intimately as possible every scrap of our community with our gentlemen of Flanders. I make such a point as this, at the same time, only to remember how, almost wherever I have tried sustainingly to turn, my imagination and my intelligence have been quickened, and to recognize in particular, for that matter, that this couldn't possibly be more the case for them than in visiting a certain hostel in one of our comparatively contracted but amply decent local Squares—riverside Chelsea having, of course, its own urban identity in the multitudinous County of London; which, in itself as happy an example, doubtless, of the hostel smoothly working as one need cite, placed me in grateful relation with a lady, one of the victims of her country's convulsion and in charge of the establishment I allude to, whom simply to "meet," as we say, is to learn how singular a dignity, how clear a distinction, may shine in active fortitude and economic self-effacement under an all but crushing catastrophe.

" 'Talk about' faces—!" I could but privately ejaculate as I gathered the senses of all that this one represented in the way of natural nobleness and sweetness, a whole past acquaintance with letters and art and taste, insisting on their present restrictedness to bare sisterly service.

The proud rigor of association with pressing service alone, with absolutely nothing else, the bare commodious house, so otherwise known to me of old and now, like most of our hostels if I am not mistaken, the most unconditioned of loans from its relinquishing owner; the lingering look of ancient peace in the precincts, an element I had already as I passed and repassed, at the afternoon hour, found somehow not at all dispelled by the presence in the central green garden itself of sundry maimed and hobbling and smiling convalescents from an extemporized small hospital close at hand, their battered khaki replaced by a like uniformity of the loose light blue, and friendly talk with them through the rails of their inclosure as blessed to one participant at least as friendly talk with them always and everywhere is; such were the hovering elements of an impression in which the mind had yet mainly to yield to that haunting force on the part of our waiting proscripts which never consent to be long denied. The proof of which universally recognized power of their spell amid us is indeed that they have led me so far with a whole side of my plea for them still unspoken.

This, however, I hope on another occasion to come back to, and I am caught meanwhile by my memory of how the note of this conviction was struck for me, with extraordinary force, many months ago and in the first flush of recognition of what the fate that had overtaken our earliest tides of arrival and appeal really meant—meant so that all fuller acquaintance, since pursued, has but piled one congruous reality after another upon the horror. It was in September, in a tiny Sussex town which I had not quitted since the outbreak of the war, and here the advent of our first handful of fugitives before the warning of Louvain and Aerschott and Termonde and Dinant had just been announced. Our small hilltop city, covering the steep sides of the compact pedestal crowned by its great church, had reserved a refuge at its highest point, and we had waited all day, from occasional train to train, for the moment at which we should attest our hospitality. It came at last, but late in the evening, when a vague outside rumor called me to my doorstep, where the unforgettable impression at once assaulted me. Up the precipitous little street that led from the station, over the old grass-grown cobbles, where vehicles rarely pass, came the panting procession of the homeless and their comforting, their almost clinging entertainers, who seemed to hurry them on as in a sort of overflow of expression or fever of charity. It was swift and eager, in the Autumn darkness and under the flare of a single lamp—with no vociferation and but for a woman's voice scarce a sound save the shuffle of mounting feet and the thick-drawn breath of emotion.

The note I except, however, was that of a young mother carrying her small child and surrounded by those who bore her on and on, almost lifting her as they went together. The resonance through our immemorial old street of her sobbing and sobbing cry was the voice itself of history; it brought home to me more things than I could then quite take the measure of, and these just because it expressed for her not direct anguish, but the incredibility, as we should say, of honest assured protection. Months have elapsed, and from having been then one of a few hundred she is now one of scores and scores of thousands; yet her cry is still in my ears, whether to speak most of what she had lately or what she actually felt, and it plays to my own sense, as a great fitful tragic light over the dark exposure of her people.

The Long Wards

$$=$$

XVII

There comes back to me out of the distant past an impression of the citizen soldier at once in his collective grouping and in his impaired, his more or less war-worn state, which was to serve me for long years as the most intimate vision of him that my span of life was likely to disclose. This was a limited affair indeed, I recognise as I try to recover it, but I mention it because I was to find at the end of time that I had kept it in reserve, left it lurking deep down in my sense of things, however shyly and dimly, however confusedly even, as a term of comparison, a glimpse of something by the loss of which I should have been the poorer; such a residuary possession of the spirit, in fine, as only needed darkness to close round it a little from without in order to give forth a vague phosphorescent light. It was early, it must have been very early, in our Civil War, yet not so early but that a large number of those who had answered President Lincoln's first call for an army had had time to put in their short period (the first term was so short then, as was likewise the first number,) and reappear again in camp, one of those of their small New England State, under what seemed to me at the hour, that of a splendid autumn afternoon, the thickest mantle of heroic history. If I speak of the impression as confused I certainly justify that mark of it by my failure to be clear at this moment as to how much they were in general the worse for wear—since they can't have been exhibited to me, through their waterside settlement of tents and improvised shanties, in anything like hospital conditions. However, I cherish the rich ambiguity, and have always cherished it, for the sake alone of the general note exhaled, the thing that has most kept remembrance unbroken. I carried away from the

From *The Book of the Homeless*, ed. Edith Wharton (New York: Scribner's, 1916) 115–25.

place *the* impression, the one that not only was never to fade, but was to show itself susceptible of extraordinary eventual enrichment. I may not pretend now to refer it to the more particular sources it drew upon at that summer's end of 1861, or to say why my repatriated warriors were, if not somehow definitely stricken, so largely either lying in apparent helplessness or moving about in confessed languor: it suffices me that I have always thought of them as expressing themselves at almost every point in the minor key, and that this has been the reason of their interest. What I call the note therefore is the characteristic the most of the essence and the most inspiring—inspiring I mean for consideration of the admirable sincerity that we thus catch in the act: the note of the quite abysmal softness, the exemplary genius for accommodation, that forms the alternative aspect, the passive as distinguished from the active, of the fighting man whose business is in the first instance formidably to bristle. This aspect has been produced, I of course recognise, amid the horrors that the German powers had, up to a twelvemonth ago, been for years conspiring to let loose upon the world by such appalling engines and agencies as mankind had never before dreamed of; but just that is the lively interest of the fact unfolded to us now on a scale beside which, and though save indeed for a single restriction, the whole previous illustration of history turns pale. Even if I catch but in a generalising blur that exhibition of the first American levies as a measure of experience had stamped and harrowed them, the signally attaching mark that I refer to is what I most recall; so that if I did n't fear, for the connection, to appear to compare the slighter things with the so much greater, the diminished shadow with the far-spread substance, I should speak of my small old scrap of truth, miserably small in contrast with the immense evidence even then to have been gathered, but in respect to which latter occasion did n't come to me, as having contained possibilities of development that I must have languished well-nigh during a lifetime to crown it with.

One had during the long interval not lacked opportunity for a vision of the soldier at peace, moving to and fro with a professional eye on the horizon, but not fished out of the bloody welter and laid down to pant, as we actually see him among the Allies, almost on the very bank and within sound and sight of his deepest element. The effect of many of the elapsing years, the time in England and France and Italy, had indeed been to work his collective presence so closely and familiarly into any human scene pretending to a full illustration of our most generally approved conditions that I confess to having missed him rather distressfully from the picture of things offered me during a series of months spent not long ago in a few American cities after years of disconnection. I can scarce say why I missed him sadly rather than gladly—I might so easily have prefigured one's delight in his absence; but certain it is that my almost outraged consciousness of our practically doing without him amid American conditions was a revelation of the degree in which his great imaging, his great reminding and enhancing function is rooted in the European basis. I felt his non-existence on the American positively produce a void which nothing else, as a vivifying substitute, hurried forward to fill; this being indeed the case with many of the other voids, the most aching, which left the habituated eye to cast about as for something to nibble in a state of dearth. We never know, I think, how much these wanting elements have to suggest to the pampered mind till we feel it living in view of the community from which they have been simplified away. On these occasions they conspire with the effect of certain other, certain similar expressions, examples of social life proceeding as by the serene, the possibly too serene, process of mere ignorance, to bring to a head for the fond observer the wonder of what is supposed to strike, for the projection of a furnished world, the note that they are not there to strike. However, as I quite grant the hypothesis of an observer still fond and yet remarking the lapse of the purple patch of militarism but with a joy unclouded, I limit myself to the merely personal point that the fancy of a particular brooding analyst *could* so sharply suffer from a vagueness of privation, something like an unseasoned observational diet, and then, rather to his relief, find the mystery cleared up. And the strict relevancy of the bewilderment I glance at, moreover, becomes questionable, further, by reason of my having, with the outbreak of the horrors in which we are actually steeped, caught myself staring at the exhibited militarism of the general British scene not much less ruefully than I could remember to have stared, a little before, at the utter American deficit. Which proves after all that the rigour of the case had begun at a bound to defy the largest luxury of thought; so that the presence of the military in the picture on the mere moderate insular scale struck one as "furnishing" a menaced order but in a pitiful and pathetic degree.

The degree was to alter, however, by swift shades, just as one's comprehension of the change grew and grew with it; and thus it was that, to cut short the record of our steps and stages, we have left immeasurably behind us here the question of what might or what should have been. That belonged, with whatever beguiled or amused ways of looking at it, to the abyss of our past delusion, a collective state of mind in which it had literally been possible to certain sophists to argue that, so far from not having soldiers enough, we had more than we were likely to know any respectable public call for. It was in the very fewest weeks that we replaced a pettifogging consciousness by the most splendidly liberal, and, having swept through all the first phases of anxiety and suspense, found no small part of our measure of the matter settle down to an almost luxurious study of our multiplied defenders after the fact, as I may call it, or in the light of that acquaintance with them as products supremely tried and tested which I began by speaking of. We were up to our necks in this relation before we could turn round, and what upwards of a year's experience of it has done in the contributive and enriching way may now well be imagined. I might feel that my marked generalisation, the main hospital impression, steeps the case in too strong or too stupid a synthesis, were it not that to consult my memory, a recollection of countless associative contacts, is to see the emphasis almost absurdly thrown on my quasi-paradox. Just so it is of singular interest for the witnessing mind itself to feel the happy truth stoutly resist any qualifying hint—since I *am* so struck with the charm, as I can only call it, of the tone and temper of the man of action, the creature appointed to advance and explode and destroy, and elaborately instructed as to how to do these things, reduced to helplessness in the innumerable instances now surrounding us. It does n't in the least take the edge from my impression that his sweet reasonableness, representing the opposite end of his wondrous scale, is probably the very oldest story of the touching kind in the world; so far indeed from my claiming the least originality for the appealing appearance as it has lately reached me from so many sides, I find its suggestion of vast communities, communities of patience and placidity, acceptance submission pushed to the last point, to be just what makes the whole show most illuminating.

"Wonderful that, from east to west, they must *all* be like this," one says to one's self in presence of certain consistencies, certain positive monotonies of aspect; "wonderful that if joy of battle (for the classic term, in spite of new horrors, seems clearly still to keep its old sense,) has, to so attested a pitch, animated these forms, the disconnection of spirit should be so prompt and complete, should hand the creature over as by the easiest turn to the last refinements of accommodation. The disconnection of the flesh, of physical function in whatever ravaged area, *that* may well be measureless; but how interesting, if the futility of such praise does n't too much dishonour the subject, the exquisite anomaly of the intimate readjustment of the really more inflamed and exasperated part, or in other words of the imagination, the captured, the haunted vision, to life at its most innocent and most ordered!" To that point one's unvarying thought of the matter; which yet, though but a meditation without a conclusion, becomes the very air in which fond attention spends itself. So far as commerce of the acceptable, the tentatively helpful kind goes, one looks for the key to success then, among the victims, exactly on that ground of the apprehension pacified and almost, so to call it, trivialised. The attaching thing becomes thus one's intercourse with the imagination of the particular patient subject, the individual himself, in the measure in which this interest bears us up and carries us along; which name for the life of his spirit has to cover, by a considerable stretch, all the ground. By the stretch of the name, moreover, I am far from meaning any stretch of the faculty itself—which remains for the most part a considerably contracted or inert force, a force in fact often so undeveloped as to be insusceptible of measurement at all, so that one has to resort, in face of the happy fact that communion still does hold good, to some other descriptive sign for it. That sign, however, fortunately presents itself with inordinate promptitude and fits to its innocent head with the last perfection the cap, in fact the very crown, of an office that we can only appraise as predetermined goodnature. We after this fashion score our very highest on behalf of a conclusion, I think, in feeling that whether or no the British warrior's goodnature has much range of fancy, his imagination, whatever there may be of it, is at least so goodnatured as to show absolutely everything it touches, everything without exception, even the worst machinations of the enemy, in that colour. Variety and diversity of exhibition, in a world virtually divided as now into hospitals and the preparation of subjects for them, are, I accordingly conceive, to be looked for quite away from the question of physical patience, of the general consent to suffering and mutilation, and, instead of that, in this connection of the sort of mind and thought, the sort of moral attitude, that are born of the sufferer's other relations; which I like to think of as being different from country to country, from class to class, and as having their fullest national and circumstantial play.

It would be of the essence of these remarks, could I give them within my space all the particular applications naturally awaiting them, that they pretend to refer here to the British private soldier only—generalisation about his officers would take us so considerably further and so much enlarge our view. The high average of the beauty and modesty of these, in the stricken state, causes them to affect me, I frankly confess, as probably the very flower of the human race. One's apprehension of "Tommy"—and I scarce know whether more to dislike the liberty this mode of reference takes with him, or to incline to retain it for the tenderness really latent in it—is in itself a theme for fine notation, but it has brought me thus only to the door of the boundless hospital ward in which, these many months, I have seen the successive and the so strangely quiet tides of his presence ebb and flow, and it stays me there before the incalculable vista. The perspective stretches away, in its mild order, after the fashion of a tunnel boring into the very character of the people, and so going on forever—never arriving or coming out, that is, at anything in the nature of a station, a junction or a terminus. So it draws off through the infinite of the common personal life, but planted and bordered, all along its passage, with the thick-growing flower of the individual illustration, this sometimes vivid enough and sometimes pathetically pale. The great fact, to my now so informed vision, is that it undiscourageably continues and that an unceasing repetition of its testifying particulars seems never either to exhaust its sense or to satisfy that of the beholder. Its sense indeed, if I may so far simplify, is pretty well always the same, that of the jolly fatalism above-mentioned, a state of moral hospitality to the practices of fortune, however outrageous, that may at times fairly be felt as providing amusement, providing a new and thereby a refreshing turn of the personal situation, for the most interested party. It is true that one may be sometimes moved to wonder which *is* the most interested party, the stricken subject in his numbered bed or the friendly, the unsated inquirer who has tried to forearm himself against such a measure of the "criticism of life" as might well be expected to break upon him from the couch in question, and who yet, a thousand occasions for it having been, all round him, inevitably neglected, finds this ingenious provision quite left on his hands. He may well ask himself what he is to do with people who so consistently and so comfortably content themselves with *being*—being for the most part incuriously and instinctively admirable—that nothing whatever is left of them for reflection as distinguished from their own practice; but the only answer that comes is the reproduction of the note. He may, in the interest of appreciation, try the experiment of lending them some scrap of a complaint or a curse in order that they shall meet him on congruous ground, the ground of encouragement to his own participating impulse. They are imaged, under that possibility, after the manner of those unfortunates, the very poor, the victims of a fire or shipwreck, to whom you have to lend something to wear before they can come to thank you for helping them. The inmates of the long wards, however, have no use for any imputed or derivative sentiments or reasons; they feel in their own way, they feel a great deal, they don't at all conceal from you that to have seen what they have seen is to have seen things horrible and monstrous— but there is no estimate of them for which they seek to be indebted to you, and nothing they less invite from you than to show them that such visions must have poisoned their world. Their world is n't in the least poisoned: they have assimilated their experience by a process scarce at all to be distinguished from their having healthily got rid of it.

The case thus becomes for you that they consist wholly of their applied virtue, which is accompanied with no waste of consciousness whatever. The virtue may strike you as having been, and as still being, greater in some examples than others, but it has throughout the same sign of differing at almost no point from a supreme amiability. How can creatures so amiable, you allow yourself vaguely to wonder, have welcomed even for five minutes the stress of carnage? and how can the stress of carnage, the murderous impulse at the highest pitch, have left so little distortion of the moral nature? It has left none at all that one has at the end of many months been able to discover; so that perhaps the most steadying and refreshing effect of intercourse with these hospital friends is through the almost complete rest from the facing of generalisations to which it treats you. One would even like perhaps, as a stimulus to talk, more generalisation; but one gets enough of that out in the world, and one does n't get there nearly so much of what one gets in this perspective, the particular perfect sufficiency of the extraordinary principle, whatever it is, which makes the practical answer so supersede any question or any argument that it seems fairly to have acted by chronic instinctive anticipation, the habit of freely throwing the personal weight into any obvious opening. The personal weight, in its various forms and degrees, is what lies there with a head on the pillow and whatever wise bandages thereabout or elsewhere, and it becomes interesting in itself, and just in proportion, I think, to its having had all its history after the fact. All its history is that of the particular application which has brought it to the pass at which you find it, and is a stream roundabout which you have to press a little hard to make it flow clear. Then, in many a case, it does flow, certainly, as clear as one could wish, and with the strain that it is always somehow English history and illustrates afresh the English way of doing things and regarding them, of feeling and naming them. The sketch extracted is apt to be least coloured when the prostrate historian, as I may call him, is an Englishman of the English; it has more point, though not perhaps more essential tone, when he is a Scot of the Scots, and has most when he is an Irishman of the Irish; but there is absolutely no difference, in the light of race and save as by inevitable variation from individual to individual, about the really constant and precious matter, the attested possession on the part of the contributor of a free loose undisciplined quantity of being to contribute.

This is the palpable and ponderable, the admirably appreciable, residuum— as to which if I be asked just how it is that I pluck the flower of amiability from the bramble of an individualism so bristling with accents, I am afraid I can only say that the accents would seem by the mercy of chance to fall together in the very sense that permits us to detach the rose with the fewest scratches. The rose of active goodnature, irreducible, incurable, or in other words all irreflective, *that* is the variety which the individualistic tradition happens, up and down these islands, to wear upon its ample breast—even it may be with a considerable effect of monotony. There it is, for what it is, and the very simplest summary of one's poor bedside practice is perhaps to confess that one has most of all kept one's nose buried in it. There hangs about the poor practitioner by that fact, I profess, an aroma not doubtless at all mixed or in the least mystical, but so unpervertedly wholesome that what can I pronounce it with any sort of conscience but sweet? That is the rough, unless I rather say the smooth, report of it; which covers of course, I hasten to add, a constant shift of impression within the happy limits. Did I not, by way of introduction to these awaiters of articulate acknowledgment, find myself first of all, early in the autumn, in presence of the first aligned rows of lacerated Belgians?—the eloquence of whose mere mute expression of their state, and thereby of their cause, remains to me a vision unforgettable forever, and this even though I may not here stretch my scale to make them, Flemings of Flanders though they were, fit into my remarks with the English of the English and the Scotch of the Scotch. If other witnesses might indeed here fit in they would decidedly come nearest, for there were aspects under which one might almost have taken them simply for Britons comparatively starved of sport and, to make up for that, on straighter and homelier terms with their other senses and appetites. But their effect, thanks to their being so seated in everything that their ripe and rounded temperament had done for them, was to make their English entertainers, and their successors in the long wards especially, seem ever so much more complicated—besides making of what had happened to themselves, for that matter, an enormity of outrage beyond all thought and all pity. Their fate had cut into their spirit to a peculiar degree through their flesh, as if they had had an unusual thickness of this, so to speak—which up to that time had protected while it now but the more exposed and, collectively, entrapped them; so that the ravaged and plundered domesticity that one felt in them, which was mainly what they had to oppose, made the terms of their exile and their suffering an extension of the possible and the dreadful. But all that vision is a chapter by itself—the essence of which is perhaps that it has been the privilege of this placid and sturdy people to show the world a new shade and measure of the tragic and the horrific. The first wash of the great Flemish tide ebbed at any rate from the hospitals—creating moreover the vast needs that were to be so unprecedentedly met, and the native procession which has prompted these remarks set steadily in. I have played too uncertain a light, I am well aware, not arresting it at half the possible points, yet with one aspect of the case staring out so straight as to form the vivid moral that asks to be drawn. The deepest impression from the sore human stuff with which such observation deals is that of its being strong and sound in an extraordinary degree for the conditions producing it. These conditions represent, one feels at the best, the crude and the waste, the ignored and neglected state; and under the sense of the small care and scant provision that have attended such hearty and happy growths, struggling into life and air with no furtherance to speak of, the question comes pressingly home of what a better economy might, or verily might n't, result in. If this abundance all slighted and unencouraged can still comfort us, what would n't it do for us tended and fostered and cultivated? That is my moral, for I believe in Culture—speaking strictly now of the honest and of our own congruous kind.

Henry James

Within the Rim

──────

XVIII

The first sense of it all to me after the first shock and horror was that of a sudden leap back into life of the violence with which the American Civil War broke upon us, at the North, fifty-four years ago, when I had a consciousness of youth which perhaps equalled in vivacity my present consciousness of age. The illusion was complete, in its immediate rush; everything quite exactly matched in the two cases; the tension of the hours after the flag of the Union had been fired upon in South Carolina living again, with a tragic strangeness of recurrence, in the interval during which the fate of Belgium hung in the scales and the possibilities of that of France looked this country harder in the face, one recognised, than any possibility, even that of the England of the Armada, even that of the long Napoleonic menace, could be imagined to have looked her. The analogy quickened and deepened with every elapsing hour; the drop of the balance under the invasion of Belgium reproduced with intensity the agitation of the New England air by Mr. Lincoln's call to arms, and I went about for a short space as with the queer secret locked in my breast of at least already knowing how such occasions helped and what a big war was going to mean. That this was literally a light in the darkness, or that it materially helped the prospect to be considered, is perhaps more than I can say; but it at least added the strangest of savours, an inexpressible romantic thrill, to the harsh taste of the crisis: I found myself literally knowing "by experience" what immensities, what monstrosities, what revelations of what immeasurabilities, our affair would carry in its bosom—a knowledge that flattered me by its hint of immunity from illusion. The sudden new tang in the atmosphere, the flagrant difference, as one

From *The Fortnightly Review* 102.608 (1 Aug. 1917): 161–71

noted, in the look of everything, especially in that of people's faces, the expressions, the hushes, the clustered groups, the detached wonderers, and slow-paced public meditators, were so many impressions long before received and in which the stretch of more than half a century had still left a sharpness. So I took the case in and drew a vague comfort, I can scarce say why, from recognition; so, while recognition lasted, I found it come home to me that we, we of the ancient day, had known, had tremendously learnt, what the awful business is when it is "long," when it remains for months and months bitter and arid, void even of any great honour. In consequence of which, under the rapid rise of presumptions of difficulty, to whatever effect of dismay or of excitement, my possession of something like a standard of difficulty, and, as I might perhaps feel too, of success, became in its way a private luxury.

My point is, however, that upon this luxury I was allowed after all but ever so scantly to feed. I am unable to say when exactly it was that the rich analogy, the fine and sharp identity between the faded and the vivid case broke down, with the support obscurely derived from them; the moment anyhow came soon enough at which experience felt the ground give way and that one swung off into space, into history, into darkness, with every lamp extinguished and every abyss gaping. It ceased quite to matter for reassurance that the victory of the North had been so delayed and yet so complete, that our struggle had worn upon the world of the time, and quite to exasperation, as could well be remembered, by its length; if the present complication should but begin to be as long as it was broad no term of comparison borrowed from the past would so much as begin to fit it. I might have found it humiliating; in fact, however, I found it of the most commanding interest, whether at certain hours of dire apprehension or at certain others of the finer probability, that the biggest like convulsion our generations had known was still but too clearly to be left far behind for exaltations and terrors, for effort and result, as a general exhibition of the perversity of nations and of the energy of man. Such at least was the turn the comparison took at a given moment in a remembering mind that had been steeped, so far as its restricted contact went, but in the Northern story; I did, I confess, cling awhile to the fancy that what loomed perhaps for England, what already did so much more than loom for crucified Belgium, what was let loose in a torrent upon indestructible France, might correspond more or less with the pressure of the old terrible time as the fighting South had had to know it, and with the grim conditions under which she had at last given way. For the rest of the matter, as I say, the difference of aspect produced by the difference of intensity cut short very soon my vision of similitude. The intensity swallowed up everything; the rate and the scale and the speed, the unprecedented engines, the vast incalculable connections, the immediate presence, as it were, of France and Belgium, whom one could hear pant, through the summer air, in their effort and their alarm, these things, with the prodigious might of the enemy added, made me say, dropping into humility in a manner that resembled not a little a drop into still greater depths, "Oh no, that surely can't have been 'a patch' on this!" Which conclusion made accordingly for a new experience altogether, such as I gratefully embrace here an occasion not to leave unrecorded.

It was in the first place, after the strangest fashion, a sense of the extraordinary way in which the most benign conditions of light and air, of sky and sea, the most beautiful English summer conceivable, mixed themselves with all the violence of action and passion, the other so hideous and piteous, so heroic and tragic facts, and flouted them as with the example of something far superior. Never were desperate doings so blandly lighted up as by the two unforgettable months that I was to spend so much of in looking over from the old rampart of a little high-perched Sussex town at the bright blue streak of the Channel, within a mile or two of us at its nearest point, the point to which it had receded after washing our rock-base in its earlier ages, and staring at the bright mystery beyond the rim of the furthest opaline reach. Just on the other side of that finest of horizon-lines history was raging at a pitch new under the sun; thinly masked by that shameless smile the Belgian horror grew; the curve of the globe toward these things was of the scantest, and yet the hither spaces of the purest, the interval representing only charm and calm and ease. One grew to feel that the nearer elements, those of land and water and sky at their loveliest, were making thus, day after day, a particular prodigious point, insisting in their manner on a sense and a wondrous story which it would be the restless watcher's fault if he didn't take in. Not that these were hints or arts against which he was in the least degree proof; they penetrated with every hour deeper into the soul, and, the contemplations I speak of aiding, irresistibly worked out an endless volume of references. It was all somehow the history of the hour addressing itself to the individual mind—or to that in any case of the person, at once so appalled and so beguiled, of whose response to the whole appeal I attempt this brief account. Roundabout him stretched the scene of his fondest frequentation as time had determined the habit; but it was as if every reason and every sentiment conducing to the connection had, under the shock of events, entered into solution with every other, so that the only thinkable approach to rest, that is to the recovery of an inward order, would be in restoring them each, or to as many as would serve the purpose, some individual dignity and some form.

It came indeed largely of itself, my main help to the reparatory, the re-identifying process; came by this very chance that in the splendour of the season there was no mistaking the case or the plea. "This, as you can see better than ever before," the elements kept conspiring to say, "is the rare, the sole, the exquisite England whose weight now hangs in the balance, and your appreciation of whose value, much as in the easy years you may have taken it for granted, seems exposed to some fresh and strange and strong determinant, something that breaks in like a character of high colour in a play." Nothing could have thrilled me more, I recognise, than the threat of this irruption or than the dramatic pitch; yet a degree of pain attached to the ploughed-up state it implied—so that, with an elderly dread of a waste of emotion, I fear I almost pusillanimously asked myself why a sentiment from so far back recorded as lively should need to become any livelier, and in fact should hesitate to beg off from the higher diapason. I felt as the quiet dweller in a tenement so often feels when the question of "structural improvements" is thrust upon him; my house of the spirit, amid everything about me, had become more and more the inhabited, adjusted, familiar home, quite big enough and sound enough for the spirit's uses and with any intrinsic inconvenience corrected long since by that principle's having cultivated and formed, at whatever personal cost (since my spirit was essentially a person), the right habits, and so settled into the right attitude for practical, for contented occupation. If, however, such was my vulgar apprehension, as I put it, the case was taken out of my hands by the fate that so often deals with these accidents, and I found myself before long building on additions and upper storeys, throwing out extensions and protrusions, indulging even, all recklessly, in gables and pinnacles and battlements—things that had presently transformed the unpretending place into I scarce know what to call it, a fortress of the faith, a palace of the soul, an extravagant, bristling, flag-flying structure which had quite as much to do with the air as with the earth. And all this, when one came to return upon it in a considering or curious way, because to and fro one kept going on the old rampart, the town "look-out," to spend one's aching wonder again and again on the bright sky-line that at once held and mocked it. Just over that line were unutterable things, massacre and ravage and anguish, all but irresistible assault and cruelty, bewilderment and heroism all but overwhelmed; from the sense of which one had but to turn one's head to take in something unspeakably different and that yet produced, as by some extraordinary paradox, a pang almost as sharp.

It was of course by the imagination that this latter was quickened to an intensity thus akin to pain—but the imagination had doubtless at every turn, without exception, more to say to one's state of mind, and dealt more with the whole unfolding scene, than any other contributive force. Never in all my life, probably, had I been so glad to have opened betimes an account with this faculty and to be able to feel for the most part something to my credit there; so vivid I mean had to be one's prevision of the rate at which drafts on that source would require cashing. All of which is a manner of saying that in face of what during those horrible days seemed exactly over the way the old inviolate England, as to whom the fact that she *was* inviolate, in every valid sense of the term, had become, with long acquaintance, so common and dull, suddenly shone in a light never caught before and which was for the next weeks, all the magnificence of August and September, to reduce a thousand things to a sort of merciless distinctness. It was not so much that they leaped forth, these things, under the particular recognition, as that they multiplied without end and abounded, always in some association at least that caught the eye, all together overscoring the image as a whole or causing the old accepted synthesis to bristle with accents. The image as a whole, thus richly made up of them—or of the numberless testifying touches to the effect that we were not there on our sea defence as the other, the harried, countries were behind such bulwarks as they could throw up—was the central fact of consciousness and the one to which every impression and every apprehension more or less promptly related themselves; it made of itself the company in which for the time the mind most naturally and yet most importunately lived. One walked of course in the shade of the ambiguous contrast—ambiguous because of the dark question of whether it was the liabilities of Belgium and France, to say nothing of their awful actualities, that made England's state so rare, or England's state that showed her tragic sisters for doubly outraged; the action of the matter was at least that of one's feeling in one's hand and weighing it there with the last tenderness, for fullest value, the golden key that unlocked every compartment of the English character.

Clearly this general mystery or mixture was to be laid open under stress of fortune as never yet—the unprecedentedness was above all what came over us again and again, armaments unknown to human experience looming all the while larger and larger; but whatever face or succession of faces the genius of the race should most turn up the main mark of them all would be in the difference that, taken together, couldn't fail to keep them more unlike the peoples off there beyond than any pair even of the most approved of these peoples are unlike each other. "Insularity!"—one had spent no small part of one's past time in mocking or in otherwise fingering the sense out of that word; yet here it was in the air wherever one looked and as stuffed with meaning as if nothing had ever worn away from it, as if its full force on the contrary amounted to inward congestion. What the term essentially signified was in the oddest way a question at once enormous and irrelevant; what it might *show* as signifying, what it was in the circumstances actively and most probably going to, seemed rather the true consideration, indicated with all the weight of the evidence scattered about. Just the fixed *look* of England under the August sky, what was this but the most vivid exhibition of character conceivable and the face turned up, to repeat my expression, with a frankness that really left no further inquiry to be made? That appearance was of the exempt state, the record of the long safe centuries, in its happiest form, and even if any shade of happiness at such an hour might well seem a sign of profanity or perversity. To *that* there were all sorts of things to say, I could at once reflect, however; wouldn't it be the thing supremely in character that England should look most complacently herself, irradiating all her reasons for it, at the very crisis of the question of the true toughness, in other words the further duration, of her identity? I might observe, as for that matter I repeatedly and unspeakably did while the two months lasted, that she was pouring forth this identity, as atmosphere and aspect and picture, in the very measure and to the very top of her consciousness of how it hung in the balance. Thus one arrived, through the succession of shining days, at the finest sense of the case—the interesting truth that her consciously not being as her tragic sisters were in the great particular was virtually just her genius, and that the very straightest thing she could do would naturally be not to flinch at the dark hour from any profession of her genius. Looking myself more askance at the dark hour (politically speaking I mean) than I after my fashion figured her as doing in her mass, I found it of an extreme, of quite an endless fascination to trace as many as possible of her felt idiosyncrasies back to her settled sea-confidence, and to see this now in turn account for so many other things, the smallest as well as the biggest, that, to give the fewest hints of illustration, the mere spread of the great trees, the mere gathers in the little bluey-white curtains of the cottage windows, the mere curl of the tinted smoke from the old chimneys matching that note, became a sort of exquisite evidence.

Exquisite evidence of a like general class, it was true, didn't on the other side of the Channel prevent the awful liability to the reach of attack—its having borne fruit and been corrected or averted again was in fact what half the foreign picture meant; but the foreign genius was other, other at almost every point; it had always in the past and on the spot, one remembered, expressed things, confessed things, with a difference, and part of that difference was of course the difference of history, the fact of exemption, as I have called it, the fact that a blest inviolacy was almost exactly what had least flourished. France and Belgium, to refer only to them, became dear accordingly, in the light I speak of, because, having suffered and suffered, they were suffering yet again, while precisely the opposite process worked for the scene directly beneath my eyes. England was interesting, to put it mildly—which is but a shy evasion of putting it passion-ately—because she hadn't suffered, because there were passages of that sort she had publicly declined and defied; at the same time that one wouldn't have the case so simple as to set it down wholly to her luck. France and Belgium, for the past, confessed, to repeat my term; while England, so consistently harmonised, with all her long unbrokenness thick and rich upon her, seemed never to do that, nor to need it, in order to practise on a certain fine critical, not to mention a certain fine prejudiced, sensibility. It was the season of sensibility now, at any rate for just those days and just that poor place of yearning, of merely yearning, vigil; and I may add with all emphasis that never had I had occasion so to learn how far sensibility may go when once well wound up. It was saying little to say I did justice easiest at once and promptest to the most advertised proposal of the enemy, his rank intention of clapping down the spiked helmet, than which no form of headgear, by the way, had ever struck one as of a more graceless, a more tell-tale platitude, upon the priceless genius of France; far from new, after all, was that measure of the final death in him of the saving sense of proportion which only gross dementia can abolish. Those of my generation who could remember the detected and frustrated purpose of a renewed Germanic pounce upon the country which, all but bled to death in 1871, had become capable within five years of the most penetrating irony of revival ever recorded, were well aware of how in that at once sinister and grotesque connection they had felt notified in time. It was the extension of the programme and its still more prodigious publication during the quarter of a century of interval, it was the announced application of the extinguisher to the quite other, the really so contrasted genius the expression of which surrounded me in the manner I have glanced at, it was the extraordinary fact of a declared non-sufferance any longer, on Germany's part, of either of the obnoxious national forms disfiguring her westward horizon, and even though by her own allowance they had nothing intellectually or socially in common save that they were objectionable and, as an incident, crushable—it was this, I say, that gave one furiously to think, or rather, while one thanked one's stars for the luxury, furiously and all but unutterably to feel.

The beauty and the interest, the now more than ever copious and welcome expression, of the aspects nearest me found their value in their being so resistingly, just to that very degree of eccentricity, with that very density of home-grownness, what they were; in the same way as the character of the sister-land lately joined in sisterhood showed for exquisite because so ingrained and incorrigible, so beautifully all her own and inimitable on other ground. If it would have been hard really to give the measure of one's dismay at the awful proposition of a world squeezed together in the huge Prussian fist and with the variety and spontaneity of its parts oozing in a steady trickle, like the sacred blood of sacrifice, between those hideous knuckly fingers, so, none the less, every reason with which our preference for a better condition and a nobler fate could possibly bristle kept battering at my heart, kept, in fact, pushing into it, after the fashion of a crowd of the alarmed faithful at the door of a church. The effect was literally, yes, as of the occasion of some great religious service, with prostrations and exaltations, the light of a thousand candles and the sound of soaring choirs—

all of which figured one's individual inward state as determined by the menace. One could still note at the same time, however, that this high pitch of private emotion was by itself far from meeting the case as the enemy presented it; what I wanted, of course, to do was to meet it with the last lucidity, the fullest support for particular defensive pleas or claims—and this even if what most underlay all such without exception came back to my actual vision, that and no more, of the general sense of the land. The vision was fed, and fed to such a tune that in the quest for reasons—that is, for the particulars of one's affection, the more detailed the better—the blades of grass, the outlines of leaves, the drift of clouds, the streaks of mortar between old bricks, not to speak of the call of child-voices muffled in the comforting air, became, as I have noted, with a hundred other like touches, casually felt, extraordinary admonitions and symbols, close links of a tangible chain. When once the question fairly hung there of the possibility, more showily set forth than it had up to then presumed to be, of a world without use for the tradition so embodied, an order substituting for this, by an unmannerly thrust, quite another and really, it would seem, quite a ridiculous, a crudely and clumsily improvised story, we might all have resembled together a group of children at their nurse's knee disconcerted by some tale that it isn't their habit to hear. We loved the old tale, or at least I did, exactly because I knew it; which leaves me keen to make the point, none the less, that my appreciation of the case for world-variety found the deeply and blessedly familiar perfectly consistent with it. This came of what I "read into" the familiar; and of what I did so read, of what I kept reading through that uplifted time, these remarks were to have attempted a record that has reached its limit sooner than I had hoped.

I was not then to the manner born, but my apprehension of what it was on the part of others to be so had been confirmed and enriched by the long years, and I gave myself up to the general, the native image I thus circled around as to the dearest and most precious of all native images. That verily became at the crisis an occupation sublime; which was not, after all, so much an earnest study or fond arrangement of the mixed aspects as a positive, a fairly sensual bask in their light, too kindled and too rich not to pour out by its own force. The strength and the copious play of the appearances acting in this collective fashion carried everything before them; no dark discrimination, no stiff little reserve that one might ever have made, stood up in the diffused day for a moment. It was in the opposite way, the most opposite possible, that one's intelligence worked, all along the line; so that with the warmth of the mere sensation that "they" were about as good, above all when it came to the stress, as could well be expected of people, there was the acute interest of the successive points at which one recognised why. This last, the satisfaction of the deepened intelligence, turned, I may frankly say, to a prolonged revel—"they" being the people about me and every comfort I had ever had of them smiling its individual smile straight at me and conducing to an effect of candour that is beyond any close notation. They didn't know how good they were, and their candour had a peculiar lovability of unconsciousness; one had more imagination at their service in this cause than they had in almost any cause of their own; it was wonderful, it was beautiful, it was inscrutable, that they could make one feel this and yet not feel with it that it at all practically diminished them. Of course, if a shade should come on occasion to fall across the picture, that shade would perhaps be the question whether the most restless of the faculties mightn't on the whole too much fail them. It beautified life, I duly remembered, it promoted art, it inspired faith, it crowned conversation, but hadn't it—always again under stress—still finer applications than these, and mightn't it in a word, taking the right direction, peculiarly conduce to virtue? Wouldn't it, indeed, be indispensable to virtue of the highest strain? Never mind, at any rate—so my emotion replied; with it or without it we seemed to *be* taking the right direction; moreover, the next best thing to the imagination people may have, if they can, is the quantity of it they may set going in others, and which, imperfectly aware, they are just exposed to from such others, and must make the best of: their advantage becoming simply that it works, for the connection, all in their favour. That of the associated outsider, the order of whose feelings, for the occasion, I have doubtless not given a wholly lucid sketch of, cultivated its opportunity week after week at such a rate that, technical alien as he was, the privilege of the great partaking of shared instincts and ideals, of a communion of race and tongue, temper and tradition, put on before all the blest appearances a splendour to which I hoped that so long as I might yet live my eyes would never grow dim. And the great intensity, the melting together of the spiritual sources so loosed in a really intoxicating draught, was when I shifted my watch from near east to far west and caught the enemy, who seemed ubiquitous, in the long-observed effort that most fastened on him the insolence of his dream and the depth of his delusion. There in the west were those of my own fond fellowship, the other, the ready and rallying partakers, and it was on the treasure of our whole unquenchable association that in the riot of his ignorance—this at least apparently armour-proof—he had laid his unholy hands.

Henry James.

Explanatory Notes

All references below to James's correspondence are to *Henry James Letters*, ed. Leon Edel, 4 vols. (Cambridge MA: Harvard Univ. Press, 1974–84).

1. THE BRITISH SOLDIER

The geopolitical events the essay refers to center on the aftermath of the Russo-Turkish War of April 1877–March 1878, in which Russia supported the independence and Pan-Slavic drives of Rumania, Serbia, Montenegro, Bosnia, and Bulgaria against Turkey. The independent Greater Bulgaria that resulted from Russia's victory so alarmed the Western European powers, especially Britain and Austria, that in the Congress of Berlin, 13 June–13 July 1878, they persuaded Russia to revise the 3 March 1878 Treaty of San Stefano (which had ended the war), returning Macedonia to Turkey and placing Bosnia-Herzegovina under Austro-Hungarian administration. There are several published letters by Henry James that refer to these events: 28 Jan. [1878] to William James (2:152–53), 1 May [1878] to William (esp. 2:173), and 29 May [1878] to Henry James Sr. (esp. 2:176), where James mentions visiting the Pakenhams at Aldershot and refers to the article "The British Solder." In a 28 February [1877] letter to William, James mentions "Mrs. Pakenham, an American married to a British general, to whom Mrs. Wister sent me a letter, (a very nice woman with a very nice husband)" (2:102). He mentions several dinners with and visits to the Pakenhams (2:124, 160, 323–24, 329).

3 Aldershot: A military training center in Hampshire, established 1854.

3 England and Russia ... reviving Turk: A reference to the aftermath of the Russo-Turkish War.

3 I exclaim. ... with Offenbach's Grand Duchess: The title character of Jacques Offenbach's 1867 operetta, *La Grande-Duchesse de Gérolstein*, with a libretto by Henri Meilhac and

Ludovic Halévy, has an aria in the first act, "Ah! j'aime les militaires!" [Oh! I love military men!].

3 Mr. Ruskin has said somewhere: In letter 10 (Oct. 1871) of *Fors Clavigera*, John Ruskin writes: "And, at this day, though I have kind invitations enough to visit America, I could not, even for a couple of months, live in a country so miserable as to possess no castles" (4 vols. [1886; rpt. New York: Greenwood, 1968] 1:132–33).

5 I should have found myself on British soil: James took up permanent residence in London in December 1876.

5 resounding to the tread of regiments: The British military raised its level of preparedness after the Treaty of San Stefano.

6 I played it with ... *conviction*: I played it with sincerity.

7 the vulgar Bulgarians ... massacred half enough: The reference is to the Turkish repression of an 1876 Bulgarian uprising (see introduction).

7 the sarcasm of some of her neighbors ... France, for instance: In a 28 January [1878] letter to his brother, William, James writes, "It has been curious to see that all the French republican papers have lately been denouncing her [England] fiercely for not pitching into Russia" (2:153).

7 The Liberal Party ... factious and hypercritical: Benjamin Disraeli's Conservative government ruled England from 1874 to 1880. The leader of the opposition Liberal Party, William Gladstone (1809–98), wrote a pamphlet in 1876, *The Bulgarian Horrors and the Question of the East*, which sold 40,000 copies in a few days, and campaigned vigorously against Disraeli's Balkan policy.

8 England has sold herself ... to "Manchester": The reference is to financial and economic interests (Manchester being an industrial city) against bellicose ones. In the same 28 January letter to William cited above, James writes of the "equally odious peace-at-any-price, 'Manchester'-minded party" (2:152). In a 15 December [1877] letter to Grace Norton, James opines that England needs to go to war, "if only to show that she still can, and that she is not one vast, money-getting Birmingham" (2:145).

8 the lady in *Dombey & Son*: The lady is Mrs. Chick, a character in Dickens's novel published in 1847–48.

8 *Londres pittoresque*, by M. Henri Bellenger: Published in 1876 by Decaux, this seems to be Bellenger's only book, though he translated Marco Polo's travels and another Italian book, on nihilism.

9 Taine ... *Notes sur l'Angleterre*: The writer is Hippolyte Taine (1828–93); Hachette published *Notes sur l'Angleterre* in 1871.

10 *lazzaroni*: The popular term refers to scoundrels or rascals.

11 *effaced*: He uses the French term to mean "erased."

12 the late prince consort: Prince Albert had died in 1861.

13 Milton's description of the celestial hosts: The description is in *Paradise Lost* 6.56–78.

2. THE AFGHAN DIFFICULTY

The article concerns the imminent outbreak of the Second Afghan War, of 1878–80 (see introduction). James refers frequently to the "Amir," "Shir Ali," or Shere Ali (1825–79), the emir of Afghanistan, who in fact was deposed in 1879, when the British occupied Kabul, and died in exile shortly thereafter. The war started in late November 1878.

14 Cyprus . . . "purchase": Britain received Cyprus from Turkey as part of the resolution of the Congress of Berlin.

14 this morning's *Times* by M. de Blowitz: Two articles about the Prince of Wales and his role in the Paris Universal International Exhibition of 1878 appear in the *Times* of 23 October 1878. Both are unsigned; one is on page 5 and one on page 9. James certainly refers to the one on page 9.

15 Sir Neville Chamberlain's very military embassy: Afghanistan had refused for years to receive a British mission, seeing it as a first step toward British domination. In 1878, a Russian mission arrived in Kabul (the degree to which Shere Ali welcomed this visit is debated, but the emir did lean more toward Russia than toward Britain). The Russian mission decided the viceroy of India, Lord Lytton (see note below), to send a mission of his own, led by Sir Neville Chamberlain.

15 the famous insult offered to Major Cavagnari: Louis Cavagnari (1841–79), deputy commissioner of Peshawar (1877–79); was a member of Chamberlain's mission and the person actually turned back at the Khyber Pass in August 1878 by Afghan border guards; he later negotiated a treaty with Yakub Khan, Shere Ali's successor as emir of Afghanistan, in May 1879, and subsequently was named British resident at Kabul, where he was killed by Afghans in September 1879.

16 The Chancellor of the Exchequer: Sir Stafford Northcote (1818–87) was chancellor of the exchequer from 1874 to 1880.

16 Mr. Gladstone . . . article in the *North American Review*: The article was "Kin Beyond Sea," *North American Review* (Sept.–Oct. 1878): 179–212. Gladstone, leader of the Liberal Party, was prime minister from 1868 to 1874, 1880 to 1885, 1886, and 1892 to 1894.

16 Prince Gortchakoff's promise in 1875: Alexander Gorchakov (1798–1883), Russian foreign minister (1856–82), ostensibly supported Pan-Slavism and Balkan independence movements, thus disguising Russia's territorial greed.

17 Lord Lytton: Edward Robert Bulwer-Lytton (1831–91), son of the novelist and playwright, was viceroy of India at time of the Second Afghan War.

17 Lord Lawrence: John Laird Mair Lawrence, first Baron Lawrence (1811–79), viceroy of India from 1864 to 1869, opposed the Second Afghan War.

17 Sir James Stephen: Sir James Fitzjames Stephen (1829–94), brother of Leslie Stephen, was an acquaintance of James's, a lawyer, legal member of the council in India (1869–72), writer, and contributor to *Cornhill Magazine* (as was James) and most often to *Pall Mall Gazette*.

18 Lord Beaconsfield . . . "peace with honor" from Berlin: Benjamin Disraeli, Lord Beaconsfield (1804–81), was the Tory prime minister (1868, 1874–80) at the moment of

the Congress of Berlin. In his 1 May [1878] letter to William James, writing about Disraeli in reference to Britain's possibly waging war against Russia in the aftermath of the Treaty of San Stefano, James says, in spite of the fact that Disraeli was a baptized and conforming Anglican: "And to think that a clever Jew should have juggled old England into it!" (2:173).

3. REVIEW OF *GRAF BISMARCK*

19 London *Times* lately published, in three instalments: The excerpts appeared on 8 Nov. 1878 (p. 8), 19 Nov. 1878 (p. 3), and 21 Nov. 1878 (p. 4); an introduction appeared on 8 Nov. 1878 (p. 7).

19 the December *Fortnightly*: This is the issue of 1 Dec. 1878 (24:144): 765–86.

19 an English translation: In 1879 Scribner's would publish an American translation and Macmillan an English one, entitled *Bismarck in the Franco-German War, 1870–1871*.

19 just out in Germany: *Graf Bismarck und seine Leute während des Krieges mit Frankreich, nach Tagebuchsblättern* was published in Leipzig by Grunow in 1878.

19 translator of those American tales: Busch (1821–99) had translated James's *Roderick Hudson*, *The American*, and *A Passionate Pilgrim and Other Tales* as well as a book of Twain's stories.

20 M. Thiers: Louis Adolphe Thiers (1797–1877), president of the French Third Republic, negotiated the treaties ending the Franco-Prussian War.

20 M. Favre: Jules Favre (1809–80) led the French government of national defense after the fall of the Second Empire; he was minister of foreign affairs under Thiers.

20 *politesse de coeur*: The phrase denotes sincere, heartfelt politeness (literally: politeness of the heart).

21 Varzin: Bismarck purchased his estate in Pomerania, 90 miles west of Danzig (now Gdansk), in 1867.

21 Napoleon III . . . in 1866: When Prussia went to war against Austria, Napoleon III could have obtained easily for France the territorial concessions in Belgium and Luxembourg he failed to obtain in 1870.

4. EARLY MEETING OF PARLIAMENT

22 The Afghan war has begun: See article 2, "The Afghan Difficulty."

23 Mr. Gladstone and his friends: The remark refers to the Liberal Party, the parliamentary opposition at that time.

23 put the Amir . . . arms of the Russians: See explanatory notes for article 2, "The Afghan Difficulty."

23 Lord Cranbrook: Gathorne Hardy, Viscount Cranbrook of Hemsted (1814–1906), was secretary for India from April 1878 to April 1880.

23 Lord Lytton: See note for p. 17, Lord Lytton.

23 Duke of Argyll: George Douglas Campbell, eighth duke and seventeenth earl of

Argyll (1823–1900), a Liberal politician, was secretary of state for India (from 1868 to 1874) and author of *The Reign of Law*.

23 incident of three months ago: See explanatory notes for article 2, "The Afghan Difficulty."

24 Lord Halifax: Charles Wood, Viscount Halifax of Monk Bretton (1800–85), a Liberal politician, was secretary of state for India from 1859 to 1866.

24 Lord Beaconsfield: See note for p. 18, Lord Beaconsfield.

25 Lord Salisbury: Robert Arthur Talbot Gascoyne-Cecil, marquess of Salisbury (1830–1903), as foreign secretary under Disraeli, was instrumental in the Congress of Berlin. He was the Conservative prime minister in 1885, 1886–92, and 1895–1902.

26 Like Topsy in the novel: In chapter 20 of Harriet Beecher Stowe's *Uncle Tom's Cabin*, the young slave, Topsy, when asked who made her, answered: "Nobody, as I knows ... I spect I grow'd. Don't think nobody never made me."

5. REASSEMBLING OF PARLIAMENT

27 lively debates upon the Afghan war: See article 4, "The Early Meeting of Parliament."

28 the military disaster in South Africa: The reference is to the Zulu defeat of the British at Isandhlwana on 21 January 1879.

28 the Indian mutiny ... twenty-two years ago: The Indian Mutiny lasted from February 1857 to March 1858.

28 Natal: The South African state was annexed by Britain in 1843 and became a Crown Colony in 1856.

28 Isandula: This is James's spelling of Isandhlwana.

28 Sir Bartle Frere: Sir Henry Bartle Edward Frere (1815–84) sat on the Indian Council from 1867 to 1877; he wanted a British resident in Kabul. Appointed high commissioner in South Africa in 1877, he declared war on the Zulus in January 1879, in spite of a request by Sir Michael Hicks Beach, the Colonial secretary, that he negotiate. He was censured and recalled in 1880.

28 massacre of Lord Chelmsford's troops: Frederic Augustus Thesiger, Baron Chelmsford (1837–1905), led the British force that invaded Zululand and was defeated at Isandhlwana.

28 Cetewayo: The king of the Zulus, Cetewayo, sometimes spelled Keshwayo (c.1836–84), led determined resistance to Boer and British encroachments into his territory; he was defeated by British troops at Ulundi in 1879.

28 Rorke's Drift: Chelmsford's troops entered Zululand at this crossing of the Buffalo River.

29 Sir Charles Dilke: Sir Charles Wentworth Dilke (1843–1911), a Liberal politician and member of parliament, was the proprietor of the *Athenaeum* and *Notes and Queries* and author of several books; he supported James's entrance to the Reform Club.

29 Sir Theophilus Shepstone: Shepstone (1817–93), secretary for native affairs and

member of executive and legislative councils of Natal, annexed Transvaal in 1877 and was administrator of Transvaal from 1877 to 1879.

29 annexing the Transvaal: Britain annexed the Boer state of Transvaal in 1877 but restored its independence in 1881.

30 Lord Beaconsfield: See note for p. 18, Lord Beaconsfield.

6. JAMES IN THE SERENE SIXTIES

36 a bit of fiction called "The Papers": James's short story satirizing newspapers had recently appeared in a collection of his tales, *The Better Sort* (London: Methuen, 1902; New York: Scribner's, 1903).

39 "The Other House": This novel was published in 1896 by Heinemann in London and Macmillan in New York.

39 "The Sacred Fount": Scribner's in New York and Methuen in London published *The Sacred Fount* in 1901.

40 "The Bostonians," "The Americans," "Daisy Miller," to mention a few, and two women in the beautiful "Wings of the Dove": *The Bostonians* was published in 1886 by Macmillan; *The American* was published in 1877 by Osgood; *Daisy Miller* was published by Harper in 1878 (after serialization in *Cornhill Magazine*). *The Wings of the Dove* was published in 1902 by Scribner's in New York and Constable in London; the two American women in the novel are Milly Theale and Susan Stringham.

40 It was in France twenty odd years ago that as a young man . . . comradeship: James resided in Paris from November 1875 to December 1876. During that time, he frequented the Sunday gatherings of writers including Emile Zola and the Goncourt brothers that Gustave Flaubert hosted. During a visit to Paris in February 1884, James visited Alphonse Daudet and thus renewed contact with the "grandsons of Balzac," as these novelists were often collectively called.

40 Balzac: James was in the process of preparing his lecture "The Lesson of Balzac."

40 Bourget's feebleness of fibre: James became increasingly annoyed with the reactionary literary tendencies of his friend, the French writer Paul Bourget (1852–1935).

7. QUESTION OF OUR SPEECH

51 vox Americana: The phrase translates "voice of America."

53 modus vivendi: The phrase is Latin for "way of life."

57 in solemn troops and sweet societies: James quotes from Milton's *Lycidas*: "There entertain him all the Saints above, / In solemn troops, and sweet Societies" (178–79).

8. SPEECH OF AMERICAN WOMEN

69 living in rooms ostensibly furnished: James resided in two furnished rooms at 102 Mount Vernon Street during March and April 1882 (he also resided during the first eight months of 1883 at 131 Mount Vernon Street, his father's house, after his father died).

69 a seminary for young ladies: This would have been St. Margaret's School, which was located from 1875 to 1888 at 5 Chestnut Street and was affiliated with the Episcopal Convent of the Society of St. Margaret, which in 1883 stood in Louisburg Square.

70 shrieking *à l'envi*: The phrase means "shrieking at will," as if to outdo each other.

76 *agrément*: The word has several meanings in French: agreement, consent, approbation, and pleasure; this last seems to fit best the context of James's sentence.

9. MANNERS OF AMERICAN WOMEN

91 When it befell me . . . those peopling it: During his visit to the United States from August 1904 to July 1905, James traveled from New York to New England, Florida, and California via Indiana, Chicago, and St. Louis.

95 *Parsifal*: Richard Wagner's opera was first performed in the United States on 24 December 1903 at the Metropolitan Opera in New York.

96 *disjecta membra*: Literally, the phrase means "scattered limbs"; the reference is to Horace's *Satires* (1.4.62): *Disjecti membra poetae*, "The scattered remnants of the poet."

96 as I moved westward: James left Chicago for Los Angeles on 20 March 1905, arriving at his destination on the evening of March 23.

99 *rari nantes in gurgite vasto*: The line is from Vergil's *The Aeneid* (1.118): *Apparent rari nantes in gurgite vasto* ("Here and there are seen swimming in the vast flood").

101 not long since . . . distinction and geniality: This probably refers to William Dean Howells and his daughter Mildred, who arrived together in England in March 1904. Howells visited James at Rye in June 1904 and was instrumental in helping to organize James's 1904–05 trip to the United States. Howells returned to America in the spring of 1905.

103 the case of a gentle relative: McEvoy Campbell, of the Cornell Medical Library, speculates on the identity of this individual. He points out that in *The American Scene*, in the final paragraph of section 2 of the first chapter, "New England: An Autumn Impression," James writes: " 'Are you the woman of the house?' a rustic cynically squalid, and who makes it a condition of *any* intercourse that he be received at the front door of the house, not at the back, asks of a *maîtresse de maison*, a summer person trained to resignation, as preliminary to a message brought, as he then mentions, from the 'washerlady' " (*Collected Travel Writings: Great Britain and America; English Hours, The American Scene, Other Travels*, ed. Richard Howard [New York: Library of America, 1993] 377).

Campbell speculates that as the passage occurs while James describes impressions from his stay at the New Hampshire vacation home of his brother, William, the "gentle relative" and "summer person" is James's sister-in-law and William's wife, Alice Howe Gibbens James.

106 the "short story" . . . hands of women: James probably has in mind the fiction of Sarah Orne Jewett and Mary Wilkins Freeman.

107 *The Kentons*: Howells's novel was published by Harper in 1902.

10. IS THERE A LIFE AFTER DEATH?

121 *déménager*: The French term means "to move," "to change residence."

122 *bête*: The French word for "beast" is used to connote a situation both beastly and stupid.

123 *portée*: The sense of the term is "reach" or "range."

11. AMERICAN VOLUNTEER MOTOR-AMBULANCE CORPS

131 Mr. Richard Norton: A son of Charles Eliot Norton, he was previously a teacher at and then director of the American School of Classical Studies at Rome.

132 *postes de secours*: This is the French term for first-aid stations.

132 *blessés assis*: The French term means "the seated wounded."

135 retreat of the Allies from Mons: The Belgian city was the site of an August 1914 battle between German and British forces.

137 Eliot Norton: He was the eldest son of Charles Eliot Norton.

137 Brown Shipley & Co.: The firm served as London bankers for the American Volunteer Motor-Ambulance Corps.

12. JAMES'S FIRST INTERVIEW

138 American Ambulance Corps: See article 11, "The American Volunteer Motor-Ambulance Corps in France."

141 A distinguished English naval expert: Leon Edel identifies this as Winston Churchill (*Henry James: The Master, 1901–1916* [Philadelphia: Lippincott, 1972] 524).

141 Derwent Wood's admirable bust: As part of the seventieth birthday gifts various friends arranged for James, the American painter John S. Sargent (1856–1925) commissioned his protegé, Derwent Wood, to sculpt a bust of James.

141 Sargent's fine portrait: Sargent painted this portrait as part of the celebration of James's seventieth birthday; it is in the National Portrait Gallery collection.

141 it's having been slashed: This occurred in May 1914. (See Fred Kaplan, *Henry James: The Imagination of Genius* [New York: Morrow, 1992] 551, and Edel, *The Master* 490.)

145 Brown Brothers: *The Observer* published a summary of the *New York Times Magazine* article entitled "Mr. Henry James and the War" (11 Apr. 1915, p. 6, col. 4), repeating this New York address for contributions. On 18 April 1915, *The Observer* published a letter by James (p. 14, col. 3), dated 14 April, providing the same London address for Brown, Shipley and Co. given in "The American Volunteer Motor-Ambulance Corps in France."

15. ALLEN D. LONEY

159 Allen D. Loney: Loney and his wife were American residents in England. Loney was an ambulance driver during the war. Only their daughter, Virginia, fourteen at the time, survived the sinking of the *Lusitania*.

159 the Lusitania: The British passenger ship was sunk by a German submarine, off the coast of Ireland, 7 May 1915. Nearly 1,200 people were drowned, including more than 100 Americans.

160 Alfred Vanderbilt: This millionaire sportsman and scion of Cornelius Vanderbilt died in the sinking of the *Lusitania* (see A. A. Hoehling and Mary Hoehling's *The Last Voyage of the Lusitania* [New York: Holt, 1956]).

16. REFUGEES IN ENGLAND

161 our so interesting and inspiring Chelsea work: See the note at the end of the *Times Literary Supplement* version of the essay (204–5).

162 our Chelsea waterside: James began residing part of the year at 21 Carlyle Mansions, Cheyne Walk, Chelsea, in 1913.

162 Crosby Hall ... transplanted a few years since ... Thomas More: Sir John Crosby built Crosby Hall around 1466; it covered part of what later became Crosby Square or Place. It was Sir Thomas More's residence c.1520. The hall was re-erected in Chelsea in 1908 and later became the center of the Federation of University Women.

168 in a tiny Sussex town: The town is Rye.

168 Louvain and Aerschott and Termonde and Dinant: These were sites of fighting and of German atrocities in Belgium during the early days of World War I.

17. THE LONG WARDS

169–70 out of the distant past ... that summer's end of 1861: James discusses this encounter with "invalid and convalescent troops," at what he remembers as Portsmouth Grove, Rhode Island, in *Notes of a Son and Brother* (see introduction).

170 I confess ... of disconnection: The reference is to James's 1904–05 visit to the United States.

175 Did I not, ... lacerated Belgians: See article 16, "Refugees in England."

18. WITHIN THE RIM

179 the old rampart of a little high-perched Sussex town: The town is Rye.

183 the most penetrating irony of revival ever recorded: After France lost the Franco-Prussian War of 1870–71, it ceded Alsace and Lorraine and paid an indemnity of five billion francs to Prussia. Since France quickly paid the indemnity, by 1875 it had rebuilt its military, which led to fear that Prussia (now Germany) would invade France in order to check growing French military power.

Textual Variants

Twelve of the eighteen essays in this collection were published only once during James's life. All five of the essays about British geopolitics have never been printed in their entirety except in their initial magazine publication. Except for "The Question of Our Speech," the four essays on gender and the American scene were published only once during James's life, in periodicals. Likewise, half of the writings on World War I ("Henry James's First Interview," "France," "Allen D. Loney—In Memoriam," and "The Long Wards") appeared in but one version during James's life (or immediately after his death, in the case of "The Long Wards").

Of the remaining six essays, two appeared in print first in a magazine and then were republished in a book ("The Question of Our Speech" and "Is There a Life After Death?"); two appeared in England in pamphlets and in the United States as newspaper articles ("The American Volunteer Motor-Ambulance Corps in France" and "The Question of the Mind"); and the remaining two were published in more than one periodical version ("Refugees in England" and "Within the Rim").

This edition reproduces in their original form the twelve essays for which there is but one text. The remaining six items all display variations among their different versions; these are listed below. The list does not include variations in conventional American as opposed to British spellings (i.e. "color" versus "colour"), except when they are part of a phrase including another change. Differences of punctuation, different wording, or deleted or added passages, all of which can have an effect upon meaning, are listed below.

This edition makes no changes to punctuation or to spelling in the original texts, except in the case of obvious errors, which have been changed as noted in the list of emendations following the variants.

There are a few instances in the texts of punctuation and spelling practices of the late nineteenth century that are no longer conventional today, such as contractions ("do n't" instead of "don't") or a comma inside a closing parenthesis; these are maintained, in this edition, in their original form. The essays in this collection were all written for magazine or newspaper publication, and as different periodicals had different in-house styles, and as part of the freelance writer's task was to conform to these various styles, it is important that the variations in the conventional practices of James's days and the differences from ours be preserved.

7. QUESTION OF OUR SPEECH

The text of James's 1905 Bryn Mawr graduation speech was first published by *Appleton's Booklovers Magazine*, with James's byline, and then in Henry James, *The Question of Our Speech; The Lesson of Balzac: Two Lectures* (Boston: Houghton Mifflin, Riverside Press, 1905). The book version is the source for this edition; it includes a number of passages not found in the periodical version. The nature of most of the changes—especially the deletion of commas, which is typical of James's revisions from periodical to book form, and the reading of "cultivation" on page 17 in the book for the less likely "civilization" in the periodical—suggests the book text is closer to James's desires.

In the periodical version of the text, the footnote on the first page reads: "Address delivered to the graduating class (young women) at Bryn Mawr College, Pennsylvania, June 8, 1905, and here printed with the restoration of a few passages omitted on that occasion."

Variants (book reading followed by periodical reading):

43 each of which branches of] each of which branches to

43 a thinkable thing should] a thinkable thing, should

44 in the fine confidence ... impute to you] in the fine confidence I impute to you

44 it suggests and expresses] it suggests and expresses,

44–45 in which a society is civilized] in which a society is civilized,

45 the Turks and the Chinese, have for] the Turks and the Chinese, have, for

45 meanwhile] mean while

45 the *whole* of the burden] the whole of the burden

45 of good breeding, above all,] of good breeding; above all,

46 how you shall speak,] how you shall speak;

46 a colloquial, a genial value] a colloquial, a genial value,

46 that reduce articulation to an easy] that reduce articulation, in short, to an easy

46 the barking or the roaring] the barking, or the roaring

46 in any at all aspiring ... immunity on the wrong side] in any at all aspiring civilization of tone, a vast mass of assured impunity, on the wrong side

47 and above all,] and, above all,

47 I mean, then, ... our language, a consideration] I mean then by speaking well, in the first place, speaking with consideration for the forms and shades of our language, speaking with a consideration

47 that have, each, an identity] that have each an identity

47 a richness, ... a value,] a richness; that have, in a word, a value

47 the whole word itself,] the whole word itself;

48 besmearing our persons;] besmearing our persons,

49 commoner than to see throughout] commoner than to see, throughout

49 another vowel alone lays] another vowel alone, lays

49 a still more questionable "Yeh-ep."] a still rather questionable "Yeh-ep."

50 in the French word.... a question of an *r,*] in the French word. It is not always a question of an r,

50 stand as a hint.... to say of those things] stand as a hint. It is enough to say of these things

51 no expert attention] no expert attention,

51 the auditor of life,] the auditor, of life,

51 It remains for the] It remains, for the

51 beyond affirming at least,] beyond saying, at least,

52 finality and felicity.] finality, and felicity.

52 to find our way] to find our *way*

53 by surprise it may] by surprise, it may

54 shrieks and yells,] shrieks, and yells,

54 of *values,* ... just appreciation,] of values of just proportion and just appreciation;

55 whether it be not ... have not in it] whether it isn't either no language at all, or only a very poor one, if it hasn't in it

55 to snort or neigh,] to snort, or neigh,

56 of a young intelligence:] of a young intelligence;

56 It is not a question ... exercise your attention on that,] It isn't a question, however, so much of simply meeting them as of attending to them, of making your profit of them, when you do meet them. If they are at all adequate representatives of some decent tradition, you will find the interest of a new world, a whole extension of life, open to you in the attempt to estimate, in their speech, all that such a tradition consists of. Begin to exercise your observation on that,

56 earnestly and without reserve, ... the imitation of formed] earnestly and without reserve, the imitation of formed

10. IS THERE A LIFE AFTER DEATH?

First published, with James's byline, in two installments in *Harper's Bazar,* 44.1 (Jan. 1910): 26; 44.2 (Feb. 1910): 128–29, and reprinted in *In After Days: Thoughts on the Future Life,* by W. D. Howells, Henry James, John Bigelow, Thomas Wentworth Higginson, Henry M. Alden, William Hanna Thomson, Guglielmo Ferrero, Julia Ward Howe, Elizabeth Stuart Phelps (New York: Harper, 1910), 199–232. The book version (which consists of two parts, corresponding to the two periodical installments) is the source for this collection.

Variants (book reading followed by magazine reading):

118 laboratory-brain] laboratory brain

120 for my full experience] for my felt experience

125 come to that), only] come to that) only

127 Above all, it takes kindly] Above all it takes kindly
127 laboratory-brain.] laboratory brain.

11. AMERICAN VOLUNTEER MOTOR-AMBULANCE CORPS

First published as Henry James, *The American Volunteer Motor-Ambulance Corps in France: A Letter to the Editor of an American Journal* (London: Macmillan, 1914), and then, greatly condensed, with James's byline, by the *New York World* (4 Jan. 1915: 2). Because of the many deletions in the *World* text, the pamphlet version is the source text for this edition.

Variants (pamphlet reading followed by newspaper reading):

Newspaper title: "Famous Novelist Describes Deeds of U.S. Motor Corps"; followed by: "Henry James Tells How Richard Norton, After Seeing Wounded in France, Got Americans to Give Their Cars. 400 Injured Men Rescued From One Village Alone. Writer Appeals to His Countrymen for Financial Aid for Ambulance Volunteers. By Henry James. (Correspondence of The World.) London, Dec. 23."

The editor and journal mentioned in the subtitle are presumably the *New York World*. James had corresponded in 1905 with Frederick A. Duneka, city editor of the *World* and then vice president of Harper Brothers.

131 Sir, [New paragraph] Several] —Several
131 excellent work ... Richard Norton] excellent work of the American Volunteer Motor Ambulance Corps in France, lately organized by Mr. Richard Norton,
    131 to express to you our] to express our
131 able to give. The idea] able to give. [New paragraph] The idea
131 course of the War, he] course of the war, we
131 others possessed of cars, who] others possessed of cars who
131 as capable chauffeurs. To ... other Cars of purchase] as chauffeurs. [New paragraph] To this equipment were at once added certain other cars of purchase
    131–32 some fifteen Cars.] some fifteen cars.
    132 Colonel A. J. Barry,] Col. A. J. Barry
132 of the Red Cross.... the American name.] of the Red Cross.
132–34 gathering in the wounded, and those disabled by illness (though ... I should mention] gathering in the wounded and those disabled by illness. [New paragraph] Worked Night and Day. [New paragraph] I should mention
134 great Army Corps, on the arrival of our first Cars on the scene,] great army corps on the arrival of our first cars on the scene
134 to this Corps ... uninterruptedly attached,] to this corps they have been as yet uninterruptedly attached
134 transfer of activity. Such an assurance] transfer of activity. [New paragraph] Such an assurance
    134 given the Commissioner] given the commissioner
    134 Colonel Barry, with] Col. Barry with

134 a four-stretcher Car,] a four-stretcher car,

134 our Volunteers in charge,] our volunteers in charge,

134 Belgian frontier.... we found one of our] Belgian frontier. [New paragraph] Very quickly we found one of our

134 Mr. Norton and Colonel Barry] Mr. Norton and Col. Barry

134 Colonel Barry had saved] Col. Barry had saved

134 Just as our Volunteers] Just as our volunteers

134 including the mayor] including the Mayor

134 behind—as in fact proved] behind—as, in fact, proved

134 we could carry. This was] we could carry. [New paragraph] Rescued 400 Wounded. [New paragraph] This was

134 one of Colonel Barry's] one of Col. Barry's

134–35 motored away—though it took the rescuing party thus three days, in the face ... Still another form] motored away, though it took the rescuing party three days. [New paragraph] Still another form

135–36 to our Corps, ... as little neutrals] to our corps in its opportunities for tracing the whereabouts and recovering the identity of the dead. [New paragraph] We Americans are as little neutral

136 is concerned. Great ... What I therefore] is concerned. What I therefore

136–37 members of the Corps ... London, *November 25th, 1914*.] members of the corps make of it is that they wish more of their friends would come and support it, either personally or financially, or, best of all, of course, both.

14. QUESTION OF THE MIND

First published, with James's byline, in *England at War: An Essay* (London: Central Committee for National Patriotic Organisations, 1915) 3–12, and subsequently under James's byline as "Mind of England at War" in the *New York Sun* 1 Aug. 1915: sec. 5, 3, and in the *Philadelphia Ledger Magazine* 1 Aug. 1915: 1. Errors in the newspaper version suggest that the pamphlet's was the more carefully prepared text, and it is the latter that provides the text for this edition.

Variants (pamphlet reading followed by *Sun* reading):

Newspaper title: "Mind of England at War." Title followed by: "Well Known Author Recently Become a British Subject Analyzes the Psychology of His Adopted Country and the Great Conflict—Describes Nation's Awakening After First Shock of Strife." This followed by an editorial note:

The following essay by Henry James on "The Mind of England at War" is the first article written by him in relation to the conflict in Europe. It possesses especial interest at the present time because Mr. James took the oath of allegiance to Great Britain last week and became a British citizen. It may be assumed that it throws light on his change of nationality and that his decision in the matter was influenced by the same course of reasoning which he follows in discussing "the whole 'psychological' mystery marking the people of Great Britain."

By Henry James.

151 great world-shocks] great world shocks
151 rise in the world,] rise in the world;
152 may often depend but] may often depend, but
152 it re-enters] it reenters
152 generalised it. He to-day] generalized it. [New paragraph] He to-day
153 ideally recoverable, or] ideally recoverable or
153 What did one after all, . . . think of the English mind"?] What did one, after all, oh what did one, as the upshot of experience, "think of the English mind?"
153 to that degree in fact as] to that degree, in fact, as
153 no *deus ex machina,*] no deus ex machina
153 comparable *portée,*] comparable portee,
153 The situation was of course that] The situation was, of course, that
153 you had to *know,*] you had to know,
153 spacious air for *that;*] spacious air for that;
153 some of them justice and] some of them injustice and
154 They had indeed, these eyes,] They had, indeed, these eyes,
154 genius signify, that is count] genius signify, that is, count
154 doubt that we *had* one—] doubt that we had one—
154 of appreciation. . . . clear; so] of appreciation. [New paragraph] These last would inevitably and probably very soon strain themselves clear so
154 our capacity for *being* on] our capacity for being on
154 every relation of course—*that*] every relation, of course—that
154 the ancient light? that] the ancient light; that
154 so goodnatured, so incorrigibly goodnatured,] so good natured, so incorrigibly good natured,
154 the incorrigible, again!)] the incorrigible again!)
154 the *comité de lecture* of the Théâtre Français] the comite de lecture of the Theatre Francais
155 And yet if it was] And yet it was
155 out-in-the-world way] out in the world way
155 and indeed one's constant,] and indeed, one's constant,
155 from *behind,* so to speak,] from behind, so to speak,
155 all so sufficing force?] all so suffering force?
156 *there* was one's golden key] there was one's golden key
156 with that *constatation*] with that contruction [*sic*]
156 because good-natured, or good-natured] because good natured, or good natured
156 to one's infinite recreation,] to one's infinite creation,

156 the exhibition, of their life.... their favourite] the exhibition of their life. They were at their ease; there it was, for their favorite

156 that is behind, ... They *kept* the idea] that is, behind, miles behind, everything else. They kept the idea

156 subtly practised, assuredly—] subtly practised assuredly—

156 intercourse, in fact] intercourse, in fact,

157 eventually and shyly, call it] eventually and shyly call it

157 about *his* remains,] about his remains,

157 the while conscious, that] the while conscious that

157 *There* was the savour,] There was the savor,

158 preparation. It grows] preparation, it grows

158 of *that* clue] of that clue

15. ALLEN D. LONEY

The article, as published in the *New York Times* 12 Sept. 1915: sec. 1, p. 4 (col. 2), has the following title: "A Tribute by Henry James. In Memory of Allen D. Loney, Who Perished on the Lusitania." The following note then precedes James's text, which appears entirely in quotation marks:

> The following article on the late Allen D. Loney, who perished on the Lusitania, was written by Henry James soon after the sinking of that vessel and was lost in transit to this country. A copy has now been received. It is headed "Allen D. Loney—In Memoriam," and is signed by Mr. James in his capacity as Chairman of the American Volunteer Motor Ambulance Corps. It reads:

The article as published in this edition adopts the title indicated in this note and eliminates the quotation marks.

16. REFUGEES IN ENGLAND

First published under James's byline in the *New York Times* 17 Oct. 1915, magazine section (sec. 4): p. 1–2; in the *Boston Sunday Herald Supplement* 17 Oct. 1915: 6, 8; and as "Refugees in Chelsea" in the *Times Literary Supplement* (*TLS*) 740 (23 Mar. 1916): 133–34. Each version of the text is significantly different from the others. The *TLS* version is the most error-free of the three versions but is a posthumous publication; many paragraph divisions are different, and it lacks an entire paragraph in the other versions. Since the *Herald* version shows even more signs of editorial intrusions (paragraph headings inserted, a sentence removed in the ninth paragraph), the *New York Times* version is the copy-text for this edition.

The *Times* and *Herald* articles have slightly different titles and subtitles: "Henry James Writes of Refugees in England: Noted Novelist Is Moved by the Interesting and Inspiring Work at Chelsea in Aid of the Belgians Driven from Their Native Country by the War"

(*Times*); "Novelist Writes of Refugees in England: Henry James is Moved by the Interesting and Inspiring Work at Chelsea in Aid of the Belgians Driven from Their Native Country by the War" (*Herald*).

The *Times* and *Herald* versions begin with the following editorial note:

"The following essay, although dealing with but one important phase of the great body of relief work, comes so to the core of national traits in their relation to the psychology of pity, that it ranks among the most important contributions to the pitiful literature of the war."

The *Herald* version also includes the following paragraph headings: Paragraph 2: "How Genius Commits Itself." Paragraph 3: "A Full Bittersweet Taste." Paragraph 4: "Time's Strange Changes." Paragraph 6: "The Testimony of Silence." Paragraph 7: "All Are Indebted." Paragraph 10: "Exquisite in Horrible." Paragraph 11: "Some Particular Instances." Paragraph 12: "The Lights in the Picture." Paragraph 13: "A Fine Example."

The *TLS* version has a different title, "Refugees in Chelsea," and a two-paragraph introduction:

Henry James, who in the measure—and indeed beyond the measure—of his health and powers was unwearied in visiting the wounded and helping those who had suffered from the war, early associated himself with the welcome given to Belgian refugees in Chelsea where he lived. He soon came to be on most friendly terms with these exiles; was always ready to listen to their stories and to act as host at their social gatherings. Anxious as he was to assist them still further, he wrote, shortly before his final illness, an account of what was being done for them by the local committee. His object was to help this committee to raise in America a special fund to start an industry for crippled Belgian soldiers; but his essay, although written for the American public, contains so much of interest to his friends and readers on this side of the Atlantic that The Times has obtained permission to print it in England. For in this paper (which was almost the last thing he wrote) he gives an account of the interests and activities which filled the last period of his life, and a vivid expression of the feelings which made the position of a neutral in this war intolerable to him.

Those who now so sadly miss the presence of that loved and honoured figure will be glad that others should see him, as they so often saw him, walking slowly out—in spite of age and illness—on his errands of sympathy; stopping (as he always stopped) to talk with wounded soldiers in the streets and squares, or standing at Crosby Hall with the refugees gathered about him. And the description, with which he ends, of the arrival in the little town of Rye, where he was then living, of the first refugees who fled thither from the desolation of their country will remain as one of the most poignant and beautiful pages in the literature of the war.

There is also a note at the end of the article: "The Chelsea War Refugees' Fund, with which Mr. Henry James's article deals, carries on its work at Crosby Hall, Chelsea. The president is the Mayor of Chelsea (the Rev. R. Hudson), and the Hon. Lady Lyttelton is the chairman. Funds are urgently needed; and subscriptions should be addressed to the Chelsea War Refugees' Fund, Crosby Hall Chelsea. Socks, gloves, mufflers, jerseys, &c.,

made by the crippled Belgian soldiers at Crosby Hall, are now on sale at 24, King's-road, Sloane-square."

Variant readings in the *Herald* and *TLS* texts from the *New York Times* text are listed here. (See Emendations, below, for *Herald* and *TLS* readings that I have adopted to correct obvious misprints in the *Times* text.)

161 This is not a report on ... Chelsea work] *TLS* reads: This is not a Report on ... Chelsea work,

161 all the preceding, and one] *TLS* reads: all the preceding; and one

161 We live into, that is we learn to cultivate,] *Herald* and *TLS* read: We live into—that is, we learn to cultivate—

161 the fortunate, and the exempt not] *Herald* reads: the fortunate and the exempt, not] *TLS* reads: the fortunate, and the exempt, not

161 surely a genius, of the most eminent kind, for] *Herald* reads: surely a genius of the most eminent kind for

161 such limits; and there] *Herald* reads: such limits, and there

161 fearless activity, that is, in high originality, as] *Herald* reads: fearless activity—that is, in high originality—as (*TLS* uses dashes)

162 Paragraph 2 from *Times* deleted in *TLS*.

162 as Reports and Tables are] *Herald* reads: as reports and tables are

162 are communicable, but I] *TLS* reads: are communicable; but I

162 of cheer, and I] *TLS* reads: of cheer; and I

162 full bittersweet taste,] *TLS* reads: full bitter-sweet taste

162 done much: the bitter ineradicably seasons the consciousness, hopes and] *TLS* reads: done much; the bitter ineradicably seasons the consciousness, hopes, and

162 fifteenth century] *Herald* reads: 15th century

162 unable to save it:] *Herald* reads: unable to—save it] *TLS* reads: unable to save it;

163 Paragraphs 3 and 4 from *Times* joined in *TLS*

163 quite despairing eyes] *TLS* reads: quite despairing, eyes

163 It is in truth still] *TLS* reads: It is, in truth, still

163 Winter and Spring] *Herald* and *TLS* read: winter and spring

163 has formed then the] *TLS* reads: has formed, then, the

163 the bewildered, and if] *TLS* reads: the bewildered; and if

163 their story it is] *TLS* reads: their story, it is

163 Hither, month after month] *Herald* reads: Hither month after month

163 after day the unfortunates have flocked, each afternoon, and] *TLS* reads: after day, the unfortunates have flocked, each afternoon; and

163 Certain afternoons, each week, have worn the character of the huge comprehensive tea party] *Herald* reads: Certain afternoons each week have worn the character of the huge, comprehensive tea party] *TLS* reads: Certain afternoons each week have worn the character of the huge comprehensive tea-party

163 been able to draw] *Herald* reads: been able ot draw [*sic*]

163 find it suggest many] *Herald* reads: find it suggests many

163 and moving order; the] *Herald* reads: and moving order, the

163 the state as of people] *Herald* reads: the state, as of people

163 ruffians, murderers, and thieves] *Herald* reads: ruffians, murderers and thieves

163 darkness mitigated but] *Herald* reads: darkness mingled but

163 incendiary torches, this has] *TLS* reads: incendiary torches—this has

164 home violated, the objects] *Herald* reads: home violated the objects

164 Paragraphs 6 and 7 in *Times* joined in *TLS*

164 moments interpose, a confused] *Herald* reads: moments interpose a confused

164 of domesticity would dash] *Herald* and *TLS* read: of domesticity, would dash

164 sisters, aligned in] *TLS* reads: sisters, alined in

164 last, round about one, was at certain hours, when] *Herald* reads: last, roundabout one, was at certain hours when] *TLS* reads: last round about one was, at certain hours when

164 Paragraphs 8 and 9 in *Times* joined in *TLS*

165 alien conditions can give them. . . . This feeling] *Herald* reads: alien conditions can give them. The feeling (*TLS* concurs with *Times*, except that it italicizes "generally")

165 rational character] *TLS* reads: national character

165 That they of all] *TLS* reads: That *they*, of all

165 horrible; so peculiarly] *TLS* reads: horrible: so peculiarly

165 self smothered society] *Herald* and *TLS* read: self-smothered society

165 this delusion; I can] *TLS* reads: this delusion: I can

165 if it too] *TLS* reads: if it, too,

166 attention ache; I think] *TLS* reads: attention ache. I think

166 of dawn; faces] *TLS* reads: of dawn—faces

166 civilized men the appreciation of] *Herald* reads: civilized men the apprehension of

166 sphere of exercise—for] *TLS* reads: sphere of exercise for

166 of them, and this even if on the whole one] *TLS* reads: of them: and this even if, on the whole, one

166 Paragraphs 11 and 12 in *Times* joined in *TLS*

166 in the picture, and] *TLS* reads: in the picture; and

166 the horde and now] *TLS* reads: the horde, and now

166 occasional visit much more for my own cheer, I apprehand [*sic*], than for theirs, express] *TLS* reads: occasional visit—much more for my own cheer, I apprehend, than for theirs—express

167 recruit them to it and,] *TLS* reads: recruit them to it, and,

167 courage and patience and] *TLS* reads: courage, and patience, and

167 our gentlemen of Flanders.] *TLS* reads: our gentleman of Flanders.

167 local Squares—riverside] *Herald* and *TLS* read: local squares—riverside

167 of London; which,] *TLS* reads: of London: which,

167 Paragraphs 13 and 14 in *Times* joined in *TLS*

167 I gathered the senses of all] *TLS* reads: I gathered the sense of all

167 old and now, like most] *TLS* reads: old and now—like most
167 relinquishing owner; the] *TLS* reads: relinquishing owner—the
167 and repassed, at the afternoon] *TLS* reads: and repassed at the afternoon
167 everywhere is; such] *TLS* reads: everywhere is: such
167 never consent to be] *TLS* reads: never consents to be
167 still unspoken. [New paragraph] This, however,] *TLS* reads: still unspoken. This, however,
167 come back to, and] *TLS* reads: come back to; and
168 the horror. It was in September] *TLS* reads: the horror. [New paragraph] It was in September
168 and here the advent] *TLS* reads: and where the advent
168 small hilltop city,] *TLS* reads: small hill-top city,
168 highest point, and we] *TLS* reads: highest point: and we
168 grass-grown cobbles, where] *TLS* reads: grass-grown cobbles where
168 almost clinging entertainers,] *TLS* reads: almost clinging, entertainers,
168 in the Autumn darkness] *Herald* and *TLS* read: in the autumn darkness
168 and but for a woman's voice scarce] *TLS* reads: and, but for a woman's voice, scarce
168 breath of emotion. [New paragraph] The note] *TLS* reads: breath of emotion. The note
168 scores of thousands; yet her cry] *TLS* reads: scores of thousands: yet her cry
168 actually felt, and it plays to my own sense, as a great fitful tragic] *TLS* reads: actually felt; and it plays, to my own sense, as a great fitful, tragic

18. WITHIN THE RIM

First published, posthumously, in England in *The Fortnightly Review* 102.608 (1 Aug. 1917): 161–71, and shortly thereafter in the United States, in *Harper's Monthly Magazine* 108.811 (Dec. 1917): 55–61. The textual differences between the two versions are limited to English vs. Americanized spellings and minor variations of punctuation. Since Elizabeth Asquith, to whom James had given the essay, might have had closer connections with the *Fortnightly Review* than with *Harper's Monthly*, the English version may be closer to James's original intentions and is the source text for this collection.

The following footnote appears on the first page of the essay:

It has been suggested to me that I should explain how *Within the Rim* came to be written.

Those who knew Henry James not as a name but as a man will approach this sketch less with the detached interest of critics than with the warm sympathy of friends, and to them these few details of its origin may be of interest. *Within the Rim* was one of the last things Henry James ever wrote, and one of the few things he wrote about the war.

In November, 1914, I organised a *matinée* which laid the financial foundations of the Arts Fund—a scheme started by Miss Constance Collier for the relief of artists in distress owing to the war.

We had naturally relied on dramatic and musical entertainments as our chief sources of income, but as all the four arts had benefited equally by our fund we wished to give to painting and literature an opportunity of making their contributions through the medium of an album. I was lunching with Henry James in February, 1915, and he promised to write something for us. "It must be about the war," he said, "I can think of nothing else." Three weeks later he asked me to lunch with him again in order that he might read me what he had written.

I can see him now sitting in front of the fire, his tongue caressing the words—conducting his verbal orchestration with his foot, as if by beating time he could force his complicated passages into a shape intelligible to the listener.

After it was over he brushed aside my thanks and began talking about the war and then the younger generation till gradually, under the spell of his conversation, lunch faded into tea, and it was time for me to go. I asked for the precious manuscript, but he told me he would send it round by messenger, as I was certain to leave it in the taxi. I assured him that I would look after and cherish it like a child. So he confided it to my care.

Ultimately the Committee of the Arts Fund abandoned the idea of an album. I told Henry James and asked him if he would like me to return him his manuscript, but he said: "It is yours, my dear child, to do what you will with."

The last time I saw him was in November, 1915, at a view of my sister's wedding presents. I again asked him whether he really wanted me to keep *Within the Rim*, and he assured me that he did. He then inquired what I would wear as a bridesmaid. "Orange," I told him. "I shall see you tomorrow as a flame," he said. Thirty-six hours later he had his stroke, and I never saw him again.

Now that he is dead I am publishing *Within the Rim* for the purpose for which he originally intended it.

It is his legacy to the literature of the war and to the English nation, for it shows him not only as a great artist, but as a great soldier fighting our battles.

Elizabeth Asquith
March, 1916

Asquith's note appears as an introduction in the *Harper's* version. *Fortnightly* italicizes the word *matinée* and the essay's title throughout the note; *Harper's* italicizes neither, putting the essay's title in quotation marks; "not as a name" in the second paragraph is set off in commas in *Harper's*; a comma follows "our fund" and a period, not a comma, comes after "he said" in the fourth paragraph in *Harper's*; a comma follows "him now" in the fifth paragraph in *Harper's*; there is no comma after "tea" in the sixth paragraph in *Harper's*; "look after" in the sixth paragraph becomes "look after it" in *Harper's*; "cherish it like a child" in the sixth paragraph becomes "cherish it as if it were a child" in *Harper's*; there is no comma after "stroke" in the eighth paragraph in *Harper's*; there is a comma after "he is dead" in the ninth paragraph in *Harper's*.

Elizabeth Asquith (1898–1945) was a friend of James's and daughter of Herbert H. Asquith (1852–1928), Liberal prime minister from 1908 to 1916. Herbert Asquith was one of the character witnesses who supported James's application for British citizenship.

Constance Collier (1880–1955) was a British theater and movie actress and later drama coach. During World War I she mounted a dramatization of George Du Maurier's *Peter Ibbetson* for charity. She wrote a memoir: *Harlequinade: The Story of My Life* (London: Lane, 1930).

James's first stroke occurred 2 December 1915 (see Edel, *The Master* 542; Kaplan, *Imagination of Genius* 561–62).

Variants (*Fortnightly* reading followed by *Harper's* reading):

178 found it humiliating; in fact, however I,] found it humiliating, in fact however I
178 contact went, but] contact went but
179 earlier ages, and] earlier ages; and
180 a person), the right] a person) the right
180 right attitude for] right attitude, for
181 doubly outraged; the action] doubly outraged: the action
182 of an extreme, of] of an extreme of
183 kept, in fact, pushing] kept in fact pushing
184 I wanted, of course, to] I wanted of course to
184 was fed, and fed] was fed and fed
184 reasons—that is, for] reasons, that is for
184 the better—the blades] the better, the blades
184 which was not, after all, so] which was not after all so
185 across the picture, that] across the picture that
185 Wouldn't it, indeed, be] Wouldn't it indeed be
185 moreover, the next best thing] moreover the next-best thing
185 such others, and] such others and
185 associated outsider, the order] associated outsider the order
185 ignorance—this at least apparently armour-proof—he] ignorance, this at least apparently armor-proof, he

Emendations

The following typographical errors in the source texts have been corrected:

1. THE BRITISH SOLDIER

13 delighful] delightful

6. JAMES IN THE SERENE SIXTIES

40 sublety] subtlety

8. SPEECH OF AMERICAN WOMEN

72 criticism in nowhere] criticism is nowhere

9. MANNERS OF AMERICAN WOMEN

86 tesified] testified
102 "... before her," Upon which] "... before her." Upon which

10. IS THERE A LIFE AFTER DEATH?

Four errors in the original book version have been replaced with readings from the periodical version.

116 it it true] it is true
119 life put on] life puts on

122 my sense of that balance] my sense of that the balance
123 contribute strangely] contributes strangely

12. JAMES'S FIRST INTERVIEW

139 greatefully] gratefully
143 plasphemy] blasphemy

16. REFUGEES IN ENGLAND

Four apparent errors in the *New York Times* text have been replaced with concurring readings from the *Herald* and *Times Literary Supplement* texts:

161 outrage than it would] outrage that it would
162 Bishopgate quarter] Bishopsgate quarter
166 familiarly stronger,) mutilated] familiarly stronger), mutilated
166 apprehand] apprehend

Four apparent errors in the *Times* and *Herald* texts have been replaced with readings from the *Times Literary Supplement* version:

163 noblest particulars and] noblest particulars; and
163 for the large house and fed and clothed] for the large housed and fed and clothed
166 but as once lighted] but at once lighted
167 tried sustainly to] tried sustainingly to

Bibliography

━━━━━━

James himself saw to press more than one version of five of the articles in this book ("The Question of Our Speech," "Is There a Life After Death?" "The American Volunteer Motor-Ambulance Corps in France," "The Question of the Mind," and "Refugees in England"), and a sixth article ("Within the Rim") was published in two different periodicals not long after James's death. For each of these articles, this bibliography lists the source text for this book first and all other printings in chronological order.

1. "The British Soldier." *Lippincott's Magazine* 22 (Aug. 1878): 214–21.
2. "The Afghan Difficulty." *The Nation* 27.698 (14 Nov. 1878): 298–99.
3. [Review of *Graf Bismarck und seine Leute während des Krieges mit Frankreich. Nach Tagebuchsblättern,* by Moritz Busch.] *The Nation* 27.703 (19 Dec. 1878): 384–85.
   Posthumous republication:
   1984. *Literary Criticism: French Writers, Other European Writers, the Prefaces to the New York Edition.* New York: Library of America. 905–06. (Only the first half of the article included.)
4. "The Early Meeting of Parliament." *The Nation* 27.704 (26 Dec. 1878): 397–98.
5. "The Reassembling of Parliament." *The Nation* 28.716 (20 Mar. 1879): 197–99.
6. "Henry James in the Serene Sixties." *New York Herald,* 2 Oct. 1904: magazine section (sec. 4), p. 1.
7. "The Question of Our Speech." *The Question of Our Speech; The Lesson of Balzac: Two Lectures.* Boston: Houghton Mifflin, Riverside Press, 1905. 3–52.
   1905. *Appleton's Booklovers Magazine* 6 (Aug.): 199–210.
   Posthumous republication:
   1960. *French Writers and American Women.* Ed. Peter Buitenhuis. Branford CT: Compass. 18–31.
   1972. *Question of Our Speech.* Rpt. New York: Haskell House. 3–52.

8. "The Speech of American Women." *Harper's Bazar* 40.11 (Nov. 1906): 979–82; 40.12 (Dec. 1906): 1103–06; 41.1 (Jan. 1907): 17–21; 41.2 (Feb. 1907): 113–17.

   Posthumous republications:

   1960. Buitenhuis, ed. *French Writers.* 32–53.

   1973. *The Speech and Manners of American Women.* Ed. E. S. Riggs. Introd. Inez Martinez. Lancaster PA: Lancaster House. 15–49.

9. "The Manners of American Women." *Harper's Bazar* 41.4 (Apr. 1907): 355–59; 41.5 (May 1907): 453–58; 41.6 (June 1907): 537–41; 41.7 (July 1907): 646–51.

   Posthumous republications:

   1960. Buitenhuis, ed. *French Writers.* 54–80.

   1973. Riggs, ed. *Speech and Manners.* 51–95.

10. "Is There a Life After Death?" *In After Days: Thoughts on the Future Life.* by W. D. Howells, Henry James, John Bigelow, Thomas Wentworth Higginson, Henry M. Alden, William Hanna Thomson, Guglielmo Ferrero, Julia Ward Howe, Elizabeth Stuart Phelps. New York: Harper, 1910. 199–233.

    1910. *Harper's Bazar* 44.1 (Jan.): 26; 44.2 (Feb.): 128–29.

    Posthumous republications:

    1947. *The James Family: Including Selections from the Writings of Henry James, Senior, William, Henry, and Alice James.* By F. O. Matthiessen. New York: Knopf. 602–14.

    1977. Howells, et al. *In After Days.* Rpt. New York: Arno. 199–233.

    1980. Matthiessen. *James Family.* Rpt. New York: Vintage. 602–14.

11. "The American Volunteer Motor-Ambulance Corps in France." *The American Volunteer Motor-Ambulance Corps in France: A Letter to the Editor of an American Journal.* London: Macmillan, 1914.

    1915. As "Famous Novelist Describes Deeds of U.S. Motor Corps." *New York World* 4 Jan., p. 2.

    Posthumous republications:

    1918. *Within the Rim and Other Essays, 1914–15.* London: Collins. 63–79.

    1968. *Within the Rim.* Rpt. Freeport NY: Books for Libraries. 63–79.

    1993. *Collected Travel Writings: The Continent; A Little Tour in France, Italian Hours, Other Travels.* New York: Library of America. 764–71.

12. "Henry James's First Interview." *New York Times,* 21 Mar. 1915: magazine section (sec. 5), pp. 3–4.

13. "France." *The Book of France in Aid of the French Parliamentary Committee's Fund for the Relief of the Invaded Departments.* Ed. Winifred Stephens. London: Macmillan, 1915. 1–8.

    Posthumous republications:

    1918. *Within the Rim.* 83–93.

    1968. *Within the Rim* [rpt.]. 83–93.

    1993. *Collected Travel Writings: The Continent.* 772–76.

14. "The Question of the Mind." *England at War: An Essay.* London: Central Committee for National Patriotic Organisations, 1915. 3–12.

    1915. As "Mind of England at War." *New York Sun,* 1 Aug.: sec. 5, p. 3.

    1915. As "The Mind of England at War." *Philadelphia Ledger Magazine,* 1 Aug.: 1.

Posthumous republication:

1993. *Collected Travel Writings: Great Britain and America; English Hours, The American Scene, Other Travels.* New York: Library of America. 309–18.

15. "Allen D. Loney—In Memoriam." *New York Times,* 12 Sept. 1915: sec. 1, p. 4 (col. 2).

16. "Refugees in England." *New York Times,* 17 Oct. 1915: magazine section (sec. 4), pp. 1–2.

1915. *Boston Sunday Herald Supplement,* 17 Oct. 1915: 6, 8.

Posthumous republications:

1916. As "Refugees in Chelsea." *Times Literary Supplement* 740 (23 Mar.): 133–34.

1918. As "Refugees in Chelsea." *Within the Rim.* 39–59.

1968. As "Refugees in Chelsea." *Within the Rim* [rpt.]. 39–59.

1993. As "Refugees in England." *Collected Travel Writings: Great Britain and America.* 319–28.

17. "The Long Wards." *The Book of the Homeless.* Ed. Edith Wharton. New York: Scribner's, 1916. 115–25.

Posthumous republications:

1918. *Within the Rim.* 97–119.

1968. *Within the Rim* [rpt.]. 97–119.

1993. *Collected Travel Writings: Great Britain and America.* 341–50.

18. "Within the Rim." *The Fortnightly Review* 102.608 (1 Aug. 1917): 161–71.

1917. *Harper's Monthly Magazine* 108.811 (Dec. 1917): 55–61.

Republications:

1918. *Within the Rim.* 11–35.

1927. *Harper Essays.* Ed. Henry Seidel Canby. New York: Harper. 219–34.

1968. *Within the Rim* [rpt.]. 11–35.

1993. *Collected Travel Writings: Great Britain and America.* 329–40.

Index